Business English in 24 Stunden

DER NEUE SCHNELL-LERN-KURS

Evan Frendo

Compact Verlag

Bisher sind in dieser Reihe erschienen:

- Englisch in 24 Stunden mit Audio-CD
- Französisch in 24 Stunden mit Audio-CD
- Spanisch in 24 Stunden mit Audio-CD
- Italienisch in 24 Stunden mit Audio-CD

Weitere Titel sind in Vorbereitung.

Chefredaktion: Dr. Angela Sendlinger
Redaktion: Grit Sperlich
Fachredaktion: Anthony Moore
Produktion: Wolfram Friedrich
Gestaltung: Axel Ganguin
Titelabbildung: zefa visual media gmbh; Getty Images, Daniel Bosler

ISBN-13: 978-3-8174-7665-7
ISBN-10: 3-8174-7665-5
7276651

Besuchen Sie uns im Internet: www.compactverlag.de

Vorwort

Gute Englischkenntnisse sind heute eine wichtige Voraussetzung für geschäftlichen und beruflichen Erfolg. Wer sich im modernen Geschäftsleben behaupten will, muss sich kompetent und professionell ausdrücken können.

Business Englisch in 24 Stunden ist der umfassende Selbstlernkurs, mit dem Sie sicher und schnell Ihre Kenntnisse erweitern und vertiefen können.

In 24 Kapiteln werden alle wichtigen Themen aus dem Wirtschaftsleben behandelt – vom Basiswissen wie Telefonate, Korrespondenz, Präsentationen und Verhandlungen bis hin zu den fachbezogenen Bereichen wie Management, Controlling, Verkauf, Marketing und Werbung.

Jede Lerneinheit enthält Mustertexte und Dialogbeispiele, die Ihnen den wichtigsten Wortschatz vermitteln. Infoboxen bieten sprachliche und kulturelle Hintergrundinformationen. Abwechslungsreiche Übungen ermöglichen ein fundiertes Sprachtraining. Ein Abschlusstest überprüft den Lernerfolg.

Auf der CD finden Sie zum Zuhören, Mitsprechen und Mitlesen alle Dialoge vertont. Hören Sie sich die Texte zunächst nur an. Sprechen Sie sie danach auch mit, um ein erstes Gefühl für die neue Sprache zu bekommen und die korrekte Aussprache zu trainieren. In einem dritten Schritt sollten die Dialoge dann im Buch mitgelesen werden, um Schriftbild und Aussprache miteinander zu verknüpfen.

Nehmen Sie sich nicht zu viel vor! Lernen Sie lieber in kleinen Einheiten, aber dafür regelmäßig!

Viel Erfolg!

Inhaltsverzeichnis

Inhaltsverzeichnis

Inhaltsverzeichnis

Begrüßen, Vorstellen und korrekte Umgangsformen 1

Korrekte Umgangsformen sind in der modernen Geschäftswelt unerlässlich. Wer wichtige Kontakte aufbauen will, muss nicht nur die Kunst des Begrüßens und Vorstellens beherrschen, sondern auch beim Geschäftsessen oder bei der Verabschiedung angemessen auftreten.

Begrüßen und Vorstellen

Der erste Eindruck zählt. Hans Meyer tritt seine neue Stelle als Revisor in einer englischen Firma an.

Hans: Good morning. My name is Hans Meyer. I'm the new auditor.

Jennifer: Hello Hans. Jennifer Smith – pleased to meet you. We've heard a lot about you.

Hans: Really. Only good things I hope.

Jennifer: Yes of course. Sorry Dave couldn't be here to show you around. He asked me to do it. Come on. Let's grab a coffee and I can introduce you to the staff.

Hans: Great. Can I leave my bag here, Ms Smith?

Jennifer: Jennifer. We're all on first names here. Yeah, put it there, behind the plant. So, this is our coffee area. Lots of people here because we're just about to have a heads of department meeting. This is Jonathan Musford. He's the IT guru. Jonathan this is Hans, the new auditor.

Jonathan: Hi Hans.

Hans: Hi.

Jennifer: And this is Caroline. She's responsible for all things financial.

Hans: Hi Caroline. I'm Hans.

Caroline: Hello Hans. I'm looking forward to working with you.

Jennifer: How do you take your coffee?

Hans: White. No sugar.

Jennifer: Here you are.

Hans: Thanks.

Jennifer: There's Norbert Longworth. He's the chief engineer.

Hans: Hello Norbert. How do you do.

Norbert: Hi. Sorry. I didn't catch your name.

Hans: Sorry. It's Hans. Hans Meyer.

Norbert: You're the new auditor, right? Come to keep us all on the straight and narrow.

Hans: Well, that's the plan.

Jennifer: And this is Andy. Andy handles sales and marketing.

Hans: Hello.

Cynthia: And I'm Cynthia, Human Resources.

1 Begrüßen, Vorstellen und korrekte Umgangsformen

Vokabeln

auditor	Revisor
heads of department	Abteilungsleiter
Human Resources	Personalabteilung
I didn't catch your name.	Ich habe Ihren Namen nicht verstanden.
I'm looking forward to working with you.	Ich freue mich darauf, mit Ihnen zu arbeiten.
She's responsible for ...	Sie ist für ... zuständig.
We've heard a lot about you.	Wir haben schon viel von Ihnen gehört.
We're all on first names here.	Wir sprechen uns hier alle mit Vornamen an.

Übung 1:

Bilden Sie sinnvolle Sätze, indem Sie die gegebenen Wörter in die richtige Reihenfolge bringen.

1. you I'm looking to working forward with

_ _

2. I name catch didn't your

_ _

3. lot heard a We've about you

_ _

4. first We're names all on here

_ _

5. things responsible for She's all financial

_ _

Übung 2:

Vervollständigen Sie die Sätze mit folgenden Wörtern: meet, pleased, from, pleasure, introduce, acquaintance, before.

1. May I _ _ _ _ _ _ _ _ _ you to Mr Meyer?
2. I'd like you to _ _ _ _ _ _ _ _ _ Hans.
3. _ _ _ _ _ _ _ _ _ _ to meet you.
4. The _ _ _ _ _ _ _ _ _ is mine.
5. Happy to make your _ _ _ _ _ _ _ _ _ _.
6. I'm _ _ _ _ _ _ _ _ _ _ Berlin.
7. I think we've met _ _ _ _ _ _ _ _ _ _.

Erste Gespräche führen

Eine positive Beziehung mit dem Geschäftspartner aufzubauen ist sehr wichtig. Dabei sind die ersten Kontakte oft am schwierigsten – hier muss erst noch „das Eis gebrochen" werden ("*break the ice*").

Harry: Excuse me. I saw you in the audience – John Hamilton's talk – just now. Did you enjoy it?

Sally: Yes, he's an excellent speaker. I like his style.

Vokabeln

conference	Konferenz
Have you come far?	Sind Sie von weit her?
investment	Anlagekapital
Pleased to meet you.	Schön, Sie kennen zu lernen.
renewable energy	erneuerbare Energie
talk	Vortrag

Harry: He's great. What did you think of the idea about renewable energy?

Sally: Well, I'm not really sure. Don't know enough about it. But it looks quite good.

Harry: Yes. But they'll need a lot of investment if it's going to work.

Sally: Yeah, sure.

Harry: Have you come far for the conference?

Sally: No, not really. I live in this town, so it took me about 20 minutes. You?

Harry: I flew in last night, but I'm staying in this hotel so it wasn't a problem.

Sally: Ah, look, there's the coffee. Fancy a cup?

Harry: Good idea. I didn't catch your name.

Sally: I'm Sally Bowers, from the Toronto Times. I work on the economics pages.

Harry: Really. That's amazing. I work in a newspaper too. I'm Harold Wilson, but people call me Harry.

Sally: Pleased to meet you.

Infobox

Here are some useful phrases to break the ice:
1. Does it always rain like this here?
2. Quite warm, isn't it?
3. It's pretty humid today, isn't it?

Übung 3:

Ordnen Sie die Antworten den entsprechenden Fragen aus der Infobox zu.

1. Yes. Good thing we're inside all day.
2. No, normally it rains harder.
3. Well, it's not cold, that's for sure.

Übung 4:

Finden Sie die in den Sätzen verborgenen Fehler und schreiben Sie die Sätze neu.

1. I see you in the audience.

____

2. Did you enjoyed it?

____

3. Don't know enough on it.

____

4. Have you far come for the conference?

____

5. It took me more or less 20 minutes.

____

6. I'm Harold Wilson, but people call I Harry.

____

7. Pleased you to meet Harry.

____

8. I catch not your name.

____

Geschäftsessen

Gespräche während eines Geschäftsessens können zu einem geschäftlichen Erfolg beitragen, ihn aber auch negativ beeinflussen. Ein amerikanischer Geschäftsmann hat seinen arabischen Gast, der erst vor kurzem in den USA angekommen ist, zum Abendessen eingeladen.

Sam: The food here is excellent. Just look at this menu. Great, isn't it. So how was your flight?

Ahmed: Not bad. We had a bit of turbulence over the mountains, but nothing to speak of.

Sam: Well you're here, and that's the main thing. Now, about the contract. There are a couple of clauses which I think we need to ...

Ahmed: Ah, there's the waiter. Perhaps we should order?

Sam: What? Oh yes. Excuse me. We'd like to order please.

Waiter: Yes certainly.

Sam: I'd like the salad to start off with, followed by the pork cutlets.

Waiter: With fried potatoes?

Sam: Yes please. And fresh vegetables.

Waiter: Of course.

And you sir?

Ahmed: I'll have the vegetarian lasagne please.

Waiter: Yes sir. Would you like the wine list?

Sam: No need for that. I recommend the Californian wine – it's first class.

Ahmed: Well actually, I don't drink.

Sam: This one's on me.

Ahmed: No really. No thank you.

Sam: How about a beer? Come on, just a small one. I insist.

Ahmed: No thank you.

Sam: Ah well, ok. Just a glass of house red for me then.

Ahmed: And I'll have a glass of mineral water please.

Waiter: Certainly.

Vokabeln

contract	Vertrag
I insist.	Ich bestehe darauf.
menu	Speisekarte
Nothing to speak of.	Nicht der Rede wert.
order	bestellen
pay	zahlen
recommend	empfehlen
tip	Trinkgeld
This one's on me.	Das geht auf meine Rechnung.

Infobox

When preparing for a business meal with a foreign guest, try to find out as much as possible about your guest and his culture. Making faux pas like those in the conversation above is unforgivable in modern business.

Übung 5:

Was weist im vorangegangenen Text darauf hin, dass die Unterhaltung eventuell negative Gefühle bei den Gesprächspartnern hinterlassen könnte?

____

____

Übung 6:

Finden Sie die richtige Definition.

1. menu	☐ someone who checks the accounts
2. clause	☐ written agreement
3. turbulence	☐ a list of food items in a restaurant
4. recommend	☐ violent, irregular motion of air
5. insist	☐ part of a contract
6. auditor	☐ suggest
7. contract	☐ demand

Infobox

Toasts

It's important to know what to say when you want to make a toast, or your business partner raises his glass.
A common form is to repeat the last phrase, like this:
A: I'd like to propose a toast. To our future cooperation.
B: To our future cooperation.

Übung 7:

Füllen Sie die Lücken im folgenden Dialog. Verwenden Sie die Wörter in der Klammer. (insist, recommend, nothing, order, menu)

John, hi. Good to see you.

Hi guys. How's it going?

Not bad. The program's nearly finished.

We're just running the tests now.

So it's time for a take-away. You're just in time to (1.) ______.

What are you having?

Don't know yet – we're still looking through the (2.) ________.

Ok. I've decided. I'll have a mushroom pizza.

And I'll have a four seasons, with extra topping.

I (3.) _______ the salami.

Good idea. I'll have that.

Me too. Although from the picture it's (4.) ________ to speak of.

Wait till you taste it. You'll see.

And I (5.) _______ on buying the beers.

What, are you crazy?

No, it's my birthday.

Verabschiedung

Zwei Geschäftspartner haben sich gerade bezüglich der Liefer- und Rechnungsbedingungen geeinigt. Nun ist es Zeit, sich voneinander zu verabschieden.

Kenneth: Well, that's about it, I guess.
Samantha: Yes, I think so. Maybe we should just summarise.
Kenneth: Good idea. So, we've agreed that the first delivery will get to us by the end of the month.
Samantha: That's right. And the rest will follow in one consignment two weeks later.
Kenneth: And payment will be by bank transfer – the total sum being 45,000 euro, payable in two instalments.
Samantha: Exactly. On the 15th and the 30th.
Kenneth: Fine. I'll put that in writing and send it to you by tomorrow.
Samantha: Ok. That's fine.
Kenneth: Is that it for you for today?
Samantha: No, unfortunately not. I have one more client to visit. Can I get a taxi near here?
Kenneth: Sure, no problem. You make your way downstairs to reception, and I'll organise it. It should be waiting for you when you get to the exit.
Samantha: Great. Thank you very much.
Kenneth: You're welcome. And I must say it's been a pleasure doing business with you.
Samantha: Yes, I've enjoyed it too. And I'm sure both our bosses will be happy with our agreement. Let's keep in touch.
Kenneth: Yes (shaking hands). Goodbye.
Samantha: Goodbye.

Vokabeln

agreement	Vereinbarung
And I must say it's been a pleasure doing business with you.	Und ich muss wirklich sagen, dass es eine Freude war, mit Ihnen Geschäfte zu machen.
bank transfer	Überweisung
Can I get a taxi near here?	Kann ich hier in der Nähe ein Taxi bekommen?
consignment	Zusendung
delivery	Lieferung
I'll put that in writing.	Ich halte das schriftlich fest.
instalment	Rate
Is that it for today?	Ist das für heute alles?
Let's keep in touch.	Lass uns in Verbindung bleiben.
Maybe we should just summarise.	Vielleicht sollten wir das noch zusammenfassen.
payment	Zahlung
reception	Rezeption
Well, that's about it, I guess.	Das war's dann wohl, glaube ich.

Übung 8:

Bilden Sie sinnvolle Sätze!

1. Can I get a	☐ it, I guess.
2. I'll put that	☐ for today?
3. Is that it	☐ doing business with you.
4. Let's keep	☐ taxi near here?
5. Maybe we should	☐ in touch.
6. It's been a pleasure	☐ just summarise.
7. That's about	☐ in writing.

Übung 9:

Bei dieser Verabschiedung ist etwas durcheinander geraten. Bringen Sie den Dialog in die richtige Reihenfolge!

1. Samantha: Exactly. On the 15th and the 30th.

2. Kenneth: Well, that's about it, I guess.

3. Samantha: Great. Thank you very much.

4. Kenneth: Good idea. So, we've agreed that the first delivery will get to us by the end of the month.

5. Samantha: That's right. And the rest will follow in one consignment two weeks later.

6. Kenneth: And payment will be by bank transfer – the total sum being 45,000 euro, payable in two instalments.

7. Kenneth: Sure, no problem. You make your way downstairs to reception, and I'll organise it. It should be waiting for you when you get to the exit.

8. Samantha: Ok. That's fine.

9. Samantha: Yes, I think so. Maybe we should just summarise.

10. Kenneth: Is that it for you for today?

11. Samantha: No, unfortunately not. I have one more client to visit. Can I get a taxi near here?

12. Kenneth: Fine. I'll put that in writing and send it to you by tomorrow.

13. Kenneth: You're welcome. And I must say it's been a pleasure doing business with you.

Lösung: _

Infobox

There are lots of ways to say goodbye. Here are some common ones:
I think I should be making a move.
Must dash.
I'm afraid I've got a plane to catch.
Is that the time? I've got an early start tomorrow.
Thank you for a delightful evening.
You must come and see us when you are in Helsinki.
We've had a great time.
I appreciate all your hard work – thank you very much.

Übung 10:

Setzen Sie die fehlenden Wörter ein:

1. Maybe we should _ _ _ _ _ summarise.
2. I'll put _ _ _ _ _ _ _ _ in writing.
3. I'm afraid I've got an early plane to _ _ _ _ _ _ _.
4. Is _ _ _ _ _ _ it for today?
5. Thank you _ _ _ _ _ a delightful evening.
6. Can I _ _ _ _ _ _ _ _ a taxi near here?
7. You must come and see us _ _ _ _ _ _ you are in Helsinki.
8. And I must say it's _ _ _ _ _ _ _ _ a pleasure doing business with you.
9. Let's _ _ _ _ _ _ _ _ _ in touch.

Übung 11:

Übersetzen Sie folgende Sätze!

1. Rufen Sie an, wenn Sie das nächste Mal in London sind.

_ _

2. Ich würde mich freuen, Ihnen unsere Firma zeigen zu können.

_ _

_ _

3. Lassen Sie wieder von sich hören.

_ _

4. Hier ist meine Visitenkarte.

_ _

5. Haben Sie meine Telefonnummer?

_ _

6. Sie können mich unter ... erreichen.

_ _

7. Ich freue mich auf Ihr Angebot.

_ _

Übung 12:

Setzen Sie die korrekte Verbform ein.
(like, talk, be, thank)

1. _ _ _ _ _ you for a very interesting discussion.
2. It _ _ _ _ _ very interesting talking to you.
3. Nice _ _ _ _ to you. Thank you so much.
4. Well, if there's anything else you _ _ _ _ _ to know, why not give me a call later?

Infobox

There are undeniably differences to be observed in business dealings with people from distinct regions of the world, such as Asia. But clichés and, of course, prejudices should be avoided at all costs. A correct appearance, politeness, consideration for a competitor's point of view are invariably sufficient in any business situation. And, of course, business cards – not only in encounters with Asian business people.

Telefonstrategien und -techniken 2

Fast jeder muss irgendwann einmal aus beruflichen Gründen auf Englisch telefonieren. Dies ist allerdings eines der schwierigeren Dinge in einer fremden Sprache, da man den Gesprächspartner nicht sehen kann und eventuell eine schlechte Klangqualität besteht. Dieser Lernschritt enthält für das Telefonieren nützliche Redewendungen und Vokabeln, die man immer wieder am Telefon braucht.

Ein Telefongespräch entgegennehmen

Eine Kundin ruft einen Lieferanten an, um sich nach dem Stand ihrer Bestellung zu erkundigen.

Laurence: Good morning. Jupiter Electronics. Laurence speaking. How can I help you?

Karen: Hi. This is Karen Preston from Fox Systems.

Laurence: Oh, hello Karen. How are you?

Karen: I'm fine, thanks. And you?

Laurence: Good, thank you. So what can I do for you, Karen?

Karen: I'm calling about our order. I wanted to ask if you had despatched it yet.

Laurence: Yes, we sent it off yesterday. You should get it tomorrow.

Karen: Great. Oh, and while I've got you on the line, there was something else I wanted to ask you. Is the documentation for your latest product line-up available on your website? We've lost the manual for one of your metres ...

Vokabeln

And you?	Und selbst?
How are you?	Wie geht es Ihnen?
How can I help you?	Wie kann ich Ihnen helfen?
I wanted to ask if ...	Ich wollte fragen ob ...
I'm calling about ...	Ich rufe an wegen ...
I'm fine, thanks.	Danke, gut.
... speaking	... am Apparat
product line-up	Produktpalette
There was something else I wanted to ask you.	Ich wollte Sie noch etwas anderes fragen.
This ... from ...	Hier ist ... von ...
What can I do for you?	Was kann ich für Sie tun?
While I've got you on the line ...	Da ich Sie gerade am Apparat habe ...

Infobox

If you are answering the phone, you say "(your name) speaking". If you are calling someone else, say "this is (your name) from (your company)". Don't say "here is (your name)" – this is German!

2 Telefonstrategien und -techniken

Übung 1:

Übersetzen Sie!

1. Hector am Apparat.

____

2. Hier ist James Zinn von Seven Systems.

____

3. Wie kann ich Ihnen helfen?

____

4. Wie geht es Ihnen?

____

5. Danke, gut. Und selbst?

____

6. Was kann ich für Sie tun?

____

7. Ich wollte fragen, ob ...

____

8. Ich rufe wegen unserer Bestellung an.

____

9. Ich wollte Sie noch etwas fragen.

____

Übung 2:

Bringen Sie die Satzglieder in die richtige Reihenfolge und bilden Sie aus den gegebenen Wörtern sinnvolle Sätze.

1. you how are?

____

2. help you can how I?

____

3. do you can what I for?

____

4. calling our I'm about order

____

5. despatched had I you to order ask if wanted our

____

6. line on while you I've the got

____

7. was you else wanted ask something there I to

____

Infobox

English speakers often begin a telephone conversation with a little small talk. This could be as simple as asking "How are you?", or they might talk about the weather, holidays, or sport. Native speakers often signal that they want to change from small talk to talking business by using words like "So ..." or "Well ...".
The correct answer to "How are you?" is "(I'm) fine thanks", not "Thanks, fine", which is a direct translation from the German.
"I wanted to ask" is more polite than "I want to ask", because it uses the past tense, which puts more distance between the speaker and his or her words.

Einen Gesprächspartner weiterverbinden

Die Controllerin Zoe Chambers ruft die Heathcoate Bank an, um mit der Investmentberaterin Frances Murphy zu sprechen. Kevin Green, der Empfangssekretär, stellt sie durch, nachdem er den Grund des Anrufs erfragt hat.

Kevin: Good morning. Heathcoate Bank. Kevin speaking.

Zoe: Hello. Can I speak to Frances Murphy in the Financial Services department, please?

Vokabeln

associate	Teilhaber
Can I speak to ..., please?	Kann ich bitte mit ... sprechen?
Could you give me the name of your company?	Könnten Sie mir bitte den Namen Ihrer Firma mitteilen?
I have a ... on the line.	... ist am Telefon.
I'd like to speak to her about ...	Ich würde gern mit ihr über ... sprechen.
I'll just put you through.	Ich stelle Sie durch.
I'm calling from ...	Ich rufe von ... an.
May I ask the reason for your call?	Können Sie mir den Grund für Ihren Anruf nennen?
May I ask who's calling?	Darf ich fragen, wer spricht?
Nice to hear from you.	Schön, von Ihnen zu hören.
One moment please.	Einen Moment, bitte.
Please hold the line.	Bitte bleiben Sie dran.

Kevin: May I ask who's calling?

Zoe: My name is Zoe Chambers.

Kevin: And could you give me the name of your company?

Zoe: I'm calling from Werner Associates.

Kevin: May I ask the reason for your call?

Zoe: I'd like to speak to her about our investment portfolio.

Kevin: Thank you, Ms Chambers. I'll just put you through. One moment, please. (calls Frances) Hello, Frances?

Frances: Hi Kevin.

Kevin: I have a Zoe Chambers on the line, from Werner Associates. Do you want to speak to her?

Frances: Sure. Put her through. (Kevin makes the connection.) Frances Murphy speaking.

Zoe: Hi Frances, it's Zoe here.

Frances: Hi Zoe. Nice to hear from you ...

Übung 3:

Vervollständigen Sie die Sätze!

1. May I ask the _ _ _ _ _ for your call?
2. One _ _ _ _ _ please.
3. Can I _ _ _ _ _ to Henry Thomson, please?
4. May I ask who's _ _ _ _ _?

5. Could you _ _ _ _ _ me the name of your company?

6. I'm calling _ _ _ _ _ Green Logistics.

7. I'd like to speak to her _ _ _ _ _ our meeting next week.

8. I'll just put you _ _ _ _ _.

9. I have a Christine Willis on the _ _ _ _ _.

10. Nice to _ _ _ _ _ from you.

Übung 4:

Bilden Sie sinnvolle Sätze!

1. May I ask	☐ for your call?
2. I have a Teresa York	☐ put you through.
3. I'd like to speak to him	☐ who's calling?
4. I'll just	☐ from you.
5. May I ask the reason	☐ of your company?
6. What's the name	☐ please.
7. Nice to hear	☐ on the line.
8. One moment	☐ about our bill.

Nachrichten übermitteln

Wenn der gewünschte Gesprächspartner nicht erreichbar ist, sollte man zumindest eine kurze Nachricht und seinen Namen hinterlassen.

Tim: Hi. Noon Consulting. Tim speaking.

Boris: Hello. This is Boris Weber from QuickClick.com. I'd like to speak to Richard, please.

Tim: Ah. I'm afraid Richard is on holiday at the moment.

Boris: When will he be back?

Tim: He'll be back on Monday. Would you like to leave a message?

Boris: Yes please. Can you tell him that I called, and that I'll call him again on Monday?

Tim: I'll do that. I'm afraid I didn't catch your name.

Boris: It's Boris Weber.

Tim: Could you spell your second name for me, please?

Vokabeln

Can you tell him that I called?	Können Sie ihm mitteilen, dass ich angerufen habe?
Could you spell your second name for me, please?	Können Sie mir bitte Ihren Familien-namen buchsta-bieren?
He'll be back on ...	Er ist am ... zurück.
I'll call him again on ...	Ich rufe ihn am ... noch einmal an.
I'll tell ... you called.	Ich sage ..., dass Sie angerufen haben.
I'm afraid ... is on holiday at the moment.	Es tut mir Leid, ... ist momentan im Ur-laub.
When will he be back?	Wann kommt er zurück?
Would you like to leave a message?	Möchten Sie eine Nachricht hinter-lassen?
You're welcome.	Bitte schön.

Boris: Sure. It's Weber, W E B E R.

Tim: That's great Boris. I'll tell Richard you called.

Boris: Thanks very much.

Tim: You're welcome. Bye now.

Boris: Bye.

Infobox

British and American people often use first names on the telephone, even with people they don't know. As a rule of thumb, wait for them to enter first into first name-terms.

Übung 5:

Vervollständigen Sie die Sätze im folgenden Telefonat!

1. I'm _ _ _ _ _ Richard is on holiday at the moment.
2. When _ _ _ _ _ he be back?
3. He'll be _ _ _ _ on Monday.
4. Would you like to a message?
5. Can you _ _ _ _ _ him that I called?
6. I'll _ _ _ _ _ him again on Monday.
7. I'm afraid I didn't _ _ _ _ _ your name.
8. Could you _ _ _ _ _ your second name for me, please?
9. I'll tell Richard you _ _ _ _ _.

Übung 6:

Bringen Sie die Wörter der folgenden Sätze in die richtige Reihenfolge.

1. moment afraid I'm is on Sarah the holiday at.

_ _

_ _

2. will when back be he?

_ _

3. be he'll afternoon back this.

_ _

_ _

4. like message to would leave you a ?

_ _

_ _

5. tell you called can that her I?

_ _

6. tomorrow him again I'll call.

_ _

7. catch I'm didn't name I your afraid.

_ _

_ _

8. for could spell please your you name me?

_ _

_ _

9. her you tell I'll called.

_ _

Um Rückruf bitten

Elizabeth Saunders, die Chefin eines Cateringservices, ruft bei KRS an, um mit ihrem Steuerberater zu sprechen. Dieser ist im Moment nicht da. Sie bittet um einen Rückruf und hinterlässt ihre Rufnummer.

Matthew: Good morning. KRS Accountancy Services. Matthew speaking.
Elizabeth: Hello. This is Elizabeth Saunders from Moulin Rouge Catering. Can I speak to Bernard Fink, please?

Vokabeln

client	Kunde
Could you ask him to call me back?	Könnten Sie ihn darum bitten, mich zurückzurufen?
He just left.	Er ist gerade weggegangen.
I'll give the number to you again.	Ich gebe Ihnen die Nummer noch einmal.
I'll make sure ... gets your message.	Ich sorge dafür, dass ... Ihre Nachricht bekommt.
I'm afraid ... isn't here at the moment.	Leider ist ... im Moment nicht da.
in case I'm not in the office	falls ich nicht im Büro bin
in that case	in diesem Fall
just in case	für alle Fälle
Let me just read those numbers back to you.	Lassen Sie mich die Nummern wiederholen.
Thanks for calling.	Danke für den Anruf.

Matthew: I'm afraid Bernard isn't here at the moment. He just left to go and meet with a client.
Elizabeth: In that case, could you ask him to call me back?
Matthew: Certainly. Your name was Elizabeth Saunders, is that right?
Elizabeth: Yes, that's right.
Matthew: Does Bernard have your number?
Elizabeth: I think so. But I'll give it to you again, just in case. It's 0170 684 7686. That's my office number. And my mobile number is 0123 799 2231, in case I'm not in the office.
Matthew: Let me just read those numbers back to you. Your office number is 0170 684 7686 and your mobile number is 0123 799 2231.
Elizabeth: That's right.
Matthew: Well, thanks for calling, Elizabeth. I'll make sure Bernard gets your message.
Elizabeth: Thank you. Bye now.
Matthew: Bye.

Übung 7:

Bilden Sie sinnvolle Sätze!

1. I'm afraid Bernard
2. He just left

3. Could you ask him

4. I'll give it to you again,

5. I'll give you my mobile number in case

6. Let me just read

7. Thanks

8. I'll make sure

☐ for calling.

☐ just in case.

☐ Bernard gets your message.

☐ isn't here at the moment.

☐ those numbers back to you.

☐ to go and meet with a client.

☐ to call me back?

☐ I'm not in the office.

Übung 8:

In folgenden Sätzen sind Fehler verborgen, korrigieren Sie diese bitte und schreiben Sie die Sätze neu!

1. I'm afraid, but he isn't here at the moment.

____

2. He just leaves to go and meet with a client.

____

3. Could you him ask to call me back?

____

4. I'll give it to you again in case.

____

5. Let me just read those numbers to you back.

____

6. Thank for calling.

____

7. I'll take sure Keith gets your message.

____

Telefongespräche beenden

Alex Gent, Chef einer Werbeagentur, und die Grafikerin Jenny Arnold beenden nach langer Diskussion über einen neuen Werbevertrag ihr Telefonat.

Alex: So, Jenny, I think that was everything. Was there anything else we need to discuss?

Jenny: I can't think of anything. So I'm going to fax you the information again.

Alex: And I'm going to tell William to call you when he knows what the final conditions for the contract are.

Jenny: That'll be great. Okay, Alex, I should really be going. I've got a pile of stuff I need to do.

Alex: Yeah, me too! Just give me a call if you've got any more questions.

Jenny: Will do! Nice speaking to you, Alex.

Alex: Likewise! Bye now.

Jenny: Bye.

Vokabeln

a pile of stuff	eine Menge Arbeit
condition	Bedingung
I'm going to fax you the information again.	Ich werde Ihnen die Informationen noch einmal faxen.
I'm going to tell ... to call you.	Ich werde ... sagen, dass er Sie anrufen soll.
Just give me a call if you've got any more questions.	Rufen Sie mich einfach an, wenn Sie weitere Fragen haben.
likewise	gleichfalls
Nice speaking to you.	Es war nett, mit Ihnen gesprochen zu haben.
Was there anything else we need to discuss?	War da noch etwas, das wir zu besprechen haben?

Infobox

English speakers don't like to finish a telephone conversation too suddenly. Often ending a call requires about six or seven "turns". Normally one person signals that he or she is ready to finish the conversation with a word like "so", "anyway", or "right". Usually people confirm what has been agreed or arranged at the end of the call, and refer to future action or the next time they will contact each other.

Übung 9:

Bei diesem Telefongespräch ist etwas durcheinander geraten. Bringen Sie den Dialog in die richtige Reihenfolge!

1. And I'm going to tell you when I have a definite date for the meeting.
2. So, Helen, I think that was everything. Was there anything else we need to discuss?
3. Will do! Nice speaking to you, Graham.
4. I can't think of anything. So I'm going to send you the order form again.
5. Bye.
6. Great. Okay, Graham, I really need to be going. I've got a pile of things I have to do.
7. Likewise! Bye now.
8. Yeah, me too! Just give me a call if you've got any more questions.

Lösung: ____________________

Übung 10:

Die Person, die Sie zu erreichen versuchen, ist gerade nicht verfügbar. Die Sekretärin geht ans Telefon.
Was tun Sie?

1. leave a message?
2. say you'll call later?
3. hang up?
4. leave a message and say you'll call later?

Lösung: ____________________

Die englische Korrespondenz folgt eigenen Regeln und Konventionen. Dieser Lernschritt betrachtet einige der wichtigsten Texttypen, die jeder im Beruf braucht, der mit englischsprachigen Geschäftspartnern zu tun hat.

Briefe und E-Mails

Egal, ob es sich um Anfragen, Einladungen oder auch Beschwerden handelt, Stil und Sprache von Briefen und E-Mails sollten stets höflich, klar und leserorientiert sein.

Mr Shawn Hannessey
KENDOS
Quanbay 153-159
53897-4 Hong Kong

19 June 2006

Dear Mr Hannessey,

It was a pleasure to meet you and your colleagues at the Berlin trade fair last week. I particularly enjoyed the presentation given by Mr Daniels, which I thought was both amusing and informative.
We spoke briefly about the possibility of Kendos becoming the main civil works contractor in the Hang San project, and you mentioned that you would like to learn more about what we do and in particular our experience in this field. I am planning to be in Hong Kong at the end of the month, and I thought this might be an ideal opportunity for us to get together and discuss the project further.
I am enclosing details of previous projects which will give you some idea of our main achievements to date. Of course if you need any additional information please feel free to contact me. I very much look forward to hearing from you.

Yours sincerely

Harold Wittenstein
Managing Director
Enc: Past projects

Vokabeln

achievements	Ergebnisse
contractor	Auftragnehmer
enclose	beifügen
in particular	vor allem
previous	vorangegangen
to date	bis jetzt
trade fair	Handelsmesse

Infobox

Opening the letter

Dear Mr Smith	Sehr geehrter Herr Smith
Dear Ms Smith	Sehr geehrte Frau Smith
Dear Miss Smith (unusual)	Sehr geehrtes Fräulein Smith
Dear Mrs Smith	Sehr geehrte Frau Smith
Dear Sirs	Sehr geehrte Herren
Dear Mesdames	Sehr geehrte Damen
Dear Sirs/ Mesdames	Sehr geehrte Damen und Herren
Gentlemen (US)	Meine Herren
Dear David (familiar)	Lieber David

Übung 1:

Bringen Sie die Sätze in die richtige Reihenfolge!

1. send it to me by not later than 17 July.
2. HR department
3. Thank you for your cv and letter of 24 June,
4. I look forward to hearing from you.
5. in which you ask about possible employment as a computer programmer.
6. is currently looking for additional staff.
7. Dear Ms Jackson
8. Could you please fill in the enclosed application form and
9. Yours sincerely
10. I am pleased to inform you that the IT department
11. Harold Maudlin

Lösung: _____________________

Infobox

Complimentary Closing

Yours sincerely/ Sincerely yours/ Sincerely	Mit freundlichen Grüßen
Cordially yours	Herzlichst Ihr/Ihre
Yours faithfully	Hochachtungsvoll
With kindest regards	Mit herzlichen Grüßen
Best regards	Liebe Grüße (eher privat)
Kind regards	Liebe Grüße (eher privat)

Note that the ending you choose depends on the way you opened the letter.

Dear Mr/Ms/ Miss/Mrs Smith	Yours sincerely
Dear Sir/Madam Sirs/ Mesdames	Yours faithfully
Dear David	Best wishes

Übung 2:

Ordnen Sie folgende Vokabeln den entsprechenden Übersetzungen zu und kreuzen Sie die richtige Lösung an!

1. achievements	☐ Handelsmesse
2. previous	☐ Auftragnehmer
3. trade fair	☐ vor allem
4. in particular	☐ vorangegangen
5. enclose	☐ bis jetzt
6. to date	☐ beifügen
7. contractor	☐ Ergebnisse

Memos

Das Versenden schriftlicher Kurznachrichten innerhalb der Firma erfolgt heutzutage oft per E-Mail. In konservativen Firmen wird noch gerne auf Papier zurückgegriffen.

MEMORANDUM

To: KLT From: JC
Date: 7 July 2006 Ref: JC/26

Subj: Office parties / Computer security / Windows

1. We need to remind staff about company regulations regarding office parties. Obviously office parties are good for morale, but we seem to be having quite a few at the moment. Besides the lost production, I believe there are health and safety implications – some staff are clearly over the limit when they go back to work. Perhaps we can suggest that the parties be held after working hours, say from 4 pm?

2. I have noticed recently that members of staff are becoming lax about computer security. I saw three monitors with passwords written on post-it stickers, and we have had two cases of virus infection in the last month. In addition I have heard that some people have been making illegal copies of software to use at home.
Please can you remind department heads of their responsibilities.

3. Could you arrange for the windows in the reception area to be cleaned – I don't think they've been touched this year!

Vokabeln

department	Abteilung
emphasize	betonen
health and safety	Gesundheit und Sicherheit
indication	Hinweis
memorandum	Kurznachricht
over the limit	über das erlaubte Maß
password	Passwort
Ref (reference)	Aktenzeichen
regulation	Regelung
responsibility	Verantwortung
Subj (subject)	Betreff
virus	Virus (Computer)
working hours	Arbeitszeit

Übung 3:

Bilden Sie sinnvolle Paare.

1. health and safety	☐ stickers
2. over the	☐ infection
3. virus	☐ parties
4. illegal	☐ implications
5. reception	☐ heads
6. computer	☐ security
7. working	☐ copies
8. office	☐ limit
9. post-it	☐ hours
10. company	☐ regulations
11. department	☐ area

Übung 4:

Füllen Sie die Lücken mit den passenden Wörtern oder Wendungen aus dem vorangegangenen Text.

1. The police said that he was _________ _______.
2. The ___________ inspector said that the restaurant was disgusting.
3. Tell the visitors to meet me in the reception ___________.
4. Please remind staff that our ________ ________ are from 9 am to 5 pm.
5. Could you ___________ for the car to be available from 8 am.
6. In addition, I would like to _________ ________ that we change the company dress policy.
7. I have ___________ that absenteeism is getting worse.

Infobox

Dates

In America it is normal to write dates like this: month – day – year. In Britain the order is usually day – month – year. This can cause problems! 5/6/2006 is 6 May in America and 5 June in Britain. It's best to play safe and write out the month in full – 5 June 2006, or 6 May 2006.

Protokolle

Protokolle können verschieden abgefasst werden, aber sie sollten alle ein Ziel verfolgen: festhalten, was besprochen wurde, passiert ist oder getan werden soll. Detailliertere Protokolle enthalten außerdem den Fortgang der Diskussion und die einzelnen Beiträge der Teilnehmer. Der folgende Text ist das Protokoll einer Besprechung mit einem Kunden.

Minutes of meeting

Date: 17 July 2006 Place: Conference room
Time: 10 – 12 am
Present: John Travers, Kenneth Jameson, Margaret Johnson, Sandra Wittington, Laura Bentley, Simon Kantaga

1. Update on new production line
John outlined the current situation regarding the new production line. The conveyor belt is now operating, and various work stations are being installed. These are expected to be completed by July 23. The shelving units have not yet been delivered, but need to be assembled by July 25. John is to contact the suppliers to confirm dates.

2. Open day
Kenneth confirmed that planning for the open day on September 25 is going well. The programme of events is almost finalised, and will be distributed to all departments by July 30 for comments. Shuttle transport to and from Sanderson Street car park will be provided by Trivers Ltd. Children will be allowed to visit the main assembly hall, but only under adult supervision. Kenneth is to check whether current insurance policies need to be adjusted.

3. Training
Margaret outlined the new induction training programme which will go into effect from September 30. New members of staff will attend seminars on company history, product lines and customer relations, as well as department specific seminars. Computer training will be outsourced, and a short list of potential suppliers will be drawn up by July 31. Margaret and Kenneth are to confirm the supplier by August 10.

Vokabeln

absent	abwesend
adjusted	angepasst
comments	Kommentare
current	aktuell
distributed	verteilt
induction	Einführung
item, point	Punkt
minutes	Protokoll
present	anwesend
report on	berichten über

Übung 5:

Sind die Sätze richtig oder falsch? Kreuzen Sie die richtige Antwort an!

1. Many production lines use conveyor belts to ensure a smooth flow.

☐ richtig ☐ falsch

2. Employees normally receive induction training at the end of their stay with a company.

☐ richtig ☐ falsch

3. "Current" means the same as "actual".

☐ richtig ☐ falsch

4. Airport shuttle transport is often provided by hotels.

☐ richtig ☐ falsch

5. Components are normally assembled together to make a product.

☐ richtig ☐ falsch

6. "Minutes" is the same as "protocol".

☐ richtig ☐ falsch

7. Minutes are always written by a secretary.

☐ richtig ☐ falsch

Übung 6:

Finden Sie die Rechtschreibfehler und verbessern Sie!

Mr Thompson reported on the actual situation regarding the new assemble line; the convey belt had now been set up and was now undergoing tests. Kommentations and suggestions for improvements were being collected from all involved, and would be distribute to heads of departments by November 12. The new staff had already received their start training on company procedures, and would be give with safety equipment by November 16.

Wichtige Abkürzungen in der Korrespondenz

Das Verwenden von Abkürzungen ist in der Geschäftskorrespondenz üblich geworden. Besonders häufig werden sie in E-Mails gebraucht.

To: Jerry Kennworth
cc: Brenda Last, Miranda Comperson
Subj: Visit of Elnos Inc reps – 5 – 7 Oct

Hi Jerry

A quick note to let you know the latest:
1. The flight details have now been confirmed as follows:
BA 889 ETA London Heathrow 2045, Dep 1150.
Could you please arrange transport to / from the hotel as we discussed. I have already made the necessary reservations.

2. The group will now total 7, incl Sen Helen Jackson and Gov Michael Folloni. The Elnos party will consist of the CEO, Larry Landrosini, CFO, Jane Baker, CIO, Sam Talkways, and Sandra Betters and John Thomas from R&D.

3. Could you also produce a draft programme for the three days. I think we will need to show them some of the production lines eg housings, instrumentation, test bed, as well as the main assembly area. I suggest you speak to Jack Harrison re meals – he will need to make sure the visitors' rooms are available.

Thanks
Bill

PS Could you also send 7 copies of our visitor's pack to Elnos, FAO Whitney Garside (Mr Landrosini's PA).

Vokabeln

cc (carbon copy)	Durchschlag
CEO (chief executive officer)	Vorstandsvorsitzender
CFO (chief financial officer)	Finanzdirektor
CIO (chief information officer)	EDV-Direktor
Dep (departure)	Abfahrt
ETA (estimated time of arrival)	geschätzte Ankunftszeit
eg (for example)	zum Beispiel
FAO (for attention of)	zu Händen von
Gov (governor)	Direktor
Inc (incorporated)	eingetragen
incl (including)	einschließlich
PA (personal assistant)	persönlicher Assistent
PS (postscript)	Postskriptum
reps (representatives)	Vertreter
re (regarding)	hinsichtlich
R&D (research and development)	Forschung und Entwicklung (F & E)
Sen (senator)	Senator
Subj (subject)	Betreff

Infobox

Sometimes you may need to sign a letter on someone else's behalf. Here you can use "pp", which stands for "per procurationem".

Übung 7:

Verwenden Sie die gebräuchlichen Abkürzungen in der folgenden E-Mail:

Subject: Visitors

The Chief Executive Officer and Chief Information Officer will be visiting this branch next Monday. They will be accompanied by Governor Timbles and Senator Collins. Their estimated time of arrival will be 12:30; departure 16:00. Department heads are asked to submit suggestions for the afternoon programme, (including names of staff members present), to my personal assistant by no later than 14:00 on Thursday.

Kenneth Sambini, Branch Manager

Übung 8:

Füllen Sie die Lücken mit den entsprechenden Abkürzungen (dep, reps, re, R&D, CFO):

1. The flights details are as follows: Arr. 1615. _ _ _ _ _ 1720.
2. The _ _ _ _ _ will be interviewing all the new accountants this afternoon. They'll be his people after all.
3. I need to talk to you _ _ _ _ _ the Xmas party.
4. The _ _ _ _ _ from Better Cars will be arriving at 3:30.
5. The _ _ _ _ _ department is always asking for more money.

Ob es sich um die Bearbeitung des Posteingangs oder -ausgangs handelt, um den Empfang von Kunden, die Terminvereinbarung oder um verwaltungstechnische Aufgaben, eine gute Büroorganisation ist in der modernen Business-Welt das A und O.

Büroausstattung

Sebastian Ryan hat sich entschlossen, seine gut bezahlte Stellung in einer internationalen Firma aufzugeben und als Berater tätig zu werden. Er macht ein eigenes Büro auf und stellt eine Liste mit den wichtigsten Anschaffungen zusammen.

Sebastian had decided to divide his list into electronic equipment, furniture, and standard office supplies. He had already ordered a few items when he got a phone call from the owners of his building. They informed him that each and every item in his office must be certified environmentally-friendly.

Vokabeln

binders	Hefter
compatible	kompatibel
counter	Ladentisch
fax	Fax
file-card box	Karteikasten
filing cabinet	Aktenschrank
folder	Aktenmappe
hole puncher	Locher
ink cartridge	Tintenpatrone
notebook	Notizbuch
office supplies	Büromaterial
paperclips	Büroklammern
pocket calculator	Taschenrechner
photocopier	Kopiergerät
stapler	Tacker

He thought it was great policy, but it left him with a few difficulties to sort out!

Firstly he had to not only return the paint he had bought, but also call all the suppliers and check that the equipment he had ordered fitted the new criteria. The light fixtures were fine, and he was able to locate some energy efficient light bulbs.

He then bought a telephone system that included a fax and was compatible with all high-speed Internet lines. Next on the list was a new photocopier with a good supply of paper and toner; hopefully it would never jam! The computer and monitor he had ordered the week before were already acceptable so he only had to change the printer. He found one which used a state-of-the-art ink cartridge, colour and black and white. He was unsure how to resolve the furniture dilemma until he learned of a company that produced counters, shelves, cupboards and filing cabinets all made out of recycled plastics such as yoghurt containers. He had to choose from several designs and managed to find a colour-coordinated package for the whole office. The company also knew of an environmentally-friendly dishwasher for sale. As for the furniture, he put in an order for 2 ergonomically designed computer chairs and 3 arm-chairs for the reception area. Then he moved on to the personalized station-ary, binders, folders, paperclips, hole puncher, and staplers.

Übung 1:

Welcher Begriff gehört nicht dazu?
Erklären Sie warum?

1. a) paperclips b) binders c) staples d) personalized stationary e) filing cabinets

____

2. a) folders b) filing cabinets c) cupboards d) shelves e) armchairs

____

3. a) jam b) switch c) ordinance d) copy paper e) toner

____

4. a) monitor b) dilemma c) ink cartridge d) state of the art e) printer

____

5. a) environmentally-friendly b) ergonomically designed c) reception area d) state of the art e) compatible with

____

6. a) light fixtures b) yoghurt containers c) dishwasher d) paint e) light bulbs

____

Übung 2:

Sind die Sätze richtig oder falsch?

1. The original light fixtures were not delivered.

☐ richtig ☐ falsch

2. He had ordered all the equipment when the phone rang.

☐ richtig ☐ falsch

3. Sebastian became a consultant before he left his job.

☐ richtig ☐ falsch

4. He had to reorder his computer.

☐ richtig ☐ falsch

5. He purchased a second-hand photocopier.

☐ richtig ☐ falsch

6. His furniture was made of wood.

☐ richtig ☐ falsch

7. He bought 5 chairs in all.

☐ richtig ☐ falsch

Übung 3:

Füllen Sie die Lücken in dem folgenden Telefonat!

A Hi Jennifer. Listen. I've just (1.) ______ the stuff for your new office.

B Great. Did you get everything?

A Not quite. You'll have to do your own dishes for a while. The (2.) __________ will be delivered some time next month.

B Ok.

A And they only had blue filling (3). _____ _______ I'm afraid. But at least they'll be large enough for all your (4) _____.

Empfang und Sekretariat

Eine der Aufgaben von Empfangssekretären ist, Kunden und Besuchern Termine mit den gewünschten Gesprächspartnern zu vermitteln. Bei der Terminabsprache gibt es bestimmte sprachliche Muster, die zu beachten sind …

Receptionist: Rotters, good morning. How may I be of help?

Caller: Hello, this is Martin Gray from Conys in San Francisco.

Receptionist: Hello, Mr Gray. Would you like to speak with Mr Avery?

Caller: Actually, yes.

Receptionist: One moment and I'll put you through.

Caller: Thank you.

Receptionist: Mr Gray, I apologize but his line is engaged at the moment. Would you like to leave a message?

Caller: That is rather unfortunate. I am in Honolulu for the week and was wondering if I could meet with him to discuss the new tender.

Receptionist: Oh, how nice. Welcome to Honolulu. I am certain that he would want to schedule an appointment. Shall I put you through to his secretary?

Caller: Thank you.

Secretary: Hello, Mr Gray. This is Cassandra speaking. How are you?

Caller: Hello Cassandra, very well, thanks. And yourself?

Secretary: Fine, thank you. How may I help you today?

Caller: I am interested in seeing Mr Avery for a few hours this week. Could you assist me on this matter?

Secretary: Yes, I am looking at his appointment book and unfortunately it looks rather full. I understand you are only here for a week, is that correct?

Caller: Yes. I could come at any time other than Tuesday from 10:30 to 3:00.

Secretary: How about Thursday at 7:30 in the morning?

Caller: Hmm, that is not ideal for me, but is that the only time he has free?

Secretary: Yes, except for today at lunch time.

Caller: Well, I could manage to be there by 12:30. Is that too late?

Secretary: No, in fact that would be a bit early for him. Why don't you come at 12:30 and you can have a coffee while you wait.

Caller: Thank you for your time.

Secretary: You're welcome. Goodbye.

Caller: Goodbye.

Later that day at the reception desk.

Mr Gray: Hello, I believe we spoke on the phone this morning, I am Martin ...

Receptionist: Mr Gray, of course! It is nice to finally meet you. How has your visit been so far?

Mr Gray: Excellent. It is so beautiful here that it is hard to get my work done.

Receptionist: I can understand that. Could I offer you something to drink while you wait?

Mr Gray: An espresso would be nice if it is no trouble.

Receptionist: No trouble at all. I'll just be a moment. Have a seat on the terrace if you like.

Mr Gray: I will, thank you.

Vokabeln

appointment	Termin
appointment book	Terminkalender
assist	assistieren
busy	beschäftigt
cancel	ausfallen lassen
engaged	besetzt
manage	schaffen
receptionist	Empfangssekretär(in)
postpone	verschieben
schedule	planen, ansetzen
secretary	Sekretär(in)

Infobox

One would note meetings, for example, in an appointment book in US American English and in a diary in British English. In the USA and in the UK writing in a diary implies keeping a daily journal of your personal thoughts and experiences. A calendar normally hangs on the wall.

Übung 4:

Finden Sie für die vorgegebenen Wörter die Entsprechungen im Text.

1. busy ________________
2. should ________________
3. able ________________
4. help ________________
5. quite a bit ________________

Übung 5:

Bringen Sie die Wörter in die richtige Reihenfolge.

1. time Thank your you for

_ _

2. help be may I of? How

_ _

3. appointment I that want he certain would schedule to an am

_ _

_ _

4. assist you matter? me Could this on

_ _

5. I spoke on morning the phone believe we this

_ _

6. this through you Shall I put secretary to

_ _

7. but the that is not time me, is Hmm, for he ideal free? only that has

_ _

_ _

8. I correct? for a you only here are, is that understand week

_ _

_ _

Übung 6:

Vervollständigen Sie die Sätze.

1. _ _ _ _ _ _ you _ _ _ _ _ _ to have a seat?
2. _ _ _ _ _ _ I take your coat?
3. Will you be _ _ _ _ _ _ at the Hilton?
4. _ _ _ _ _ _ is it _ _ _ _ _ _ for you to come?
5. Can you _ _ _ _ _ _ to make it at 3:00?
6. Monday is not _ _ _ _ _ _ for us.
7. _ _ _ _ _ _ me this way, please.

Übung 7:

Finden Sie die korrekten Formulierungen:

1. It me, Troy.

_ _

2. I will not get up that early to meet her!

_ _

3. I must see him today!

_ _

4. He has been chattering on the phone all morning.

_ _

_ _

5. You have to sit and wait.

_ _

6. Get me a tea.

_ _

Posteingang und -ausgang

Ein neuer Büroangestellter wird in seinen Aufgabenbereich eingeführt.

Good morning, Henry, I am pleased to welcome you to Gabbletry. We are happy to have you on board. We should begin because we have many points to cover. First, we will discuss your responsibilities with the mail. The volume of incoming and outgoing mail per day may be surprising to some of you, at first. We deal with around 2000 letters a day.

Now, the following process is very important, so please pay attention. The mail is delivered between 10:00 and 11:00 daily. It is to be stamped with the time and date of arrival and then sorted. Then it is to be placed in the pigeonholes for each department. If you have a large delivery for any one department arrange for the runners to pick it up immediately. It is essential that this task be performed carefully. A deal could be lost with just one misplaced package.

Now, for the outgoing mail. You are required to weigh and add postage to each item. This must be finished by 3:30 pm each day. There will be another delivery at that time and you are to follow the aforementioned procedure.

The internal post, or house mail, is rather simple. You are to deliver any envelopes or packages twice a day. If there is an item for a different branch in the city, it must be placed in this crate and will be picked up at 5:00 pm daily.

This is a general overview, so when questions arise don't hesitate to phone me at extension 4332.

Vokabeln

arise	sich ergeben
delivery	Zustellung
envelope	Briefumschlag
house mail	Hauspost
internal post	interne Post
incoming mail	Posteingang
outgoing mail	Postausgang
package	Paket
pigeonholes	Fächer
postage	Porto
registered mail	Einschreiben
sort	sortieren
weigh	wiegen

Übung 8:

Ordnen Sie zu!

1. incoming mail	☐ Fach
2. arise	☐ sich ergeben
3. package	☐ wiegen

4. delivery	☐ Posteingang
5. internal	☐ Postausgang
6. outgoing mail	☐ Paket
7. pigeonhole	☐ Zustellung
8. weigh	☐ intern

Übung 9:
Formulieren Sie die Sätze im Passiv.

1. We must pay the postage.

_ _

2. They should lower the rates.

_ _

3. You should pick up the parcels today.

_ _

4. Heather weighs the outgoing mail.

_ _

5. Jerome will stuff the envelopes.

_ _

6. They have finished their task.

_ _

7. When will they install the pigeonholes?

_ _

Übung 10:
Welche Wörter gehören in die Lücken?

Before you are able to leave today, you must (1.) _ _ _ _ _ the incoming mail. It must be (2.) _ _ _ _ _ in the (3.) _ _ _ _ _ by 6:00 pm. Once that has (4.) _ _ _ _ , you must contact headquarters and report that the (5.) _ _ _ _ has been (6.) _ _ _ _ _ late four consecutive days. Find out how such a problem could (7.) _ _ _ _ _ at the end of the fiscal year. We need the (8.) _ _ _ _ _!

Datenbankverwaltung, Krankmeldung und Urlaubsanträge

Im folgenden Ausschnitt unterhalten sich zwei Angestellte einer großen Firma darüber, wie Urlaubstage und Krankmeldungen korrekt in die Datenbank eingegeben werden sollen.

Wes: Hi Winston. Well, I have been reading up on the database but I still would like to take you up on your offer to give me some pointers.
Winston: Ok, why don't we work through the sick-leave, paid and unpaid vacation updates together.
Wes: I understand the mail merge process necessary for coordinating the letters and the envelopes. So, this new information would be helpful.
Winston: First, we take the forms filled out for those out sick and take the

letters from the doctors and enter the dates of absences. Then we're able to inform the necessary people when someone is over the allotted number of sick days. Then we can send that information to the payroll department. Now, these databases must be updated regularly. The laws here are very strict about how many hours of overtime one can acquire before the year comes to an end. This program monitors each employee's absences, discerns if an excuse is valid and if the correct number of vacation days were taken.

Vokabeln

absence	Abwesenheit
accurate	akkurat
allotted	zugewiesen
database	Datenbank
excuse	Entschuldigung
overtime	Überstunden
sick-leave	krankgeschrieben
valid	gültig

Übung 11:

Bilden Sie sinnvolle Paare.

1. to give some	☐ number of
2. valid	☐ excuse
3. fill out	☐ forms
4. allotted	☐ pointers
5. work	☐ through
6. comes to	☐ an end

Übung 12:

Füllen Sie die Lücken mit passenden Wörtern aus dem Text.

1. Please update your files to make sure they are _ _ _ _ _.
2. We had to work _ _ _ _ _ today, I am so tired!
3. The project leader said there would be no _ _ _ _ _ accepted for missed deadlines.
4. Were you out on _ _ _ _ _ yesterday?
5. They only _ _ _ _ _ twenty tickets for the concert.
6. You must have a _ _ _ _ _ passport to enter!
7. You are required to fill out forms before you go on _ _ _ _ _.

Übung 13:

Sind die Sätze richtig oder falsch?

1. Databanks must be regularly maintained.

☐ richtig ☐ falsch

2. Overtime is welcomed in all societies.

☐ richtig ☐ falsch

3. Mail merge requires hand addressing of letters.

☐ richtig ☐ falsch

In der heutigen Geschäftswelt werden Besprechungen und Konferenzen immer wichtiger. Dabei finden sie im Zuge der Globalisierung immer häufiger auf Englisch statt. Ist man mit den notwendigen Redemitteln vertraut, lassen sie sich auch auf Englisch problemlos meistern.

Die Tagesordnung

Eine gut durchdachte Tagesordnung und eine optimale Vorbereitung helfen dabei, die Besprechung effektiv zu gestalten und sie zu einem Erfolg werden zu lassen ...

Peter: David, can you come in here for a moment, please?
David: What can I do for you, Peter?
Peter: Our monthly meeting with the steering committee is next Monday. Have you prepared the agenda for circulation yet?
David: Um. No. I've had all these other things to do, and I thought writing an agenda for this meeting would be last on the priority list. You know how these meetings run.

Vokabeln

accomplish	erreichen
agenda	Tagesordnung
allocate	zuteilen
circulation	Verteilung
keep everybody on track	jeden in der Spur halten
pay attention	auf etwas achten
steering committee	Lenkungsausschuss
timeframe	Zeitrahmen

Peter: Yes, I know exactly how these meetings run, and that's why we need an agenda. It'll be easier to keep everybody on track, if they know beforehand what we need to accomplish, and we need to consider what we need to do to be properly prepared.
David: Yeah, ok. I'll write it now.
Peter: And please be sure to allocate time for each item on the agenda. Also pay particular attention to the order. We should be able to create a fairly logical sequence which will also help us to achieve the goals of the meeting.
David: You think that'll work?
Peter: Absolutely. It's the only chance we have of making sure we don't spend all night talking about unnecessary things. If everybody knows the timeframe for each item, and if the goals of the meeting are clear, then maybe we can avoid some of the problems we had last time.
David: Ok. I will prepare and bring it in for you to look at right away.
Peter: Thanks.

Infobox

A typical agenda has the following items:
- Name of the chair and the recorder.
- Follow-up points from the last meeting.
- Objectives of the meeting.
- The actual items themselves, together with the time allocated for each item, and the presenter.
- Attendees.

Übung 1:
Wie lauten die Sätze richtig?

1. David, for you come moment in can a here, please?

_ _

2. Have circulation prepared the for yet agenda you?

_ _

3. It'll everybody on easier keep be track to.

_ _

4. Also order particular to pay the attention.

_ _

5. Think you work that'll?

_ _

Übung 2:
Schreiben Sie besser!

1. Do you prepare the agenda for circulation yet?

_ _

2. It'll be easier to hold everybody on track.

_ _

3. Yeah, ok. I'm writing it now.

_ _

4. I prepare and bring it in for you to look at right away.

_ _

5. A typical agenda is having the following items.

_ _

Besprechungen leiten

Wer Besprechungen erfolgreich leiten und die angestrebten Ziele erreichen will, sollte neben festem Zeitplan und straffer Tagesordnung auch ein angenehmes Gesprächsklima im Auge behalten.

The person who chairs a meeting has the most important, and perhaps most difficult, job in the room. He/she is responsible for the meeting's success. Hopefully every participant will have an agenda, and a clear picture as to what has to be achieved during the meeting. The leader must then control the meeting, and ensure that everybody sticks to the agenda. A clear structure of the

meeting has to be given, so that all the participants know at which item they are, what is to be discussed, and the goal of the particular item.
At the same time, the chair should be aware of the time allocated to each item, and to keep the discussion on track he/she should insist that the time given for each item be observed. This is of course part of the preparation for the meeting; sufficient time for each item has to be given. The chairperson has to control the participants, and remember that he/she is dealing with the human element. Fiery discussions can lead to disgruntled participants. Interruptions must be handled in a way that all participants have a chance to get their ideas across.
The minutes must also be taken by one of the participants, and after the meeting sent to each participant. The minutes should include what actions have been decided upon in the meeting, and who is responsible for each action.

Vokabeln

chair	leiten
chairperson	Leiter(in), Vorsitzende(r)
disgruntled	unbefriedigt
ensure	darauf achten
insist	insistieren
interruption	Unterbrechungen
minutes	Protokoll
the human element	menschliches Element

Infobox

It is often difficult for the chairperson of a meeting to be totally unbiased, because of his/her position in relation to the other participants. The time spent by company employees in meetings is also increasing. Therefore many companies are looking for alternative methods to run meetings. One possible answer is the use of a moderator, who can be an impartial member of the meeting or even a professional external moderator.

Übung 3:

Formulieren Sie die Sätze im Passiv!

1. What do the participants have to achieve in the meeting?

_ _

2. The meeting organiser has to give a clear structure of the meeting.

_ _

3. The chair must give sufficient time to each item on the agenda.

_ _

4. One of the participants takes the minutes of the meeting.

_ _

5. Sometimes, companies use professional external moderators.

_ _

Übung 4:
Übersetzen Sie und enträtseln Sie das Lösungswort!

1. Protokoll, 2. Unterbrechung, 3. unbefriedigt, 4. ausreichend, 5. leiten, 6. zuteilen, 7. insistieren, 8. erreichen, 9. darauf achten

1. ☐ _ _ _ _ _ _

2. _ _ _ _ _ _ _ _ _ _ _ ☐ _

3. ☐ _ _ _ _ _ _ _ _ _ _ _

4. _ _ _ _ _ _ _ _ ☐ _ _

5. _ _ _ _ _ ☐

6. ☐ _ _ _ _ _ _ _ _

7. _ _ _ _ _ _ ☐

8. _ _ _ _ ☐ _ _ _ _ _ _ _

9. _ _ _ _ _ ☐ _

Mystery Word ☐ ☐ ☐ ☐ ☐ ☐ ☐ ☐ ☐

Übung 5:
Ergänzen Sie mit Wörtern aus dem Text.

1. The leader must then control the meeting, and ensure that everybody sticks _ _ _ _ _ _ _ _ _ _ _ _ the agenda.

2. The meeting must be structured, so that all the participants know _ _ _ _ which item they are.

3. All participants must be able to get their ideas _ _ _ _ _ _ _ _ _ _ _ .

4. The human _ _ _ _ _ _ _ _ _ _ _ plays a big part in most meetings.

5. Every participant needs a clear _ _ _ _ _ _ _ _ _ _ as to what should be achieved.

6. The time _ _ _ _ _ _ _ _ _ _ _ by company employees in meetings is also increasing.

7. Many companies are looking for alternative methods to _ _ _ _ _ _ _ _ _ _ _ meetings.

Argumente und Kompromisse

Effiziente Geschäftsgespräche setzen voraus, dass Standpunkte klar und verständlich vertreten, Überzeugungen zum Ausdruck gebracht, aber auch Kompromisse vorgeschlagen und Gegenbedingungen aufgestellt werden.

Customer: Would you be able to deliver the goods by the end of each week?
Supplier: That's out of the question, I'm afraid. We would have to keep such large stocks that we couldn't afford the costs.
Customer: It's very important for us. You do realise that our customers are always demanding quicker and quicker delivery. What delivery time could you agree to?
Supplier: With the current orders you place with us, we can't do better than

once a month. If you increase the orders, then perhaps we could consider a faster delivery date.

Customer: Unfortunately that won't be possible.

Supplier: Then perhaps you could take on some of the costs. I hope you agree that we have always met your demands, and we would certainly like to maintain the relationship.

Customer: But higher costs?

Supplier: In my opinion, it's not unreasonable to ask that at least for the initial stages, you accept a slightly higher price. We would then have time to work out another solution.

Customer: Yes, that's fair enough. But this price increase is only short term!

Supplier: Yes, of course. When we have found another solution, the price will return to normal.

Vokabeln

agree	annehmen
convince	überzeugen
demand	Forderung
I'm afraid	ich befürchte
increase	vergrößern
in my opinion	meiner Meinung nach
maintain	fortsetzen
negotiate	verhandeln
outcome	Ergebnis
position	Standpunkt
price increase	Preiserhöhung
solution	Lösung, Einigung
take on	übernehmen

Infobox

The ability to negotiate solutions is crucial in today's business world. In the case of conflict, partners have to be able to present their arguments, and convince the other of their position. The best outcome is one where both parties are satisfied with the result. To achieve this, both parties should know the interests of the other, and try to reach a settlement which is optimal for both sides. This will lead to long and rewarding business partnerships.

Übung 6:

Ordnen Sie die Übersetzungen zu!

1. outcome	☐ überzeugen
2. take on	☐ verhandeln
3. convince	☐ fortsetzen
4. increase	☐ Ergebnis
5. optimal	☐ vergrößern
6. negotiate	☐ optimal
7. maintain	☐ übernehmen

Übung 7:

Übersetzen Sie folgende Sätze:

1. Ich bin der Meinung, dass Sie auch einen etwas höheren Preis akzeptieren können.

____

2. Ich habe den Eindruck, dass Sie unsere Beziehung gerne fortsetzen würden.

____

3. Die Fähigkeit, Lösungen herbeizuführen, ist entscheidend.

_ _

4. Wenn wir eine andere Lösung gefunden haben, wird der Preis wieder seine alte Höhe erreichen.

_ _

_ _

5. Konfliktparteien versuchen, die anderen von ihrer Position zu überzeugen.

_ _

_ _

6. Vielleicht könnten Sie einige der Kosten übernehmen?

_ _

Übung 8:

Finden Sie für die vorgegebenen Wörter die Entsprechungen im Text.

1. persuade _ _ _ _ _ _ _ _ _ _ _ _ _ _ _
2. merchandise _ _ _ _ _ _ _ _ _ _ _ _ _ _ _
3. think about _ _ _ _ _ _ _ _ _ _ _ _ _ _ _
4. best (solution) _ _ _ _ _ _ _ _ _ _ _ _ _ _ _
5. in my view _ _ _ _ _ _ _ _ _ _ _ _ _ _ _
6. keep _ _ _ _ _ _ _ _ _ _ _ _ _ _ _
7. result _ _ _ _ _ _ _ _ _ _ _ _ _ _ _

Zusammenfassen und Schließen der Besprechung

Es liegt in der Verantwortung des Vorsitzenden sicherzustellen, dass alle Teilnehmer nach der Besprechung sich klar darüber sind, was erreicht wurde und was noch getan werden muss. Es folgen zwei Zusammenfassungen, die die Gesprächsergebnisse bei den Teilnehmern sichern sollen.

So that's it for today. Before we disappear I'd just like to go over the decisions reached if I may. We have agreed that this project must be finished by the end of year. We have also agreed the budget and the time-scale for the various parts. Sally will provide us with a list of the computing requirements we need. Tom and his team will research the market, and report his findings to us at the next meeting. So, if everybody agrees, I'd like to wrap up the meeting at this point. Thank you all for coming. I´m grateful for your input. And let's keep each other informed as to our progress. We´ll see each other at the next meeting.

If there are no other points, I think that brings us to the end of the meeting. If I could just summarise the main points that we´ve covered. We are all now agreed that the marketing strategy proposed by The Clever Company is the most suitable. We decided that Christmas will be the best time to start. The accounting department will present to us our projected earnings and the effect on our accounts. And finally, the research department will keep us updated as the progress of the next release. If there is nothing more, I would like to thank you all for your participation. You will all receive a copy of the minutes by Friday. As I said at the start, I would like to ask you for your comments on the effectiveness of this meeting. Perhaps after reading the minutes, you can get back to me. And please contact me if you have any further questions or comments.

Vokabeln

alternatively	Eine andere Möglichkeit ist ...
budget	Budget, Etat
compromise	Kompromiss
crucial	wesentlich, entscheidend
decision	Entschluss
earnings	Ertrag
go over	besprechen
item	Tagesordnungspunkt
project	projizieren (hier: vorausplanen)
report findings	Ergebnisse/Befunde berichten
summarise	zusammenfassen
wrap up	beenden (wörtlich: einpacken)

Infobox

Many meetings in English start and/or end with a period of small talk. As people wait for every participant to arrive, they might discuss non-business related topics with each other. Alternatively, at the end of the meeting some people may remain to talk with colleagues and business partners who they have not seen for a while. This small talk is a crucial part of the business relationship for many native English speakers.

Übung 9:

Bringen Sie die Wörter in folgenden Sätzen in die richtige Reihenfolge.

1. If we´ve I just main covered summarise could points that the.

_ _

_ _

2. I decisions go to like today the over would reached.

_ _

_ _

3. Thank for you coming all.

_ _

4. You Friday all the will a minutes copy of receive by.

_ _

_ _

5. I like to ask you on the effectiveness would of this meeting for your comments.

_ _

_ _

6. That's today for it.

_ _

7. Many English with a in start period of small meetings talk.

_ _

_ _

Übung 10:

Füllen Sie die Lücken in folgenden Sätzen mit den passenden Vokabeln aus dem Text.

Before and after many meetings, the participants may engage in (1.) _ _ _ _ _ _ _ _ _ _ _. This is a (2.) _ _ _ _ _ _ _ _ _ _ _ part of many English meetings.

At the end the (3.) _ _ _ _ _ _ _ _ _ _ _ of the meeting will (4.) _ _ _ _ _ _ _ _ _ _ _ the main points of the meeting. He/she will (5.) _ _ _ _ _ _ _ _ _ _ the main points discussed, and after the meeting a copy of the (6.) _ _ _ _ _ _ _ _ _ _ will be sent to each participant.

Übung 11:

Vervollständigen Sie die Sätze!

1. So, I'd like to wrap up the meeting _ _ _ _ _ _ _ _ _ _ this point.
2. We'll see each other _ _ _ _ _ _ _ _ _ _ _ the next meeting.
3. I'm _ _ _ _ _ _ _ _ _ _ _ for your input.
4. Let me _ _ _ _ _ _ _ _ _ _ _ over the decisions reached today.
5. I would like to _ _ _ _ _ _ _ _ _ _ _ the points discussed today.
6. Please _ _ _ _ _ _ _ _ _ _ _ me if you have any further questions or comments.
7. This small talk is a _ _ _ _ _ _ _ _ _ _ _ part of the business relationship for many native English speakers.

Infobox

In France and Italy, some conference participants may feel less bound by the discipline of a meeting than others. They may leave a meeting to make phone calls or attend paperwork if the discussion is not directly relevant to them.
In the UK it is not acceptable to leave a meeting half-way through.

Präsentationen in einer Fremdsprache zu halten ist eine große Herausforderung. Damit einem nicht die passenden Worte fehlen, sollten Präsentationen gut vorbereitet sein und bestimmten Grundsätzen folgen.

Präsentationsmedien

Wer eine Präsentation organisiert, muss sich zunächst um die notwendigen Präsentationsmedien kümmern ...

Clair: Hi Andrew. How are you?

Andrew: Hello, Clair. I'm fine. I am glad I ran into you. Do you have time to tell me exactly what equipment you will need for your presentation? The hotel has asked me to send them a list so they can begin setting up the rooms.

Clair: Actually, I would like to know what equipment they normally provide in the conference rooms.

Andrew: Makes sense. I'll just get the list out. Yes, they'll provide the standard gear: podium, flip chart and whiteboard.

Clair: Good, but do they mention dry-erase markers for the whiteboard and presentation markers for the flip chart?

Andrew: I'll ask them. Now, on to more technical devices, will you require a slide projector or an OHP?

Clair: An OHP please! I've got lots of nice OHTs to show.

Andrew: And do you need any erasable or permanent markers for those?

Clair: Er no. I'll take my own.

Andrew: They also offer DVD players and VCRs, or video recorders, if you want.

Clair: No, I'll be taking my laptop so I'll need a multimedia projector and a laser pointer.

Andrew: Ok. Good. Hopefully everything will be there when you arrive.

Clair: I hope so. Oh, Andrew, could you also ask them to check and see that all of the extension cords and outlets are functioning properly. I would hate to go through that again!

Andrew: Of course! Last time was a disaster.

Vokabeln

DVD player	DVD-Spieler
extension cord	Verlängerungskabel
flip chart	Flipchart
laser pointer	Laserzeiger
multimedia projector	Beamer
OHT (Overhead transparency)	Folie
outlet	Steckdose
overhead projector	Tageslichtprojektor
podium	Podium
presentation markers	Stifte für Flipcharts
slide projector	Diaprojektor
video recorder	Videorekorder
white board	Whiteboard

6 Präsentationen, Vorträge und Referate

Infobox

The term Beamer is well known in English, but as a slang term for a BMW and not for a multimedia projector. This could cause confusion if you asked to have a car available for your presentation!

Übung 1:

Ordnen Sie den folgenden Kategorien Wörter aus dem Text zu.

1. writing utensils:

____

2. places to write:

____

3. machines used to present information:

____

4. electrical components:

____

5. items to help the audience follow the presentation:

____

Übung 2:

Entnehmen Sie dem Gespräch Verben, die ähnliche Bedeutungen haben.

to need:

1. ________________________

2. ________________________

3. ________________________

to make available:

4. ________________________

5. ________________________

6 ________________________

Übung 3:

Welche der oben benutzten Phrasen bedeutet dasselbe wie:

1. to accidentally see someone

____

2. to examine/test something

____

3. to be reliable, trustworthy

____

4. to experience

____

5. to tell someone something

____

6. to prepare a room/equipment

____

Übung 4:

Das Gespräch hat Ihnen gezeigt, wie Sie die folgenden Sätze höflicher sagen können. Finden Sie die Entsprechungen.

1. Just wait! __________________

2. Stop what you are doing and give me some facts! ______________________

3. Huh? What did you call that thing? ____

____

4. You have to tell me ... ___________

5. They have to give me ... __________

6. Do you like ... _______________

Eine Präsentation beginnen

Beim Präsentationsbeginn gibt es eine bestimmte Struktur, die eine Englisch sprechende Zuhörerschaft erwartet. Lesen Sie die folgende Einleitung einer Präsentation und beachten Sie die notwendigen Phasen: Begrüßung, Vorstellung der eigenen Person, Einführung in das Thema, Erläuterung zum Ablauf.

Good Morning! I hope everyone has refilled their coffee cups but if not, I intend to provide you with some information that will get your blood flowing. I would like to introduce myself to those of you who might not already know me. My name is Bradley Marra and I have been with Checktilers Ltd for a bit over 3 years. I was hired to help ensure the successful unification of Checkers and Tilers. However, I know most of you are familiar with the many unforeseen difficulties we have had during our recent merger. Therefore, this morning I would like to discuss three main points with you, the last of which will disclose the inspiring news I have for you today. First, I'd like to run through the annual report from Checktilers Ltd's first year. Then I will select some vital statistics from year one to compare with the corresponding figures from year two. And finally, after analyzing the annual report from our third year together since the merger, I'd like to report some exciting news based on some key figures from the profit and loss statement. There will be a question/answer session following my talk. So, if you could hold all questions, other than brief clarification questions, until the end, I would greatly appreciate it. There will then be a short reception on the terrace to commemorate your triumphant efforts.

Vokabeln

annual report	Jahresbericht
clarification	Klarstellung
compare with	vergleichen mit
disclose	bekannt geben
inspiring	ermutigend
loss	Verlust
merger	Fusion
statistics	Statistik, Statistiken
profit	Gewinn, Profit, Erlös
triumphant	triumphierend
unforeseen	unerwartet

Übung 5:
Setzen Sie die richtige Verbform in die Lücke und kreisen Sie „for" oder „since" ein, so dass ein richtiger Satz entsteht.

1. Bradley Marra _ _ _ _ _ (work) for Checktilers Ltd since / for three years.

2. Checktilers Ltd _ _ _ _ _ only _ _ _ _ _ (exist) since / for a few years.

3. Marra _ _ _ _ _ (employed) by Checktilers Ltd since / for the merger began.

Übung 6:
Lesen Sie nochmals die Einleitung der Präsentation. Bringen Sie dann die folgenden Sätze in die richtige Reihenfolge.

1. Tell the audience when to ask questions.

2. Introduce and give a brief history of yourself.

3. Greet your audience and possibly tell a short joke.

4. Introduce your topic.

5. Announce your main points in order of appearance.

Lösung: _

Übung 7:
Finden Sie die richtige Definition und kreuzen Sie an:

1. corresponding

a) agreeing with

b) opposite

c) to answer

2. compare

a) copy

b) to examine likenesses or differences

c) to choose

3. disclose

a) keep secret

b) announce

c) shut

4. inspiring

a) depressing

b) motivating and amazing

c) interesting

Interesse wecken und halten

Es gibt viele Wege, Interesse zu wecken und zu halten. Wer eine gute Rede halten will, sollte sich zunächst einmal selbst in die Rolle des Zuhörers versetzen. Ist die Rede wirklich adressatengerecht? Oder stellt sie nur die Persönlichkeit des Redners zu stark in den Mittelpunkt?

So, I would like to begin with the first point I mentioned in the introduction. The historical background of the Circle program has brought us the success we are currently enjoying. The Circle program was conceived in 1973. It was born after the founders managed, but just barely, to evade succumbing to bankruptcy. They held a company-wide weekend gathering at a nearby lake. The

members of the company were encouraged to come to the retreat to offer their personal input on how to preserve the existence of their company. They arrived to find a whiteboard consisting of a chart with rows and columns listing the times for the weekend's workshop sessions. There were no names and no topics listed! How did they fill these spaces? Easy. By asking for volunteers, by handing out blank sheets of paper and pens, and by showing pie charts demonstrating the plunge in departmental motivation. Risky? Maybe, however, these actions proudly lead us to my next point. Survival. Evolution of the information flow from top-down to The Circle, which we maintain today, can be attributed to the end-product of the workshop. Now, I would ask each of you to draw a circle on your handout.
Now pass your circle to another person. And what do you see, Sir? "A circle." Obviously. Neither a beginning, nor an end. The Circle program operates on this simple principle. Each and every employee of this company, each of you, is required to turn in a minimum of one anonymous Circle per quarter. The Circle can be filled in with as many or as few suggestions, grievances, comments, rumours, fears, successes, diagrams ... All input is welcomed, or should I say required to preserve the Circle. Summaries of the information garnered is published in The Circle Newsletter and inevitably incorporated into company policy. Now, I will move on to the final and most inspiring part of my presentation to report on the developments since that fateful weekend. If I could draw your attention to this slide, you will see that profits began to fluctuate slightly then shot up in 1977. As we speak they are higher, more consistent, and climbing more rapidly than ever before. Need I say more?

Vokabeln

attribute to	jdm etw zuschreiben
bankrupt	bankrott
bankruptcy	Konkurs
chart	Diagramm, Schaubild
column	Spalte
company policy	Unternehmenspolitik
demonstrate	zeigen
development	Entwicklung
fluctuate	fluktuieren
pie chart	Kreisdiagramm
plunge	Sturz
quarter	Vierteljahr
row	Zeile
shoot up	hochschnellen
slide	Dia
succumb	erliegen

6 Präsentationen, Vorträge und Referate

Infobox

Some tips for presenters
Pronunciation can make or break you. Practice difficult words often. Once you are confident with pronunciation, begin developing your ability to control the pace, how fast or slowly you speak. Add pauses after a main point to allow your audience time to ponder or take notes. Remember to enunciate clearly, no mumbling! Try taping your presentation and listen carefully for areas to improve.

Übung 8:

Welches Wort aus dem Text ist hier jeweils gemeint?

1. give credit to someone for the work they have done

_ _

_ _

2. the process and results of change

_ _

3. to show

_ _

4. close to

_ _

5. to give into

_ _

6. a three month period in a year

_ _

Übung 9:

Füllen Sie die Lücken in folgenden Sätzen mit den passenden Vokabeln aus dem Text.

1. A _ _ _ _ _ _ _ _ _ is round and shows percentages in pieces.

2. The CEO was furious after sales _ _ _ _ _ _ _ _.

3. Trends rise quickly and sharply when they _ _ _ _ _ _ _ _.

4. It can be stressful for shareholders when their shares' values _ _ _ _ _ _ _ _ randomly.

5. Any variety of _ _ _ _ _ _ _ _ can be placed on the table and examined by the group. They can see the horizontal _ _ _ _ _ _ _ _ _ and the vertical _ _ _ _ _ _ _ _ _.

Übung 10:

Beantworten Sie die folgenden Fragen, um einige Präsentationstaktiken, die im Text vorkamen, zu wiederholen.

1. List the three expressions that announce the presenter is changing to the next topic.

a) _

b) _

c) _

2. How does the speaker engage the audience? Why?

_ _.

3. Find the question to which the presenter awaits no answer from the audience.

________________________? Easy.

4. Fill in the three answers the speaker provides to his redundant question in question three.

a) By ____________, b) by __________, c) and by __________________.

5. Which single words are used for emphasis?

a) _________________________

b) _________________________

c) _________________________

6. How is status of the current profits described?

a) ________, b) ________,

c) ________ then d) ________.

7. Why does the presentation end with the question "Need I say more?" __________

____

____

Infobox

Effective delivery of your presentation is essential for success. Make eye contact with your audience. To do this well it is impossible to read your speech. Make note key words and transition phrases on an index card to guide you through the talk. This will also deter you from memorizing the text. Research the culture of your audience so you can avoid making any hand gestures which may offend them.

Zusammenfassung, Rückfragen und Feedback

Es ist wichtig, die Hauptpunkte der Präsentation nochmals zusammenzufassen. Die Zuhörerschaft kann das Gehörte dann nicht nur mit den Notizen vergleichen, sondern auch besser im Gedächtnis behalten.

I believe I have covered everything. Now I would just like to recap the main points from today. I first spoke about the value of investing in high quality merchandise. The examples I gave to you will hopefully help you remember what my grandfather always told me, "A cheap product is twice purchased!" The second point I made pertained to consumer rights and your personal responsibility to enquire about your rights that may not be common knowledge. Thirdly, and finally, I led you through a case study which exemplified the process of bringing a consumer rights case to court. So, I would like to conclude by thanking you for your attendance and especially your attention throughout the day.
I would be glad to answer any questions or entertain any comments that you might have at this time. Ah, yes, the gentleman in the far corner ...

"I was wondering if you could elaborate on the percentage of cases that are actually won by the consumer."
Certainly. I have a handout in the back of the room which lists the cases won verses those lost over the past two years. Owing to the multitude of cases, I would ask you to take one of these handouts and we could discuss it in detail over coffee later.
"Ah, this one. Ok. I'll peruse it now."
Are there any further questions? Yes, go ahead.
"I am interested in the case study. Have the positive results of that specific case encouraged other consumers to take a stance?"
Excellent question. As a matter of fact there has been great publicity of this case which has in turn motivated those involved to create a website stocked with tips for those interested. The address is ...

Vokabeln

case study	Fallstudie
consumer rights	Verbraucherrecht
elaborate on	näher ausführen
pertain to	etwas betreffen
peruse	sorgfältig durchsehen
recap	rekapitulieren
stocked with	gut eingedeckt mit
take a stance	eine Haltung einnehmen

Übung 11:

Bringen Sie die Wörter in die richtige Reihenfolge.

1. have everything I I covered believe

____

2. I and you finally, Thirdly, through led a case study

____

____

3. points would just main like Now recap the today to from I

____

____

4. pertained to made second The I point consumer rights

____

____

5. about first spoke I investing value of the

____

____

Infobox

Keep the K.I.S.S. Principle in mind when you prepare your next presentation: Keep It Short and Simple. Different cultures have unique styles of presentations. Be sure to limit detailed facts and figures to OHTs when speaking to US American audiences.

Stellenanzeigen, Bewerbungen und Weiterbildung

Für Arbeitsplatzsuchende wird Englisch immer wichtiger. International agierende Firmen annoncieren freie Stellen immer häufiger auf Englisch. Es ist dann üblich, die Bewerbung auf Englisch zu verfassen und das Bewerbungsgespräch in der Fremdsprache zu führen.

Stellenanzeigen

In der folgenden Stellenanzeige sucht ein Pharmaunternehmen einen Leiter für die Personalabteilung.

Director of Human Resources

Hughes Pharmaceuticals is looking for a Director of Human Resources. Your responsibilities will include developing, implementing, updating and co-ordinating strategic human resources policies and managerial issues. This position is ideal for an ambitious, well-qualified candidate, with at least 5 years experience working in Human Resources. Fluency in English is essential. Remuneration dependent on experience and qualifications. Candidates should apply to:
Mxwell@hughespharm.com.
Closing date for applications: 02.03.06

Vokabeln

ambitious	ehrgeizig
candidate	Bewerber
dependent	abhängig
essential	unentbehrlich
experience	Erfahrung
look for	suchen
position	Stelle
qualification	Qualifikation
remuneration	Bezahlung
responsibility	Verantwortung
well-qualified	hoch qualifiziert

Übung 1:

Vervollständigen Sie die Sätze!

1. We need to ___________ a new Personnel Manager, the old one is leaving.
2. The new manager is very ___________, he wants to move up in the company very quickly.
3. IT skills are ___________ for this position.
4. ___________ is linked to your experience.
5. In my opinion, Craig Fraser is the best ___________ of the three – we should give him the job.
6. I want to find a new ___________, I'm bored with my current job.
7. This job carries a lot of ___________, you will be running a department with more than 50 people.
8. This candidate is very ___________, he has an engineering degree and an MBA.
9. How many years ___________ do you have?

+1 Lebenslauf

Der Lebenslauf ist neben dem Anschreiben das wichtigste Dokument der Bewerbungsunterlagen. So könnte ein typischer englischer Lebenslauf aussehen:

CURRICULUM VITAE

Name	Henry Fox
Address	98 Lockhurst Lane, Coventry CV6 5SF
Telephone	024 7670 3412
Email	henry.fox@coolmail.com

CAREER GOAL
A position in Marketing and Promotions with an emphasis on Sales.

SUMMARY OF QUALIFICATIONS
- Over 10 years experience in marketing, promotions and sales, with a talent for communicating with people from all backgrounds
- Excellent organisation and co-ordination skills

PROFESSIONAL EXPERIENCE
Oxford Training Ltd
Sales and Marketing Consultant 2000 – present
- Worked with promotional teams in coordinating opening events at new training centres in Aylesbury and Banbury
- Researched market trends and advertising opportunities

Mercury Electronics
Sales representative 1994 – 2000
- Analysed sales reports to identify market trends
- Created marketing campaigns for new products

EDUCATION
B.A. Business Studies, Warwick University, 1991-1994

OTHER SKILLS
Computer: MS Word, Excel, PowerPoint, Lotus Notes

REFERENCES: Available on request.

Vokabeln

career	Karriere
career objective	Karriereziel
curriculum vitae	Lebenslauf
education	Ausbildung
energetic	energisch
goal	Ziel
hard-working	fleißig
internship	Praktikum
trend	Trend, Tendenz
professional experience	Berufserfahrung
qualification	Qualifikation
references	Referenzen
skill	Fähigkeit
summary	Zusammenfassung
talent	Begabung
team player	Teamplayer

Infobox

A modern curriculum vitae (US: résumé) normally consists of only one page, or two pages maximum. They often begin with a "career goal" or "career objective" statement, followed by a brief summary of qualifications, relevant professional experience, and relevant education. Information should be in reverse chronological order. Photographs are almost never included in a British or American CV, and personal information such as marital status, nationality and even date of birth can be left out if not relevant to the position being applied for. Use bullet points and headings to make your CV easier to read. CVs often finish with the sentence "references available on request" – it is no longer necessary to include contact details for references. If possible, ask a native speaker to proofread your CV for style and grammar or spelling mistakes.

Übung 2:

Übersetzen Sie und enträtseln Sie das Lösungswort!

1. Erfahrung, 2. fleißig, 3. Zusammenfassung, 4. ausgezeichnet, 5. Karriere, 6. energisch, 7. Fähigkeit, 8. Ziel, 9. Begabung

1. _ _ _ □ _ _ _ _ _ _

2. _ _ _ □ _ _ _ _ _ _ _

3. _ □ _ _ _ _ _

4. _ _ □ _ _ _ _ _ _

5. _ □ _ _ _ _

6. _ _ _ _ _ _ □ _ _

7. _ _ □ _ _

8. _ □ _ _

9. _ _ _ _ □ _

Mystery Word

□ □ □ □ □ □ □ □ □

Übung 3:

Welche Wortgruppen gehören zusammen?

1. More than 10 years

2. Computer skills

3. Certificate in

□ include: MS Office, Internet

□ Office Management

□ experience as an executive secretary.

Blindbewerbung

Eine Blindbewerbung (*cold application*) bei einer Firma kann sehr erfolgreich sein, wenn sie an die richtige Person adressiert ist und zu einem guten Zeitpunkt im Unternehmen eintrifft.

Ms Margaret Hill
Human Resources
Macintyre Corp.

9 January 2006

Dear Margaret Hill

IT costs are a major burden for any company. Good management and effective controlling processes are imperative for minimising these costs.

I would like to offer your company help in this important area.

My extensive skills and experience include:

- Management of IT systems in several Fortune 500 companies.
- Planning and executing capital investment programmes to the value of €4 million in my current company.
- Reducing maintenance costs by 13 per cent in my last company.

I would be pleased to meet you to discuss how I could contribute to your company.

Yours sincerely

Joy Dixon

Vokabeln

burden	Belastung
cold application	Blindbewerbung
cover letter	Anschreiben
execute	ausführen
extensive	umfangreich
imperative	erforderlich
major burden	Hauptbelastung
reduce	senken
speculative letter	Blindbewerbungsanschreiben

Anschreiben

Das Anschreiben (*cover letter*) ist die Visitenkarte eines jeden Bewerbers. Es muss kurz und aussagekräftig sein. Die Eignung für den Job muss an dieser Stelle klar zum Ausdruck kommen.

Mr Victor Kowalski
Human Resources
GreneLabs

7 June 2006

Project Manager vacancy at GeneLabs

Dear Victor Kowalski

I have always followed your company's progress with interest, as I believe it is one of the most dynamic and innovative working in the biotechnology field. That's why I was so excited to discover on your website that you are looking for a project manager.
I feel that I could use my considerable experience and skills as a project manager to help GeneLabs face the challenges that arise in today's uncertain economic climate. I believe that my background in IT would give me a unique perspective on managing projects in the biotechnology field. In my previous position I consistently completed projects in time and often under budget, and I would welcome a chance to discuss my ideas for implementing project management best practice at GeneLabs. I will call your secretary next week to see if it is convenient for me to see you.
Thank you in advance for taking the time to consider my application.

Yours sincerely
Mike Prentice

Vokabeln

application	Bewerbung
background	Werdegang
best practice	optimales Verfahren
challenge	Herausforderung
economic climate	Konjunkturlage
face	sich stellen
field	Gebiet
implement	realisieren
in advance	im Voraus
innovative	innovativ
progress	Fortschritt
vacancy	offene Stelle

Das Vorstellungsgespräch

Das Vorstellungsgespräch – die große Kür für jeden Bewerber. Jessica Rodman, die sich um die Stelle als Chefdesignerin in einer Grafikfirma bewirbt, steht dieser große Auftritt bevor.

Hugh: Ah, hello. Good morning. You must be Jessica Rodman. Nice to meet you. I'm Hugh Smith.

Jessica: Nice to meet you, too.

Hugh: Please take a seat. So, Jessica, I've had a good look at your CV, and I must say it's very impressive. Naturally I have a few things I'd like to ask you. For example, why do you want to leave your current job? It looks like a great position in a good company.

Jessica: It is. I've really enjoyed my time working at Gopher Design. But it's time to move on. Basically I feel I'm ready to become a head designer, and there aren't really any prospects for promotion at Gopher.

Hugh: That makes sense. Let's talk a little more about your time at Gopher. What would you say have been your greatest achievements there?

Jessica: Well, one of the things that I'm proud of is an innovative design that I produced for a corporate website for a leading car manufacturer. It was actually my presentation that won us the contract, and that company has gone on to become one of Gopher's major clients. Something that gave me great personal satisfaction was the corporate design that I did for the local transport company here. I received an award from the German Design Council for that work.

Hugh: That must have been very satisfying. Moving on, what would you say are your greatest strengths?

Jessica: First of all, I can work well under pressure, and you know for yourself how important that is when there are deadlines to be met. Secondly, I always try to produce quality work – I set very high standards for myself. And one other thing is I am very detail-oriented, which is naturally essential for design work.

Hugh: And your weaknesses?

Jessica: In the past, I would say time management was my weakness. I would spend very long hours in the office, and my personal life suffered. But this is something I've been trying to change. I recently took a course in time management, and since then I've become more productive and I can now achieve a better balance between my work and personal life.

Hugh: Yes, that's very important. I've seen so many young designers burn themselves out for exactly that reason. Let's think about the future for a moment. What would you like to be doing five years from now?

Jessica: My ambition is to become a project manager, leading teams of designers and dealing with clients. I think I would find that kind of work very rewarding. I can envisage myself doing that within the next 5 years.

Hugh: Interesting. Okay Jessica, I'd like to ask you some more specific questions about projects you've worked on in the past, but before I do, have you got any questions for me?

Jessica: Only one. About salary actually. Would you like to discuss that now or later?

Hugh: What sort of sum were you expecting?

Jessica: That's difficult to answer without knowing exactly what the job entails. But I would certainly be looking at over $60,000.

Hugh: Hmm. That's quite a lot. We were thinking more around $50,000, but don't forget bonuses and perks. And of course an increase after the first six months if everything was satisfactory.

Jessica: Maybe we should talk about the job and then come back to this?

Hugh: Yes, good idea. This is all probably a bit premature anyway.

Vokabeln

achieve	erreichen
achievement	bedeutende Leistung
ambition	Ehrgeiz
award	Stipendium, Auszeichnung
burn oneself out	sich völlig verausgaben
deadline	Abgabetermin
detail-oriented	detailverliebt
It's time to move on.	Es wird Zeit, sich weiterzuentwickeln.
pressure	Druck
productive	produktiv
project manager	Projektmanager
promotion	Beförderung
prospect	Aussicht
rewarding	lohnend
satisfying	befriedigend
strength	Stärke
weakness	Schwäche

Infobox

There are many standard interview questions you can expect to be asked during an English job interview. Try to anticipate these questions in advance and prepare possible answers. One way to prepare for a job interview is to act it out as a role-play with a friend, preferably one who speaks good English.

7 Stellenanzeigen, Bewerbungen und Weiterbildung

Weiterbildung

Der folgende Artikel erklärt, warum Fortbildung für Firmen heute wichtiger ist als je zuvor.

Training has never been as important as it is today. In our knowledge-based economy, it is essential that workers continually develop and update their skills. Training has benefits both for companies and employees. For companies, investment in training results in higher quality standards, better customer satisfaction, and a more motivated and productive staff. For the employee, training leads to personal development and increased job satisfaction. Many companies strive to be "learning organisations".

In a learning organisation, knowledge-sharing, innovations and productivity improvements are routine, resulting in higher profits. Learning organisations often benchmark other companies to learn about industry best practices. Learning organisations typically spend around 20 per cent more than average on training, providing 20 per cent more training to employees. Around 90 per cent of learning organisations use mentoring programmes, where senior staff coach junior staff. They are also more likely to use learning technologies, such as web-based training.

Vokabeln

benefit	Vorteil
benchmark	vergleichen
coach	trainieren
develop	entwickeln
improvement	Verbesserung
knowledge-based	wissensbasiert
motivated	motiviert
personal development	Personalentwicklung
result in	führen zu
strive	sich bemühen
training	Weiterbildung
update	aktualisieren

Übung 4:

Bilden Sie sinnvolle Paare.

1. develop	☐ other companies
2. invest	☐ development
3. result in	☐ junior staff
4. coach	☐ skills
5. benchmark	☐ satisfaction
6. customer	☐ higher profits
7. personal	☐ in training

Branchen, Unternehmensformen, Organisation und Personalstruktur

8

In der Geschäftswelt wird die Arbeit von Menschen durch Unternehmen organisiert. Dieser Lernschritt untersucht verschiedene Branchen, Unternehmensformen und die Personalstruktur im englischsprachigen Raum.

Branchen

Wirtschaftliche Aktivität lässt sich in drei Kategorien unterteilen: eine primäre, eine sekundäre und eine tertiäre ...

Let's look at each category in turn. Primary economic activity has to do with natural resources like mining, oil, and agriculture. Secondary activity is basically the manufacturing sector, in other words making things from what we get from the primary activities. Here we are looking at the construction industry, for example, or engineering, chemicals, and pharmaceuticals. The tertiary activities group services together, so this includes retailing for example, as well as financial sectors like banking and insurance. It also includes education, healthcare, communication, entertainment industry and the leisure industries.

Of course there are problems dividing economic activity this way. Many industries do not fit neatly into the categories. In fact, many large companies fit across all three, and so find it difficult to define their particular sector.

Vokabeln

agriculture	Landwirtschaft
banking	Bankwesen
chemicals	Chemieindustrie
construction	Baugewerbe
education	Erziehung
entertainment industry	Unterhaltungsindustrie
healthcare	Gesundheitswesen
insurance	Versicherung
leisure industry	Freizeitindustrie
mining	Bergbau
natural resources	Rohstoffe
pharmaceutical industry	Pharmaindustrie
primary	primär
retailing	Einzelhandel
secondary	sekundär
tertiary	tertiär

Übung 1:

Finden Sie die korrekte Übersetzung:

1. education	☐ Bau
2. insurance	☐ im Grunde
3. construction	☐ Freizeit
4. healthcare	☐ Erziehung
5. basically	☐ Gesundheitsfürsorge
6. leisure	☐ Versicherung

Übung 2:

Sind die Sätze inhaltlich richtig oder falsch? Kreuzen Sie an:

1. Banking is part of the primary economic sector.

☐ richtig ☐ falsch

2. It is easy to categorise industries into economic sectors.

☐ richtig ☐ falsch

3. Healthcare belongs in the tertiary sector.

☐ richtig ☐ falsch

4. Large companies are easier to categorize into sectors.

☐ richtig ☐ falsch

5. The tertiary sector is growing at present.

☐ richtig ☐ falsch

6. Fishing belongs in the primary sector.

☐ richtig ☐ falsch

Übung 3:

Bringen Sie die Sätze in die richtige Reihenfolge!

1. so this includes retailing for example, as well as
2. financial sectors like banking and in-surance.
3. Let's look at each category in turn.
4. or engineering, chemicals, and pharmaceuticals.
5. It also includes education, healthcare, communication
6. mining, oil, and agriculture.
7. Primary economic activity has to do with natural resources like
8. Secondary activity is basically the manufacturing sector,
9. The tertiary activities group services together,
10. in other words making things from what we get from the primary activities.
11. Here we are looking at the construction industry, for example,
12. and the leisure industries.

Lösung: ____________________

Unternehmensformen

Im englischen Sprachraum sind Unternehmen in den verschiedensten Rechtsformen organisiert, die nicht immer mit den deutschen gleichgesetzt werden können.

> Sole proprietor – One person owns and runs the business. In the UK this is called a sole trader.

Partnership – This can take various forms, but the basic idea is that the risks and profits from the business are shared between more than one person. In a limited partnership a partner's liability may be limited by the amount of capital invested.
Corporation – Here the business has a separate legal identity. In the USA the three main types of corporation are S-corporations, C-corporations and limited liability companies (LLC).
The main differences have to do with the way tax and risk are handled. In the UK public companies raise capital by selling shares, with profits being distributed as dividends. Private companies cannot raise capital in this way.

Vokabeln

C-corporation (US)	Gesellschaft mit beschränkter Haftung (GmbH)
corporation	Körperschaft
limited liability company (UK)	Gesellschaft mit beschränkter Haftung (GmbH)
partnership	Partnerschaft
proprietor	Inhaber
public company (UK)	Aktiengesellschaft (AG)
S-corporation (US)	Aktiengesellschaft (AG)
sole trader	Einzelunternehmer

Übung 4:

Passen Sie die Wörter in Klammern in der Wortart dem jeweiligen Satz an und setzen Sie ein.

1. (basic) There are _ _ _ _ _ _ _ three problems.
2. (partnership) This is Chris, our _ _ _ _ _ _ _.
3. (private) The public transport system is much better since it was _ _ _ _ _ _ _.
4. (capital) A venture _ _ _ _ _ _ _ invested a lot of money in our company.
5. (invest) We need new equipment but it's such a big _ _ _ _ _ _ _.
6. (limited) We should _ _ _ _ _ _ _ spending – we're over budget already.
7. (own) The company has a new _ _ _ _ _ _ _.

Übung 5.

Bilden Sie sinnvolle Paare aus den folgenden Wörtern:

1. sole	☐ partnership
2. raise	☐ resources
3. limited	☐ activities
4. handle	☐ capital
5. economic	☐ risk
6. tertiary	☐ trader
7. natural	☐ sector

Infobox

When a company is to be listed on the stock exchange we say it is to go public or to be floated on the stock exchange.

Übung 6:

Übersetzen Sie!

1. Körperschaft ______________
2. beschaffen ______________
3. Partnerschaft ______________
4. Einzelunternehmer ______________
5. beschränkt ______________
6. Inhaber ______________
7. Dividende ______________
8. Haftung ______________

Infobox

Some common abbreviations:
plc – public limited company
corp – corporation
Inc – incorporated
Ltd – Limited

Unternehmensorganisation

In der modernen Welt verändern sich Unternehmen ständig, um sich dem schnell wandelnden Markt anzupassen. Umso mehr muss die innere Struktur eines Unternehmens für reibungslose Abläufe sorgen.

An organisation can be defined as a group of people who work together in a systematic way to achieve common goals. The structure of the organisation describes the system which is used to coordinate and direct the way the employees work together in order to achieve these goals.
Many companies use organisational charts to show the reporting relationships between different people, although communication within an organisation is never this straightforward. Tasks are often coordinated through divisions, departments, sections and teams according to function (e.g.

Vokabeln

achieve	erreichen
charts	Schaubilder
coordinate	koordinieren
department	Abteilung
division	Abteilung, Geschäftsbereich
empowered	ermächtigt
enforced	durchgesetzt
function	Funktion
manufacturing	Herstellung
marketing	Marketing
organisational chart	Organigramm
section	Unterabteilung, Sektion
staff	Belegschaft
systematic	systematisch
team	Arbeitsgruppe, Team

marketing, manufacturing, finance), process (e.g. milling, painting, assembly), product (e.g. cars, vans, trucks), customer (or market), project or by geographical region. Many companies use a combination of these methods. The reporting structure can be centralized, with most decisions coming from the management, or decentralized, where employees are empowered to make decisions at lower levels. The structure can be formal or informal, depending on how strictly rules and regulations are defined and enforced.

Übung 7:

Füllen Sie die Lücke mit der richtigen Präposition.

1. I am responsible _ _ _ _ _ marketing.
2. I report _ _ _ _ _ the head of sales.
3. The structure _ _ _ _ _ the organisation has changed.
4. He's in charge _ _ _ _ _ production.
5. Departments are often organised _ _ _ _ _ geographical location.
6. Most decisions come _ _ _ _ _ the boss.
7. We're planning _ _ _ _ _ go public next year.

Infobox

Downsizing is used to describe how companies reduce costs by reducing the size of their workforce; often middle management jobs are the first to go. Reengineering describes how companies redesign their processes in order to become more efficient. A virtual organisation refers to a temporary situation where two or more organisations come together to achieve a specific objective.

Übung 8:

Übersetzen Sie folgende Wörter ins Englische und enträtseln Sie das Lösungswort!

1. erreichen, 2. dezentralisiert, 3. Bericht, 4. Beziehung, 5. systematisch, 6. durchsetzen, 7. Funktion, 8. Methode, 9. Arbeitnehmer

1. _ _ ☐ _ _ _ _
2. _ _ _ _ _ _ _ _ _ _ ☐ _ _ _
3. _ ☐ _ _ _ _
4. ☐ _ _ _ _ _ _ _ _ _ _ _
5. _ _ _ _ _ _ ☐ _ _ _
6. _ _ _ _ ☐ _ _
7. _ _ _ ☐ _ _ _ _
8. _ _ _ ☐ _ _
9. _ _ _ _ _ ☐ _ _

Mystery Word

☐ ☐ ☐ ☐ ☐ ☐ ☐ ☐ ☐

Infobox

A parent or holding company owns more than half of another company's shares. The latter is known as a subsidiary.

Übung 9:

Sind die Sätze inhaltlich richtig oder falsch? Kreuzen Sie an:

1. A department is part of a company.

☐ richtig ☐ falsch

2. A sole proprietor is where two or more people own the company.

☐ richtig ☐ falsch

3. A corporation has a separate legal identity.

☐ richtig ☐ falsch

4. Profits in a public company in the UK may be distributed as dividends.

☐ richtig ☐ falsch

5. A company owned by another company is called a daughter.

☐ richtig ☐ falsch

6. In the USA, LLC stands for Lots of Liability Corporation.

☐ richtig ☐ falsch

7. A parent company is similar to a holding company.

☐ richtig ☐ falsch

Übung 10:

Unterstreichen Sie die inhaltlichen Fehler:

Downsizing is used to describe how companies increase costs by reducing the size of their workforce; often top management jobs are the first to go. Reengineering describes how companies redesign their products in order to become more efficient. A virtual organisation refers to a permanent situation where two or more organisations come together to achieve a specific objective.

Personalstruktur und Karriere

Im folgenden Dialog unterhalten sich zwei Rentner über ihre unterschiedlichen Berufserfahrungen und Karriereverläufe.

Archie: I left school at 15, and went straight into an apprenticeship. My plan was to become a welder, work for a few years, qualify as a foreman and have a guaranteed job for the rest of my life. Of course, it didn't work out quite like that.
Bertram: What happened?
Archie: Well the apprenticeship went well, and I came out with high marks. After a couple of years the company

decided to sponsor me through evening college and later through university, and I ended up as a qualified mechanical engineer at the age of thirty.

Bertram: Sounds good. What happened then?

Archie: Oh, well, I worked on various projects, and I was a member of the workers' council for a while, but I had to leave that when I was promoted to management level. I then went back to university to do a doctorate. I became a department head, and eventually took over as managing director of the company when the owner died.

Bertram: I see.

Archie: Of course the company then went bust – no-one wanted to buy typewriters any more. I was unemployed for a while, and then I found another job in a different firm. Much bigger than my first company – a multinational in fact.

Bertram: Right.

Archie: That gave me the chance to travel and to try things I had only dreamt about. Anyway to cut a long story short, I ended up on the board as a director. Amazing really.

Bertram: Sounds like a dream career! A bit different to my story.

Archie: Go on.

Bertram: I went from school to university, read accountancy, and from there to my first job in the city. I was a stock analyst at first. I advised people on what to buy. From there I became a financial consultant, and I was quite lucky with a couple of clients. I was a millionaire by the time I was 35.

Archie: Wow. What happened then.

Bertram: Oh, I enjoyed the good life for a bit, you know fast car, parties, that sort of thing.

Archie: And then?

Bertram: And then I invested badly and lost everything I owned. I became bankrupt. I had to sell my house and my cars; it was a hard time.

Archie: Ok. But you obviously picked yourself up again.

Bertram: Yes, I was lucky. I worked in a restaurant for a while, and eventually

Vokabeln

apprenticeship	Lehre
board (of directors)	Vorstand
break even	ausgeglichener Geschäftsabschluss
department head	Abteilungsleiter
estate	Besitz
foreman	Vorarbeiter
managing director	Vorstands vorsitzender
promoted	befördert
read	(hier) studieren
workers'council	Personalrat

paid off all my debts. Then I inherited some land in Australia, which just happened to be full of minerals. I set up a company, mined the land for all it was worth, and sold out a couple of years later. Basically I had more money than I needed. I came back to Europe, and bought the estate where I now live. I have about a dozen employees who manage the place and do all the day-to-day administration, and we break even most years. It's great.

Übung 11:

Setzen Sie die Begriffe so zusammen, dass sinnvolle Formulierungen entstehen:

1. work	short	a story
2. take	up	a solution
3. cut	out	a debt
4. pay	over	as a manager
5. end	on	a company
6. work	off	a project

1. _
2. _
3. _
4. _
5. _
6. _

Übung 12:

Füllen Sie die Lücken mit Wörtern aus dem Text.

After I left (1.) _ _ _ _ _ I worked in a bar for a few months and then I went to university and (2.) _ _ _ _ _ engineering. When I graduated I went (3.) _ _ _ _ _ into a managerial (4.) _ _ _ _ _ with CFX Systems. The company grew dramatically and became a (5.) _ _ _ _ _. I was transferred to the USA where I was (6.) _ _ _ _ _ to area manager. After 10 years with the company I had made a lot of money, which I (7.) _ _ _ _ _ in dot-com companies. I was (8.) _ _ _ _ _ enough to get out before the bubble burst and by then I was a (9.) _ _ _ _ _.

I retired last year at 35!

Infobox

In the UK, a company secretary is the person responsible for the legal and financial affairs of a company. In the US he or she is known as a corporate secretary.

Übung 13:

Übersetzen Sie!

1. Lehre _ _ _ _ _ _ _ _ _ _ _ _ _ _ _
2. Personalrat _ _ _ _ _ _ _ _ _ _ _ _ _ _ _
3. Vorstand _ _ _ _ _ _ _ _ _ _ _ _ _ _ _

Zeit- und Projektplanung

Zeit ist Geld! In der heutigen Geschäftswelt ist es wichtiger denn je, sich selbst und die einzelnen Arbeitsprozesse optimal zu organisieren. Der folgende Lernschritt macht mit den wichtigsten Begriffen und Wendungen aus den Bereichen Zeit- und Projektplanung vertraut.

Zeitplanung

Effektives Selbstmanagement ist eine der Grundvoraussetzungen für beruflichen Erfolg. Um alle Aufgaben in der zur Verfügung stehenden Arbeitszeit zu bewältigen, müssen Prioritäten gesetzt und Wichtiges von Unwichtigem unterschieden werden.

How often have you said: This year is flying by. Or perhaps at work, you have commented on how much there is to do in so little time. Perhaps you need to take a serious look at your time management. Have you ever taken the time to work out what is of value to you? The important first step is to decide what is important, rather than what is urgent. This involves the setting of priorities, and changing them when unforeseen events influence what is important.

Your priority list can then be converted into goals. Your goals should be flexible, because the future does not always bring what we expect. Goals can then be broken down into smaller pieces, called objectives. This gives you a chance to record your progress, and determine whether your goal is realistic. To achieve the objectives, you may need an action plan.

This provides the framework you will use in order to accomplish your goal. Within this framework, you can decide on your "to do" list. You can then review your action plan on a short term basis.

After setting your priorities, you should consider your performance level during a normal day. Most people function better early in the morning, when they are fresh. Successful time management will enable you to perform the tasks which are important to you, and therefore give you the sense that there is exactly enough time to get what you want from life.

Vokabeln

accomplish	erreichen
action plan	Aktionsplan
goal	Ziel
objective	Absicht, (Teil-)ziel
of value	von Wert
perform	ausführen
performance	Leistung
priority list	Prioritätenliste
review	überarbeiten
time management	Zeitplanung
unforeseen	unvorhergesehen

9 Zeit- und Projektplanung

Infobox

After setting priorities, and breaking down goals into daily tasks, remember the Pareto Principle: 20% of my effort produces 80% of my results. We should concentrate on this 20%, and consider which of our tasks will fall into this range. This may require more prioritisation, and a realistic look at which tasks are really important, and which might eventually end up in the waste paper basket.

Übung 1:

Benutzen Sie nun die Verben des Textes, um die Lücken in der folgenden Übung zu füllen!

The first step in time management is to (1.) __ _______ priorities. At the same time, you might consider the time of day when you (2.) _________ best. You can then (3.) __ _______ the tasks with the highest priority in this time. This will help you (4.) _______ __ your goals. Remember to periodically (5.) _________ your goals, and analyse whether you have (6.) __________ what you wanted.

Übung 2:

In den folgenden Sätzen verbergen sich einige Fehler. Verbessern Sie:

1. This year flies by.

____

2. Are you ever taking the time to work out what is of value to you?

____

____

3. The future is not always bringing what we expect.

____

____

4. Most people function better early in the morning, if they are fresh.

____

____

5. You should consider your performance level while a normal day.

____

____

6. 20% of my effort is producing 80% of my result.

____

____

Übung 3:

Ordnen Sie folgende Vokabeln den entsprechenden Übersetzungen zu!

1. objectives	☐ überlegen
2. realistic	☐ Rahmen

3. of value	☐ unvorhergesehen
4. unforeseen	☐ von Wert
5. consider	☐ realistisch
6. framework	☐ Ziele
7. accomplish	☐ überarbeiten
8. review	☐ erreichen

Ideensammlung

Wenn eine Firma ein neues Projekt plant, kann es sinnvoll sein, Ideen von Mitarbeitern aus den verschiedensten Arbeitsbereichen zu sammeln. Bei einem Brainstorming werden diese Ideen zunächst zusammengetragen, aber noch nicht auf Tauglichkeit geprüft. Jeder Teilnehmer muss seine Einfälle äußern können, ohne zu befürchten, dass sie als unangemessen zurückgewiesen werden.

Lisa (Manager): As you all know, we have this new product which has to be supported by our computer system. What I would like to hear from you all today are your ideas and thoughts, although at this stage, I'm only concerned with ideas. So, no analysis, please. Nothing is out of bounds. I've drawn a mind map here on the board around the topic "New Product", so I'll write up your ideas around this topic.

Tim: Perhaps we can modify our software.

David: Yeah. How about waiting to see how the product develops. Maybe, our existing software will be able to handle it.

Lisa: Ok. Any other ideas?

Paul: We could buy an existing software program already on the market.

Rachel: Yes, and if we don't find exactly the right product, we could have it customised for our purposes.

Tim: What if we developed the program in-house?

Trevor: Or we could hire externals to develop the program.

Paul: That will be too expensive.

Rachel: Right. We can't afford that.

Lisa: Hang on, please. Remember, only ideas at this stage.

Vokabeln

applicable	umsetzbar
brainstorming	Brainstorming, Gedankenaustausch
have it customised	den Bedürfnissen angepasst
imaginative	kreativ
inappropriate	unangemessen
input	Beitrag
market	Markt
mind map	Mind Map, Gedankendiagramm
modify	modifizieren
out of bounds	verboten
provoke	provozieren
work environment	Arbeitsatmosphäre

Infobox

Brainstorming sessions are a great way to bring out creativity in employees. However, it is very important to first build a work environment where people feel free to give their input, without thinking that there will be a negative response. Managers use brainstorming sessions to provoke unusual ideas. Imaginative and applicable solutions are sometimes found in the ideas, which at first glance, appear ridiculous or inappropriate.

Übung 4:

Wie lauten die Sätze richtig?

1. I topic ideas write up will around your this.

_ _

2. Perhaps can software our modify existing we.

_ _

3. We could customised it have purposes our for.

_ _

_ _

4. That too expensive be will.

_ _

5. We program hire develop externals to could the.

_ _

_ _

Übung 5:

Übersetzen und entscheiden Sie: Welcher der folgenden Begriffe gehört zum Thema „Ideensammlung“?

1. imaginative

_ _

2. glance

_ _

3. out of bounds

_ _

4. input

_ _

5. inappropriate

_ _

6. provoke

_ _

7. brainstorming

_ _

Übung 6:

Übersetzen Sie und enträtseln Sie das Lösungswort!

1. umsetzbar, 2. Arbeitsatmosphäre, 3. Rahmen, 4. Beitrag, 5. Blick, 6. Ideen, 7. unangemessen, 8. provozieren, 9. unvorhergesehen, 10. kreativ

1. _ _ _ _ _ _ _ ☐ _ _

2. _ _ ☐ _   _ _ _ _ _ _ _ _ _ _ _

3. _ _ ☐ _ _ _ _ _ _

4. ☐ _ _ _ _

5. _ _ _ ☐ _ _

6. _ _ _ _ ☐

7. _ _ _ _ _ _ _ _ _ _ _ _ ☐ _

8. _ _ ☐ _ _ _ _

9. _ _ _ _ ☐ _ _ _ _ _

10. _ ☐ _ _ _ _ _ _ _ _ _ _

Mystery Word ☐ ☐ ☐ ☐ ☐ ☐ ☐ ☐ ☐ ☐

Projektplanung

In diesem Abschnitt werden einige Aspekte der Projektplanung betrachtet. Eine gut strukturierte Herangehensweise an ein Projekt ist von äußerster Wichtigkeit, will man es effektiv durchführen.

A project is a goal oriented form of co-operation between people, and is limited by a specified time period. Due to the long term nature of projects, the preparation is extremely important.

In the preparation phase, it is important firstly to determine the goal of the project, and the budget which can be allocated to the project. It is also necessary to analyse the skills and resources required. Finally, the general time frame for the project is considered.

After these general constraints are worked out, the project is planned in more detail. The overall time frame can be broken down into specific dates, by when each part of the project should be completed. The human resources are allocated, so that the people with the necessary skills are included at the right stage of the project.

After the planning of the project is completed, comes the implementation stage. The plans and preparation are now carried out. This phase also requires constant review, to ensure that all parts of the project are working well with each other, and that the project is on course as planned. Hopefully the project will be completed in accordance with the plan.

It is then a good idea to evaluate the project, and to compare the results with goals as stated in the preparation phase.

Vokabeln

allocated	zugeteilt
assess	einschätzen
constraint	Beschränkung
dependencies	Abhängigkeiten
embark	anfangen
human resources	Personal
in accordance with	in Übereinstimmung
oriented	orientiert
plot	aufzeichnen
skills	Fähigkeiten

Infobox

In order to assess the running of a project, many people use a Gantt chart. This is a graphical tool, which plots the time span of the project against the tasks which must be performed. However, a Gantt chart does not allow you to analyse task dependencies. Therefore, some project managers prefer to use the PERT (Program Evaluation Review Technique) or CPM (Critical Path Method) chart. These charts allow the project manager to plot the tasks which are dependent on others, and therefore can only be completed in a certain order. Other tasks which are not dependent, can be completed in any order.

Übung 7:

Formulieren Sie die Sätze im Passiv!

1. The project manager plans resources before embarking on a project.

____

2. It is important to allocate the budget.

____

3. We must break down the time frame into specific dates.

____

4. The project manager allocates human resources.

____

5. The project team now carries out the plans and preparations.

____

6. To assess the running of a project, many people use a Gantt, PERT or CPM chart.

____

Übung 8:

Bringen Sie die Sätze in die richtige Reihenfolge!

1. After completion, it is a good idea to evaluate the project.
2. In the planning stage, human resources are allocated, and more specific time frames worked out.
3. The first step is to define the goal of the project, and the budget which can be allocated.
4. After the planning of the project is completed, comes the implementation stage.
5. This is the preparation stage.
6. The project can then be planned in more detail.

Lösung: ____________________

Übung 9:

Bilden Sie sinnvolle Paare.

1. in accordance	☐ dependencies
2. human	☐ phase
3. implementation	☐ oriented

4. graphical	☐ frame
5. goal	☐ term
6. task	☐ resources
7. time	☐ with
8. long	☐ tool

Phasen eines Projekts

Der folgende Text untersucht die Hauptphasen eines Projekts. Ein erfahrener Projektleiter legt die Schritte fest, die er bei jedem Projekt der Firma angewendet wissen will. Diese Schritte geben die Prioritäten bei der Bearbeitung des Projekts vor.

Our internal customers provide us with the job specification. They have already analysed the need, and together we work out the goal of the project. We should then conduct a risk analysis. After this, the project team should, in my opinion, follow the following guidelines:

1. The project has to be controlled, and instruments should be established for this purpose.
2. Work out the skills needed to complete the project, and the human resources needed to perform those skills.
3. Establish the structure of the team, including the nomination of the project leader. This step also requires a clear division of responsibilities. Tasks should be delegated, and thought given as to how the project will be co-ordinated. The motivation of staff and communication between the team members should also be considered.
4. Plot the expected progress of the project. What are the milestones? Are there any particular deadlines that must be met?
5. The project is now in the implementation phase. During the course of the project, reviews must be carried out. The project leader should conduct status meetings, so that the progress is charted. Procedures for change requests should be in place. Communication is the key, because not all factors are within the control of the team. The lines of communication must be clear.

Vokabeln

change request	Änderungswunsch
conduct	durchführen, einberufen
establish	festlegen
guideline	Richtlinie
implementation stage	Realisierungsphase
milestone	Meilenstein
preparation stage	Vorbereitungsphase
review	nochmalige Prüfung
risk analysis	Risikoanalyse
status meeting	Projektbesprechung

6. Upon completion of the project, the initiator/sponsor should be consulted. Together, an evaluation of the project can be carried out, to ensure the original goal has been met.

Infobox

Most projects will involve many people from different areas of the enterprise. For the purposes of the project, they work in a team, even when normally they do not work together. A crucial part of any project is therefore the teamwork between the project members. The project leader should take careful consideration of the members of the team, and how the team will work together. The approach from all parties to teamwork could mean the success or failure of the project.

Übung 10:

Sind die Sätze richtig oder falsch?

1. A project will run itself. There is no need for control.

☐ richtig ☐ falsch

2. The project leader needs to delegate tasks.

☐ richtig ☐ falsch

3. Reviews should only be carried out after the completion of the project.

☐ richtig ☐ falsch

4. Communication between project members is not important, because everyone has their own job.

☐ richtig ☐ falsch

5. Projects should be evaluated at the end.

☐ richtig ☐ falsch

6. Teamwork is crucial to the success of a project.

☐ richtig ☐ falsch

Übung 11:

Vervollständigen Sie die Sätze mit Wörtern aus dem Text!

1. Here are the ___________ for managing projects in our company.

2. We will carry out a risk ___________.

3. Please ___________ a structure for the project, including the lines of communication.

4. The head of our department will ______ _____ the project leader.

5. The project leader should ___________ tasks to the team members.

6. We will have regular meetings to discuss the current ___________ of the project.

7. After the project is finished, we will _____ _____ it, to ensure the sponsor is satisfied.

Computer, Internet und E-Commerce 10

Viele Firmen haben firmeneigene Netzwerke und der größte Teil der Geschäftskommunikation findet per E-Mail statt. Darüber hinaus ist das Internet ein unersetzliches Werkzeug bei der Vermarktung, der Forschung und dem elektronischen Handel. Auf dem gesamten Gebiet der elektronischen Datenverarbeitung ist die englische Sprache dominierend.

Computer

Der Student Grant Smith möchte endlich seinen ersten Computer kaufen und bittet die Computerspezialistin Susan um Hilfe.

Grant: Hi Susan. Do you have a moment? I wanted to ask you some questions.
Susan: Sure. Fire away!
Grant: Well, I'm thinking about buying a computer to use at home. The problem is, I don't know anything about computers! What should I buy?
Susan: Well, you're going to need the computer itself, obviously. It normally comes in a tower. That contains the processor, memory, a hard disk drive, a floppy disk drive, and a CD-ROM drive.

Vokabeln

cartridge	Patrone
CD-ROM drive	CD-ROM-Laufwerk
floppy disk drive	Floppy-Laufwerk
graphics card	Grafikkarte
hard disk drive	Festplatte
keyboard	Tastatur
memory	Speicherplatz
mouse	Maus
printer	Drucker
processor	Prozessor
scanner	Scanner
sound card	Soundkarte
tower	Tower

It usually contains a graphics card and a sound card as well. The standard packages you can buy at these big electronics stores are normally quite good.
Grant: Okay. What else do I need?
Susan: Naturally you need a monitor as well. And a keyboard and a mouse, otherwise you won't be able to use your computer!
Grant: What about a printer? Is that important?
Susan: I would say so. Most people need to print things at some time. You can either get an inkjet printer or a laser printer. Laser printers are faster and give better quality, but are more expensive. But one problem with inkjet printers is that the ink cartridges are normally quite expensive.
Grant: Is there anything else I should buy?
Susan: You might want to think about getting a scanner as well. They can be very useful if you want to transfer printed text or images to your PC.
Grant: Well Susan, thanks a lot!
Susan: You're welcome.

10 Computer, Internet und E-Commerce

Infobox

The capacity of a hard disk drive is often measured in gigabytes (GB). One gigabyte is approximately 1 million kilobytes. One kilobyte is enough to store about 1000 characters, for example a short text. Processor speed is measured either in megahertz (MHz) or gigahertz (GHz). This describes how many calculations the processor can perform in one second. A 1MHz processor can perform 1 million calculations per second. A 1GHz processor can perform 1 billion (1 000 000 000) calculations per second.
Monitor size is often measured in inches. Typical monitor sizes are 17 or 19 inches. This measurement refers to the distance between the bottom left and top right corners of the screen.

Übung 1:

Welche Wörter gehören zusammen?

1. hard disk	☐ keyboard
2. printer	☐ card
3. type on a	☐ drive
4. scan in a	☐ disk
5. graphics	☐ intelligence
6. floppy	☐ cartridge
7. artificial	☐ commerce
8. data	☐ processor
9. electronic	☐ page
10. home	☐ picture
11. word	☐ traffic

Übung 2:

Vervollständigen Sie die Sätze!

1. You need a _ _ _ _ _ _ _ if you want to make a paper copy of a text.
2. A _ _ _ _ _ _ _ is useful if you want to put a photograph into your computer.
3. If you have an inkjet printer, you will need to buy a new ink _ _ _ _ _ _ _ every few months.
4. You type with a _ _ _ _ _ _ _.
5. You use a _ _ _ _ _ _ _ to display output from your computer.
6. If you want to store information on a floppy disk, you need a _ _ _ _ _ _ _.
7. If you want to listen to music on your computer, then a good _ _ _ _ _ _ _ is important.
8. Normally a PC comes in a kind of box, called a _ _ _ _ _ _ _.
9. You use a _ _ _ _ _ _ _ to move a pointer or cursor on the screen.
10. Most software comes on CD, so you need a _ _ _ _ _ _ _ to install it.
11. A good _ _ _ _ _ _ _ is essential if you want to do graphics work on your PC.
12. You can connect to the Internet using a _ _ _ _ _ _ _.

Internet

Gegenwärtig wird das Internet immer wichtiger. Fast jede Firma hat eine eigene Website und die Angestellten ihre eigenen Internetadressen, über die sie Informationen einholen oder aber Geschäfte anbahnen und abwickeln.

Derek: So, let me give you my business card.
Gillian: Thanks. And here's mine.
Derek: That's great. Sorry, do you have an email address?
Gillian: I do, actually. It's not on the card because we didn't have email when the cards were printed. It's very easy – gillian.smith@bomens.com. I'll just write it on the back of the card for you. I also have a web-based email account. It's gillian.smith@hitmal.com. But I don't look at that account very often.
Derek: Oh, that is easy. And what's the URL of the Bomens home page?
Gillian: Again, it's very simple – www.bomens.com. And I see your email address is derek.thorn@fanbury.com. That's easy to remember as well. And the company website is www.fanbury.co.uk.
Derek: So Gillian, I'll send you an email within the next few days, with that information we talked about.
Gillian: That's great. The only thing is, I don't check my email very often, so don't worry if you don't get a reply immediately!

Vokabeln

account	Konto
business card	Visitenkarte
check	überprüfen
email address	E-Mail-Adresse
home page	Homepage
reply	Antwort
send	schicken
URL	URL-Adresse (Website-Adresse)
website	Website

Infobox

Email adresses and websites
The email address gillian.smith@bomens.com is read "Gillian dot Smith at bomens dot com". The website www.fanbury.co.uk is read "W (double you) W W dot Fanbury dot co dot UK".

Übung 3:

Wie lauten die Sätze richtig?

1. give let card me business you my

____

2. you address email do have an?

____

3. home the your page what's URL of?

____

4. account I that look often at don't very

____

5. send within next an I'll days few email you the

_ _

_ _

6. don't often very email I check my

_ _

Übung 4:

Bilden Sie sinnvolle Paare.

1. company	☐ page
2. check	☐ card
3. send	☐ your email
4. email	☐ website
5. business	☐ email account
6. get	☐ address
7. home	☐ an email
8. web-based	☐ a reply

Intranet

Interne Nachrichten werden in vielen Firmen heute über das firmeneigene Intranet verbreitet. So wird im Vergleich zu den herkömmlichen Memos und Rundschreiben viel Zeit und Papier gespart.

So what is an intranet exactly? Well, basically it's a network based on the same protocols as the Internet, with the difference being that an intranet belongs to an organization, usually a company. That means it's only accessible by the organization's members, employees, or anyone else who has authorization. An intranet has a firewall around it, which stops unauthorized people accessing it. So what do people actually use intranets for? Well, just like the Internet itself, intranets are used to share information. An intranet has websites which look and behave just like the websites you find on the World Wide Web. These websites could contain information about a company's products, technical documentation, company news, useful resources for employees, or even just information about the company football team!

Vokabeln

access	zugreifen
accessible	zugänglich
authorization	Berechtigung
firewall	Zugangsschutzsystem
network	Netzwerk
password	Passwort
protocol	Protokoll
resource	Hilfsmittel
share	verteilen
unauthorized	unberechtigt
user	Benutzer

Übung 5:
Sind die Sätze richtig oder falsch? Kreuzen Sie an:

1. An intranet is a kind of network.

☐ richtig ☐ falsch

2. Intranets use different technology from the internet.

☐ richtig ☐ falsch

3. Anyone can access an intranet.

☐ richtig ☐ falsch

4. A firewall protects an intranet.

☐ richtig ☐ falsch

5. Intranets are used to give information to people.

☐ richtig ☐ falsch

6. Intranet websites look different from internet websites.

☐ richtig ☐ falsch

7. Intranet websites only contain information on company products.

☐ richtig ☐ falsch

Übung 6:
Vervollständigen Sie die Sätze!

1. An intranet is a kind of _ _ _ _ _.

2. It is used to _ _ _ _ _ information within a company.

3. An intranet often has many useful _ _ _ _ _.

4. Only a person with _ _ _ _ _ can use a company intranet.

5. An intranet is normally only _ _ _ _ _ to employees of the company.

6. Employees are allowed to _ _ _ _ _ the company intranet.

7. _ _ _ _ _ users are not allowed to use a company intranet.

8. An intranet is protected by a _ _ _ _ _.

Suchmaschinen

Da das Internet ständig weiter wächst, werden Suchmaschinen immer wichtiger. Der folgende Artikel beschreibt, wie Suchmaschinen funktionieren.

An Internet search engine is a special website designed to help users find information located on other sites.
A search engine searches documents on the World Wide Web for specified keywords, and then produces a list of the documents where the keywords were found. Some well-known search engines are Google, Excite and Alta Vista.
A search engine normally works by sending out a program called a "spider"

to gather as many documents as possible from the Web. The spider works by following links from one document to another. When the spider finds a document, it sends it back to the search engine. These documents are then read by another program called an indexer. The indexer creates an index which is based on the words contained in each document.

When a user submits a query, the search engine uses the index to find which pages match the query. The query can be a single word, or several words. Many search engines allow you to refine your search using Boolean operators such as AND, OR and NOT. In addition, some search engines allow natural-language queries which allow you to write queries as simple questions.

Vokabeln

Boolean operators	Boole'sche Operatoren
document	Dokument
gather	sammeln
keyword	Schlüsselwort
link	Verknüpfung
match	entsprechen
provider	Anbieter
query	Anfrage
refine	verbessern
search engine	Suchmaschine
submit	vorlegen
website	Website

Übung 7:

Welche Wörter gehören in die Lücken? (match, gather, refine, keywords, submit, documents, query)

John: So how do search engines work?

Fiona: Well, first of all they (1.) _ _ _ _ _ (2.) _ _ _ _ _ from the web and index them. Then, when you (3.) _ _ _ _ _ your (4.) _ _ _ _ _ they use the index to find the relevant sites. It will then give you a list of sites that (5.) _ _ _ _ _ your query.

John: But how do I make a query?

Fiona: Well, you have to choose (6.) _ _ _ _ that you think might be in the website you're looking for. So if you're looking for a site about holidays in Thailand, you would choose words like "holiday", "Thailand", "tourism", and so on. If your first try doesn't work, you can (7.) _ _ _ _ _ your search by adding more words.

Übung 8:

Finden Sie Wörter mit ähnlicher Bedeutung im Text.

1. question _ _ _ _ _ _ _ _ _ _ _ _ _ _ _ _
2. connect _ _ _ _ _ _ _ _ _ _ _ _ _ _ _ _
3. collect _ _ _ _ _ _ _ _ _ _ _ _ _ _ _ _
4. send _ _ _ _ _ _ _ _ _ _ _ _ _ _ _ _

5. fit together ________________

6. purify ________________

7. data ________________

Online-Banking und E-Commerce

Zwei wichtige Anwendungsgebiete des Internets sind Online-Banking und E-Commerce. Der folgende Auszug aus einer Präsentation gibt Informationen zu beiden Themen.

... Now I want to look at two different uses of the Internet. First of all, online banking. This is a service provided by many banks, which allows customers to use bank services via a webpage. These services can include viewing your current balance, checking your transaction history, or paying bills online. To make online banking secure, all the information that is sent backwards and forwards between your computer and the bank's server is encrypted. The great advantage of online banking is that you can do your banking from home, at any time of the day or night.

Now let me move on to e-commerce, also known as e-business. This refers to the buying and selling of goods and services over the Internet. For example, a company might use its website to sell directly to customers. Again, security is very important, as often customers need to enter credit card numbers online. Much e-commerce is referred to as "B2B", which stands for business-to-business. For example, a company might buy products from a supplier using the Internet – this is known as online procurement. This brings me on to my next point ...

Vokabeln

balance	Kontostand
bill	Rechnung
credit card	Kreditkarte
encrypted	verschlüsselt
procurement	Beschaffung
secure	sicher
security	Sicherheit
transaction	Transaktion

Infobox

The German word "sicher" can be translated into English in at least 3 different ways, as "safe", "secure", or "sure". "Safe" is the opposite of dangerous, for example:
Are you sure this car is safe?
We use "secure" for things like banks and computer networks, meaning that the data or other valuable things in them are protected.
E.g. This network has a firewall, so it's reasonably secure.
We use "sure" when we are certain something will happen, or to mean "of course".
E.g. Can you help me? Sure!
We are sure to win the contract.

Übung 9:

Sind die Sätze richtig oder falsch? Kreuzen Sie die korrekte Antwort an:

1. You can only check your balance with online banking.

☐ richtig ☐ falsch

2. It is possible to pay bills online.

☐ richtig ☐ falsch

3. The information you send to your bank is protected.

☐ richtig ☐ falsch

4. A company can sell its products over the internet.

☐ richtig ☐ falsch

5. With B2B e-commerce, companies sell products or services to other companies.

☐ richtig ☐ falsch

6. Selling directly to normal customers is known as online procurement.

☐ richtig ☐ falsch

Übung 10:

Übersetzen Sie und enträtseln Sie das Lösungswort!

1. Rechung, 2. Transaktion, 3. Kreditkarte, 4. sicher, 5. Sicherheit, 6. Kontostand, 7. Beschaffung, 8. verschlüsselt

1. _☐_ _

2. _ _ _☐_ _ _ _ _ _ _

3. _ _ _ _ _☐ _ _ _ _

4. _☐_ _ _ _

5. _ _ _ _☐_ _ _

6. _ _ _ _☐_ _

7. _ _ _ _ _ _☐_ _ _ _

8. _ _ _ _ _ _☐_ _

Mystery Word ☐☐☐☐☐☐☐☐

Übung 11:

Vervollständigen Sie die Sätze:

1. Oh no! I forgot to pay my telephone _ _ _ _ and now they've cut off my telephone!

2. I don't know if I have enough money to pay for the trip myself – I need to check my bank _ _ _ _ _.

3. At our company _ _ _ _ _ is very important. That's why we all have our own user names and passwords.

4. Online _ _ _ _ _ is saving companies money – it's now much easier and cheaper to deal with suppliers.

5. A: I can't open this email!

B: That's because it's _ _ _ _ _. You need a special software to read it.

Forschung und Entwicklung sollen die Wettbewerbsfähigkeit eines Unternehmens sichern. Dabei beziehen sich die Innovationsprozesse sowohl auf das Produkt als auch auf die Produktionsverfahren. Der folgende Lernschritt liefert hierzu wichtige Begriffe.

Produkt

Der folgende Artikel informiert über die verschiedenen Lebenszyklen von Produkten.

A product life cycle can be divided into four parts. First there is the design and production, which includes making decisions about investment. Next comes the growth stage: here the product is launched onto the market, and begins to sell. Hopefully at some point the initial investment is recouped, and the product begins to generate profits. After a while the product goes into its third stage, which is where the product reaches maturity. It produces steady income, and might go through various improvements or modifications. Finally the product goes into decline and eventually stops being produced; this is the fourth and final stage.
Examples from the real world show just how different this life cycle can be, depending on the product. Every year the entertainment industry produces new films, shows and music. Most of these have a very brief life cycle and go into decline after only a few months. Similarly clothing is sometimes produced for a single season. Cars may have life cycles of five to ten years before a model is replaced by a newer design. Some foodstuffs, however, were introduced onto to the market place over a hundred years ago, and show no sign of going into decline.

Vokabeln

assortment	Auswahl
brand	Sorte, Marke
by-product	Neben-/ Abfallprodukt
consumer durables	langlebige Gebrauchsgüter
core product	Haupterzeugnis
decline	(hier) nachlassender Bedarf
design	Design, Gestaltung
feature	Merkmal, Bestandteil
finished product	Fertigerzeugnis
foodstuff	Nahrungsmittel
generate	erzeugen
growth	Wachstum
manufactures	Industrieware
maturity	Reife
modification	Änderung
life cycle	Lebenszyklus
semifinished product	Halberzeugnis

11 Produkt, Forschung, Entwicklung und Herstellung

Übung 1:

Bringen Sie die Wörter der Sätze in die richtige Reihenfolge.

1. A divided product life into four cycle can be parts.

_ _

2. stage production involves design The first and.

_ _

3. stage onto the the product is During the growth launched market.

_ _

_ _

4. The stops being product eventually produced

_ _

_ _

5. into product goes Finally the decline.

_ _

6. season Clothing is produced for a sometimes single.

_ _

_ _

7. show no into sign Some foodstuffs of going decline.

_ _

_ _

Übung 2:

Füllen Sie die Lücken mit Wörtern aus dem Text.

1. A product life cycle can be _ _ _ _ _ _ _ _ _ _ _ _ into four parts.

2. The first stage _ _ _ _ _ _ _ _ _ _ _ _ _ _ _ design and production.

3. During the growth stage the product is _ _ _ _ _ _ _ _ _ _ _ _ _ _ onto the market.

4. The product _ _ _ _ _ _ _ _ _ _ _ _ _ _ _ stops being produced.

5. Finally the product goes into _ _ _ _ _ _ _ _ _ _ _ _ _ _ .

6. Clothing is sometimes _ _ _ _ _ _ _ _ _ _ _ _ _ _ _ _ _ for a single season.

7. Some foodstuffs show no _ _ _ _ _ _ _ _ _ _ _ _ _ _ of going into decline.

Übung 3:

Finden Sie die richtige Definition und kreuzen Sie an:

1. foodstuff	☐ technical changes
2. decline	☐ no ups or downs
3. mature	☐ to get back
4. modifications	☐ fully developed
5. to recoup	☐ going down
6. steady	☐ something you eat

Forschung

Forschung und Entwicklung spielen in modernen Unternehmen eine wichtige Rolle. Sie sollen die Wettbewerbsfähigkeit sicherstellen. Bestimmte Industriezweige, wie z. B. die pharmazeutische oder biotechnische Industrie, geben einen großen Teil ihres Etats für Forschungszwecke aus.

Research involves developing new knowledge and ideas which may be of benefit to the company. Basic research looks at how we can improve our understanding of fundamental principles, whereas applied research aims to acquire knowledge in order to solve a particular problem or meet a specific need.

Most research follows a basic pattern. First researchers ask the question and review the literature to see what is already known. They then formulate a hypothesis, which is a statement of what they expect to find. This allows researchers to design the research, which could be a case study, a field survey, a laboratory experiment or even a field experiment. Once the data has been collected it must be analysed and interpreted.

There are three key issues which must be addressed by research. First of all there is the question of ethics. Some companies do not carry out research which may benefit the defence industry, for example, or harm the environment. Research which harms human participants is also ethically questionable. Next there is the question of reliability. Are the results consistent? Will other researchers come up with the same data? Finally there is the validity issue – do the results of the research really mean what the researchers claim?

Vokabeln

applied research	angewandte Forschung
acquire	erwerben
basic research	Grundlagen-forschung
case study	Fallstudie
data	Daten
environment	Umwelt
field experiment	Feldexperiment
field survey	Feldstudie
formulate	formulieren
hypothesis	Hypothese
improve	verbessern
issue	Thema, Frage
knowledge	Kenntnis
laboratory	Labor
reliability	Zuverlässigkeit
researcher	Forscher
review	durcharbeiten
validity	Gültigkeit

Übung 4:

Übersetzen Sie die folgenden Sätze!

1. Mein Auto ist sehr zuverlässig.

____

2. Wir führen Experimente in dem Labor durch.

____

3. Die Hauptangelegenheit hat mit dem Honorar zu tun.

____

____

4. Sind die Daten gültig?

____

5. Zuerst müssen wir eine Hypothese formulieren.

____

6. Lassen Sie uns die Literatur nochmal durcharbeiten.

____

7. Kinder erwerben Wissen in der Schule.

____

Übung 5:

Welche Wörter gehören in die Lücken?
(analysed, review, laboratory, formulate, find)

First researchers ask the question and (1.) __________ the literature to see what is already known. They then (2.) __________ a hypothesis, which is a statement of what they expect to (3.) __________. This allows researchers to design the research, which could be a case study, a field survey, a (4.) __________ experiment or even a field experiment. Once the data has been collected it must be (5.) __________ and interpreted.

Infobox

Reverse engineering is about examining competitors' products in detail to see how they are made.

Entwicklung

Die Entwicklung eines Produkts geht Hand in Hand mit der Forschung. Bevor ein Produkt auf den Markt kommt, werden von der Produktidee bis zur Herstellung alle Schritte konzipiert. Entwicklung beinhaltet aber mehr, als lediglich Konzepte zu generieren.

Ideas are not the same as concepts. Concepts explain the form of the product or service, the way in which it will operate, the market need it will satisfy, and the benefits to the customer. Once

this has been formulated, the next stage is to screen the concept, to make sure that it is feasible. Such a feasibility study will look at financial aspects such as how much investment is required and how much profit can be expected (ROI). It will also consider technical issues – can the product actually be made, and what technology will be necessary. Finally it will examine what will happen if things go wrong, in other words, the vulnerability of the design.
Products go through several other stages before they are released onto the market. Preliminary design allows developers to evaluate and improve a basic concept before prototyping and final design.

Vokabeln

benefit	Vorteil
concept	Konzept
evaluate	evaluieren, bewerten
feasible	möglich
market need	Nachfrage
operate	operieren, funktionieren
preliminary	vorläufig
prototyping	Entwicklung eines Prototyps
ROI (return on investment)	Kapitalrendite
screen	überprüfen
release on to the market	auf den Markt bringen
vulnerability	Anfälligkeit

Infobox

Part of process design involves designing the jobs which people have to do. Questions to be asked at this stage include:
Where will the job take place?
What skills are required?
Who will do what tasks?
What will be the order of the tasks?
What facilities will the workforce need?
What decisions will staff be allowed to take?

Übung 6:

Bringen Sie diese Stadien der Entwicklung in die richtige Reihenfolge: concept, final design, feasibility study, evaluation and improvements, idea, preliminary design, prototyping

1. ________________________
2. ________________________
3. ________________________
4. ________________________
5. ________________________
6. ________________________
7. ________________________

Übung 7:

Füllen Sie die Lücken mit dem jeweils richtigen Fragewort.

1. ___________ decisions will staff be allowed to take?
2. ___________ will the job take place?

3. ___________ will be the order of the tasks?

4. ___________ skills are required?

5. ___________ facilities will the workforce need?

6. ___________ will the workforce be needed?

7. ___________ will do ___________ ___________ tasks?

Herstellung

Eine Besuchergruppe besichtigt eine Fabrik der Metallindustrie. Ms Allen, Mitarbeiterin der PR-Abteilung des Spezialwerkzeugherstellers Binfurt, leitet die Führung durch die Werkhallen.

"Right, before we go in there are one or two safety points I'd like to mention. First of all please don't touch any of the machines or talk to any of the operators. And we'll need to wear these helmets in the main assembly hall.
And these safety glasses in the machine shop.
Ok, if you'd like to follow me. Oh, one more thing. Please keep to the walkways. – They're marked in yellow.
Right, can everybody hear me? What you can see in front of you now is what we call incoming. This is where we unload all the trucks and unpack all the items that come in from our sub-suppliers. All the raw materials and some of the basic components come in through here. You can see a truck just coming in now. Behind me are some of the offices which are involved in the supply management chain. Over there is inventory control, and next door is part of the purchasing department. We use a just-in-time system which allows us to keep our inventory levels low.
If you follow me through this door, we'll just cross the yard into the machine shop. This is where we manufacture various metal items which we need for the assembly later. We also keep any special tools, jigs and fixtures which may be needed in the assembly area.
This is the assembly area. This is where all the components are put together to

Vokabeln

assembly	Montage
cast	gießen
conveyor belt	Förderband
forge	schmieden
jigs and fixtures	Vorrichtungen
lathe	Drehbank
milling machine	Fräsmaschine
operator	Bediener
shop	Werkhalle
tool	Werkzeug
walkway	Fußweg

make the final product. You can see the finished products in the cardboard boxes at the end of the conveyor belt over there.
I'd just like to point out some of the machines we have. Over there is a lathe. And next to it you can see a milling machine. We also do our casting and forging on-site, but we do that in another building."

Übung 8:

Welche Wörter gehören zusammen?

1. safety	☐ management
2. machine	☐ points
3. special	☐ department
4. raw	☐ area
5. supply	☐ materials
6. inventory	☐ tools
7. purchasing	☐ control
8. assembly	☐ shop

Übung 9:

Übersetzen Sie!

1. Montage _______________
2. Werkhalle _______________
3. Fräsmaschine _______________
4. Drehbank _______________
5. Vorrichtungen _______________
6. Förderband _______________
7. gießen _______________
8. schmieden _______________
9. Fußweg _______________

Qualität

Die Qualitätssicherung von Produkten hat in den letzten Jahren immer mehr Managementspezialisten beschäftigt. Dieser Artikel erklärt einige Schlüsselbegriffe.

Final quality inspections are based on a traditional view of quality, where a product is made and then inspected for defects. Quality control has to do with checking what has been produced, but normally looks at the product at various stages of manufacture. The aim is to catch the defects at an early stage. Quality assurance moves away from the idea of looking at what has been produced, and instead looks at how it has been produced. The key is to look at the methods affecting production, and finding the best way to do things. This is sometimes known as setting up a quality system.

TQM stands for Total Quality Management. Here are some of the key principles:
1. Focus on the customer: it is the requirements of the customer which are paramount.
2. Continuous improvement: the aim is to achieve "zero defects".
3. Excellent communication and training: all members of staff, from senior management to shop floor workers, must be fully aware of what the aims are and how they are to be achieved.
4. Measurement of results: methods must be put in place to see exactly what has been achieved, so that improvements can be made.
5. Everyone is responsible for quality: quality is not only about products, it is also about everything to do with the organisation.

Vokabeln

check	kontrollieren, testen
comply with	entsprechen, erfüllen
defect	Mangel
final quality inspection	Endkontrolle
flawed	fehlerhaft, defekt
paramount	ausschlaggebend
quality assurance	Qualitätssicherung
quality control	Qualitätskontrolle
sample check	Stichprobe
Total Quality Management, TQM	totales Qualitätsmanagement

Übung 10:

Sind die Sätze inhaltlich richtig oder falsch?

1. Quality assurance looks at the how, quality control looks at the what.

☐ richtig ☐ falsch

2. TQM stands for Training Quality Managers.

☐ richtig ☐ falsch

3. The search for zero defects is part of the continuous improvement philosophy.

☐ richtig ☐ falsch

4. Quality systems try to find the best way of doing things.

☐ richtig ☐ falsch

5. One of the principles of TQM is that the interests of the customer must come first.

☐ richtig ☐ falsch

6. Another TQM principle is that the quality manager is responsible for quality.

☐ richtig ☐ falsch

Im Zeitalter der Globalisierung wächst die Bedeutung von Handel und Logistik. Dieses Kapitel stellt einige der wichtigsten Ausdrücke dieser Sachgebiete vor.

Import und Export

Der globale Handel wächst jedes Jahr und fördert das Wirtschaftswachstum der einzelnen Länder. Import und Export sind daher entscheidende Faktoren der Volkswirtschaft.

Importing and exporting basically consists of selling goods originating in one country (the source country or country of origin) in a second country (the target country or destination country). A company may decide to export directly to another country, or it may work with a trading partner. This trading partner could be a representative or agent working on a commission basis, and also possibly receiving a retainer, or it could be a wholesaler, distributor or retailer. Many countries place restrictions on the import of certain goods. These restrictions could be tariff barriers or quotas. Imports are generally also subject to import duties. On the other hand, some governments encourage the export of certain goods by using incentives such as tax breaks. If a company is importing or exporting goods, it must have the correct import or export licence.

Vokabeln

agent	Repräsentant
commission	Provision
country of origin	Herkunftsland
destination country	Bestimmungsland
distributor	Zwischenhändler
import duty	Einfuhrzoll
incentive	Anreiz
quota	Quote
representative	Vertreter
restriction	Beschränkung
retailer	Einzelhändler
retainer	Vorschuss
source country	Herkunftsland
target country	Bestimmungsland
tariff barrier	Zollbarriere
tax break	Steuervergünstigung
trading partner	Handelspartner
wholesaler	Großhändler

Übung 1:

Sind die Sätze richtig oder falsch?

1. The source country is the same as the target country.

☐ richtig ☐ falsch

2. Export companies work with trading partners.

☐ richtig ☐ falsch

3. There are different kinds of trading partners.

☐ richtig ☐ falsch

4. A tariff barrier is a kind of import restriction.

☐ richtig ☐ falsch

5. You normally have to pay import duties on imported goods.

☐ richtig ☐ falsch

6. Tax breaks are used to encourage the import of certain goods.

☐ richtig ☐ falsch

7. You must have an import licence to import goods.

☐ richtig ☐ falsch

Übung 2:

Bilden Sie sinnvolle Paare!

1. trading	☐ trade
2. tariff	☐ exports
3. target	☐ partner
4. tax	☐ commission basis
5. subject to	☐ on imports
6. import	☐ country
7. work on a	☐ outflow
8. place restrictions	☐ break
9. balance of	☐ duty
10. invisible	☐ barrier
11. currency	☐ import duty

Übung 3:

Finden Sie die sieben Rechtschreibfehler in den folgenden Sätzen und verbessern Sie das jeweilige Wort.

1. A holesaler buys products in bulk and sells them to retailers.

____

____

2. There are often restriction on what you can import.

____

____

3. When you import something you normally have to pay extra dutee.

____

____

4. You need a handling partner to do business.

____

5. An agent normally works for a Kommission.

____

6. Another word for target is destiny.

____

7. The country where goods are produced is called the country of original.

____

____

Zoll und Dokumente

Wenn man Waren im- oder exportieren will, muss man sicherstellen, dass die Waren ohne Probleme den Zoll passieren. Der folgende Artikel betrachtet Vorgänge beim Zoll.

It is not always easy to obtain permission to import goods into a country. There may be an embargo, which means a ban against importation of goods from a specific country, or high tariffs imposed to favour local businesses; alternatively some goods may be classed as illegal or contraband (such as drugs).

Customs agencies spend a lot of time and effort trying to prevent the movement of such goods across their borders. If a business traveller is carrying samples to show a potential business partner, these count as imports, and have to follow specific procedures. There are two main ways to bring samples into a country. The first involves simply paying the necessary duty or tax upon arrival. Normally if the goods are later exported in the same condition it is possible to claim these duties back – this is known as drawback.

Another option is to obtain some sort of permission to import goods for a specific period of time. Such temporary importation documents are sometimes called carnets, and are issued by authorities such as local business associations or chambers of commerce. In this case it is not necessary to pay any duty.

Other documents often required by customs are a customs invoice, which describes the goods and gives information about the consignor, consignee and value of the shipment, and a certificate of origin, which shows where the goods were produced.

Vokabeln

ban	Verbot
carnet	Zollbegleitschein
certificate of origin	Ursprungs-zeugnis
claim back	zurückfordern
condition	Zustand
consignee	Warenempfänger
consignor	Verfrachter
contraband	Schmuggelware
customs invoice	Zollfaktura, ~rechnung
customs officer	Zollbeamter
drawback	Rückerstattung
embargo	Handelsverbot
impose	verhängen
issue	ausstellen
permission	Genehmigung
regulation	Regelung
sample	Warenprobe
search	Suche
shipment	Versandeinheit
value	Wert

Übung 4:

Sind die Sätze richtig oder falsch?

1. An embargo is a kind of ban.

☐ richtig ☐ falsch

2. Legal goods are known as contraband.

☐ richtig ☐ falsch

3. Samples are not classified as imports.

☐ richtig ☐ falsch

4. "Drawback" refers to reclaiming duties paid on imported goods.

☐ richtig ☐ falsch

5. A carnet lets you pay lower import duties.

☐ richtig ☐ falsch

6. A certificate of origin shows where the goods come from.

☐ richtig ☐ falsch

Übung 5:

Übersetzen Sie ins Englische.

1. Suche ______________
2. Wert ______________
3. Warenempfänger ______________
4. Zollbegleitschein ______________
5. verhängen ______________
6. Warenprobe ______________
7. ausgeben ______________

Transportmittel

Das folgende, einer Website entnommene Werbematerial beschreibt die Aktivitäten einer typischen Logistikfirma.

ABOUT US

Reliance Shippers, Inc. is one of North America's leading providers of global logistics and transportation services. We are an integrated intermodal transportation company serving domestic and international customers countrywide from origin to destination with our own rail, truck, and terminal operations. With more than 80 regional and international operational and sales facilities

Vokabeln

carrier	Spediteur
container	Container
destination	Ziel
door-to-door	von Haus zu Haus
facility	Einrichtung
fleet	Flotte
intermodal transportation	Transport mit mehreren Verkehrsmitteln
origin	Herkunft
rail	Eisenbahn
reach	Reichweite
shipper	Befrachter
single-source	einzelne Quelle
terminal	Endstelle
tracking and tracing facilities	Nachvollziehbarkeit des Transportwegs
trailer	Anhänger
transcontinental	transkontinental
truck	Lastkraftwagen

in North America, we offer global shippers a single-source team approach with modern rail, road, sea and air transportation services.
We serve more key markets than any other carrier. Our countrywide network of terminals ensures the widest-possible reach in the United States, in Canada and in Mexico. Our services include:
- Transcontinental container service
- Door-to-door services between key markets
- Large fleet of vehicles, including 40-foot and 20-foot containers, trailers, and insulated equipment
- 24-hour tracking and tracing facilities

Infobox

The word "truck" is American English. In British English it is normally "lorry".

Übung 6:
Bilden Sie sinnvolle Paare.

1. intermodal	☐ source
2. tracing	☐ container
3. single-	☐ service
4. wide	☐ shipper
5. 40-foot	☐ transportation
6. door-to-door	☐ reach
7. leading	☐ markets
8. global	☐ facilities
9. key	☐ provider

Übung 7:
Übersetzen Sie!

1. Befrachter _______________
2. Ziel _______________
3. Flotte _______________
4. Spediteur _______________
5. Lastkraftwagen _______________
6. Einrichtung _______________
7. Reichweite _______________
8. Anhänger _______________
9. Herkunft _______________

Groß- und Einzelhandel

Groß- und Einzelhandel verändern sich zurzeit rapide. Die folgende Präsentation beschreibt aktuelle Trends in den USA.

Good morning everyone. Thanks for coming. Today I'm going to be talking to you about trends in food wholesaling and retailing. Let's start with a couple

of definitions. First of all, what exactly do food wholesalers do? Well, basically they buy large amounts of goods from manufacturers and sell them on to retailers in smaller, more desirable quantities.
And what about retailers? Retailers buy goods from wholesalers and sell them to consumers. They basically decide what goes on store shelves but their decisions must ultimately be driven by consumers. Food is the largest retail sector in the USA, accounting for around $900 billion in sales every year.
So what are the trends? Let's look at wholesaling first. There are three main trends. First of all, the number of food service distributors is growing – this includes restaurants, fast-food outlets, airlines, and even schools. Secondly, wholesale food clubs are becoming more popular – these allow the end-consumer to buy food at wholesale prices. Thirdly, the wholesale industry is growing through a process of consolidation – mergers are becoming more and more common.
In the retail trade we can also see three main trends. First of all, the number of retail outlets is declining, but at the same time the average outlet size is increasing. Secondly, there is an increasing amount of foreign investment, mainly from Europe and Asia. Thirdly, the format of stores is becoming more diverse – as well as the traditional supermarket and Mom and Pop store, we now have very large retail outlets, the so-called "supercenters", as well as small convenience stores.
Another important development for both wholesale and retail is the increasing use of ECR, or Efficient Consumer

Vokabeln

checkout	Kasse
commodity market	Warenbörse
consolidation	Konsolidierung
consumption	Verbrauch
convenience store	24-Stunden-Geschäft
distributor	Zwischenhändler
end-consumer	Endverbraucher
manufacturer	Hersteller
merchandise	Ware
merger	Fusion
Mom and Pop store	Tante-Emma-Laden
outlet	Verkaufsstelle
retailing	Einzelhandel
sector	Branche
shelf (pl: shelves)	Regal
stockist	Fachhändler, ~geschäft
store	Laden
supply chain	Lieferkette
up-to-date	aktuell
warehouse	lagern
wholesaler	Großhändler
wholesaling	Großhandel

Response. ECR aims at developing a responsive, consumer-driven system which allows wholesalers, distributors, and retailers to work together to maximize consumer value and minimize supply chain costs. This requires a smooth, continual product flow matched to consumer consumption. And to maintain the flow of products, both wholesalers and retailers need up-to-date, precise information flowing electronically between the retail checkout and the manufacturing line.

ECR has two main advantages – it maximizes consumer satisfaction, and it minimizes the cost of marketing, through increased efficiency.

Infobox

Be aware of language differences:
"Store" is American English. In British English it is "shop".

Übung 8:

Sind die Sätze richtig oder falsch?

1. Retailers sell goods to wholesalers.

☐ richtig ☐ falsch

2. Food is the biggest retail industry in the USA.

☐ richtig ☐ falsch

3. American wholesalers are currently merging with each other.

☐ richtig ☐ falsch

4. The average size of retail outlets is getting bigger.

☐ richtig ☐ falsch

5. Mom and Pop stores are replacing convenience stores.

☐ richtig ☐ falsch

6. Efficient Consumer Response aims at minimizing consumer value.

☐ richtig ☐ falsch

7. Efficient Consumer Response increases the cost of marketing.

☐ richtig ☐ falsch

Übung 9:

Bilden Sie aus den gegebenen Buchstaben sinnvolle Wörter. Die Zahl in Klammern gibt die Anzahl der Wörter an.

1. no icon so tidal (1) ____________
2. steer on nice coven (2) ____________
3. i not a fascist (1) ____________
4. chins play up (2) ____________
5. oh real slew (1) ____________
6. bistro id rut (1) ____________
7. run me a cat fur (1) ____________

12 Vertrieb, Handel und Logistik

Direktvertrieb

Produkte werden oft auch ohne Einzelhändler direkt an die Kunden verkauft. Der folgende Artikel beschreibt Möglichkeiten hierfür.

There are several ways in which producers can sell directly to consumers, without intermediaries such as retailers. This benefits both producers and consumers. "Direct selling" refers to the person-to-person sale of a consumer good or service, away from a traditional retail location. Goods are mainly sold by sales representatives at in-home product demonstrations or parties. Some examples of direct selling goods are cleaning products, kitchen implements, or clothing. Sales representatives generally work part-time and normally receive commission based on the quantity of goods sold. The internet is becoming an important element in direct selling, allowing direct sellers to have (at least in theory) a global customer base. Another variation is known as "direct marketing", where a producer sells directly to the consumer, for example through mail-order catalogues or via the internet. Goods can also be sold via teleshopping channels on cable television. Factory shops are another possibility. These are generally located close to where the goods are actually produced, and sell "seconds", namely goods which do not quite meet the company's quality standards. Clothing and kitchenware are two examples of goods commonly sold through factory shops.

Vokabeln

channel	Kanal
commission	Provision
customer base	Kundenstamm
direct marketing	Direktvertrieb
doorstep selling (UK)	Haustürverkauf
factory shop	Fabrikverkauf
intermediary	Zwischenhändler
mail-order catalogue	Versandhauskatalog
representative	Vertreter
seconds	Waren zweiter Wahl
teleshopping	Teleshopping

Übung 10:

Vervollständigen Sie die Sätze!

1. With direct selling, manufacturers sell directly to customers, without an ______ .

2. __________ are normally located near where the goods are made.

3. With the internet, a direct seller can have a worldwide __________ .

Kunden zu werben und ihnen Produkte zu verkaufen ist selbst in der eigenen Sprache nicht einfach. In einer fremden Sprache ist es noch schwieriger. Dieser Lernschritt vermittelt die wichtigsten Redemittel für das erfolgreiche Verkaufsgespräch auf Englisch.

Kundenakquisition

Kunden zu akquirieren und sie an sich zu binden ist der Schlüssel zum Erfolg. Im folgenden Text beschreibt ein Berater die Techniken, die er sich zu Nutzen macht.

First of all you've got to make sure that clients know about you. This means that your marketing has got to be first class. There are lots of ways to do this – they all cost time and money, but think of it as an investment. For example, you can get yourself known by giving talks, writing to the press, getting yourself published, or simply by having your name on people's lists. You might even consider advertising. I use a very simple brochure that leads people to my website. Networking is about using other people to lead you to clients. Get to know people and let them know what you do. The more people you know the greater the chance of finding that client. What you are looking for is someone with MAN.

M stands for money, A for authority, and N for need. In other words, the decision maker who can give you work. Sometimes it's worth getting a third party to do your selling for you. An agent earns a commission on the work he gets for you, so it doesn't cost you much. And some companies will be happy to keep you on their books on a freelance basis. They may recommend you to other companies if your work is good.

Vokabeln

agent	Vertreter
brochure	Broschüre
client	Kunde/Kundin
commission	Provision
decision maker	Entscheidungsträger
freelance	freiberuflich
on someone's books	in einer Kartei
prospectus	Prospekt
publish	veröffentlichen
recommend	empfehlen

Übung 1:

Sind die Sätze inhaltlich richtig oder falsch?

1. There are many ways to market a product.

☐ richtig ☐ falsch

2. You can become known by writing newspaper articles.

☐ richtig ☐ falsch

3. When you network you should always try to sell your product to your contacts.

☐ richtig ☐ falsch

4. The more people you know, the more chance you have to make a sale.

☐ richtig ☐ falsch

5. You need to find a person with money, authority and need.

☐ richtig ☐ falsch

6. Using an agent is expensive.

☐ richtig ☐ falsch

7. Your current customers may recommend you to other companies.

☐ richtig ☐ falsch

Übung 2:

Bilden Sie sinnvolle Paare zwischen diesen Wörtern.

1. decision	☐ books
2. on someone's	☐ a commission
3. third	☐ published
4. earn	☐ maker
5. get	☐ basis
6. give	☐ party
7. write	☐ talks
8. on a freelance	☐ to the press

Übung 3:

Übersetzen Sie!

1. freiberuflich ___________
2. Dritte ___________
3. veröffentlichen ___________
4. Provision ___________
5. Kunde/Kundin ___________
6. Entscheidungsträger ___________
7. in einer Kartei sein ___________
8. Vertreter ___________

Verkaufspsychologie

Beim Verkauf geht es darum, potenzielle Kunden zu überzeugen. Im folgenden Text gibt ein erfahrener Verkäufer jungen Kollegen einige Tipps. Wie er betont, wurden einige dieser Punkte schon vor 2500 Jahren von Aristoteles erwähnt, und sie werden noch heute von Verkäufern beachtet.

Ok, so you have a problem. You need to sell. Well, let me tell you that the answers have been around for over two and a half thousand years. You want to know more? Aristotle suggested that there are four main ways to persuade people. Either you persuade people to do something by producing clear evidence, or you do it by strength of character, or by logical argument or by passion. Let's go through each of these in turn. The first one is easy. If your product or service is the best on the market, show the customer the proof. Produce facts. Give them the evidence. Sometimes, however, your product is not quite as superior as you would like it to be. But no problem. You can still sell it. All you have to do is connect with your customer's heart, head or soul. Heart first. Let me give you an example. Some people have a certain charisma – you want to believe what they say. You can develop this charisma. One way is to build up your reputation, to convince the customer that you can be trusted.

The customer must be confident that what you have to say is correct and fair, and carries weight.
Alternatively you can go for the head – use logic. Use reasoned argument to make your point. Organise your sales pitch so that it shows the customer not only the problem he or she is facing, but also the solution to the problem that you can provide. Don't forget to stress the benefits. The last method is to use passion. Being interested in a product is not enough. You have to believe in what you are saying, and you have to be committed. And your customer must feel this – no pretending.
But please don't forget – you are selling to people. Make people feel good about what you are selling, and the rest will be a piece of cake. Believe me. I know.

Vokabeln

a piece of cake	ein Kinderspiel
benefit	Nutzen
charisma	Charisma, Ausstrahlung
committed	engagiert
confident	selbstbewusst
convince	überzeugen
evidence	Beweis
hard sell	aggressive Verkaufstaktik
persuade	überreden
pitch	zum Kauf drängen
pretend	vortäuschen
proof	Beweis
reputation	guter Ruf
sales pitch	Kundenansprache
soft sell	diskrete Verkaufstaktik
trust	vertrauen

Übung 4:
Sind die Sätze inhaltlich richtig oder falsch?

1. Aristotle said there are three main ways to persuade people.

☐ richtig ☐ falsch

2. If your product is the best show your customer evidence of this.

☐ richtig ☐ falsch

3. Charisma is not important for selling.

☐ richtig ☐ falsch

4. You should emphasize the benefits to the customer in your sales pitch.

☐ richtig ☐ falsch

5. You need to be passionate about your product, not just interested.

☐ richtig ☐ falsch

6. You should pretend to be committed to your product.

☐ richtig ☐ falsch

7. If you get your customer feeling good about your product, the sale will be easy.

☐ richtig ☐ falsch

Infobox

Some rhetorical techniques you can use to persuade your customer

- Tripling: Describe your product using three elements. Our product is affordable, efficient and reliable. Our service teams are well-trained, experienced, and motivated.
- Ask rhetorical questions (questions which do not expect an answer from the listener): So, how did we get such high profits? What do you need to do to solve this problem? Who cares?
- Build rapport: by using "we" and "us" rather than "me" and "you". We have the same objective – to make this project succeed. Both of us have a lot of experience in this field. We're looking for a win-win solution.

Übung 5:

Füllen Sie die Lücken, indem Sie die folgenden Wörter verwenden: evidence, pretending, convinced, reputation, pitch, persuasive, benefited, confident, cake.

A: Hi Sally. How's it going?

B: Great thanks. Hey, I really liked your presentation. Excellent sales (1.) ____________.

A: Really? Thanks. I wasn't very (2.) ________________.

B: You made it look like a piece of (3.) ______________.

A: But do you think I (4.) __________________ them?

B: You were very (5.) ________________. You presented the (6.) ____________________ clearly. And you looked committed too – the bit about how your family has (7.) ________________ was first class. And I think the manufacturer has a good (8.) ________________, which always helps.

A: Maybe. Actually I think the product is terrible. Still, at school they always said I was good at (9.) ________________.

Übung 6:
Welche Wörter gehören zusammen?

1. a piece	☐ point
2. sales	☐ your reputation
3. reasoned	☐ the benefits
4. strength of	☐ weight
5. clear	☐ argument
6. make your	☐ of cake
7. stress	☐ pitch
8. carry	☐ evidence
9. build up	☐ character

Kundenberatung

Eine Verkäuferin in einem Laden für Mobiltelefone berät einen Kunden. Das Gespräch endet erfolgreich – mit dem Verkauf eines Telefons.

Shop assistant: Good morning. Can I help you?
Customer: Actually, yes. I'm looking for a mobile phone.
Shop assistant: Well, you've come to the right place! First of all, can you tell me what you plan to use your phone for?
Customer: Well, I travel around a lot for my job, so I need to be reachable while I'm away from the office.
Shop assistant: Are you planning to make calls as well as receive calls?
Customer: Yes, I suppose so. But I'll probably receive more calls than make them.
Shop assistant: So it's mainly for business? Or do you think you'll use it for friends and family as well?
Customer: I would say mainly business, but of course I'll use it to call friends and family, for example if I'm on a business trip.
Shop assistant: Are you interested in using the internet or email with your phone?
Customer: Yes, I am, actually. Especially email – it would be good if I could check my email while I'm on the move.

Vokabeln

bargain	günstiger Kauf
charge	Gebühr
concession	Zugeständnis
discount	Rabatt, Preisnachlass
estimate	Kostenvoranschlag
kindly	freundlicherweise
make sense	einen Sinn ergeben
on approval	zur Ansicht
on the move	unterwegs
peak times	Hauptbelastungszeit
sale	Ausverkauf
sale or return	Kauf mit Rückgaberecht
special offer	Sonderangebot
suggest	vorschlagen, empfehlen
suit	passen
without obligation	unverbindlich

And I often need to check the company website when I'm visiting customers, to check the status of their orders.
Shop assistant: In that case, I would suggest this model – the Erika 150. You can open it up like this, then you have a normal keyboard for writing emails. And notice the large screen – makes visiting websites much easier.
Customer: Wow – that's really very impressive. I've never seen that one before.
Shop assistant: And the best thing is, it's actually on special offer at the moment – there's a 30 per cent discount on the price.
Customer: That sounds good.
Shop assistant: Let me tell you about the different charge plans we offer. Plan A is good if you're going to be making most of your calls during peak times, that is, from 8am until 6pm. Plan B has slightly higher charges during peak times, but very good rates in the evenings and weekends. I would say plan A will suit you better, seeing as most of your calls will be for business.
Customer: Yes, that would make sense.
Shop assistant: Shall I make out the contract for you?
Customer: Um ... actually yes. That sounds like just what I need.

Übung 7:

Wie lauten die Sätze? Bringen Sie die Wörter in die richtige Reihenfolge.

1. sense would that make

_ _

_ _

2. price there's 10 a on per discount cent the

_ _

_ _

3. this in I model suggest would that case

_ _

_ _

4. phone your me you can plan use tell what to you for?

_ _

_ _

5. out contract make the shall I you for?

_ _

_ _

6. just what that need like sounds I

_ _

_ _

7. product suit I would this say better will you

_ _

_ _

Infobox

Make sure you find out about your customer's needs before you try to sell them anything. Ask them questions to discover what they really need!

Übung 8:

Bilden Sie sinnvolle Paare.

1. peak	☐ discount
2. special	☐ need
3. slightly higher	☐ move
4. in that	☐ offer
5. a 30 per cent	☐ times
6. make	☐ case
7. on the	☐ charges
8. just what I	☐ sense

Übung 9:

Übersetzen Sie und enträtseln Sie das Lösungswort!

1. Rabatt, 2. vorschlagen, 3. da, 4. ein bisschen, 5. Sonderangebot, 6. hauptsächlich, 7. besonders, 8. Gebühr

1. _ _ _☐ _ _ _ _

2. _☐ _ _ _ _ _

3. ☐ _ _ _ _ _ _ _

4. _ _ _ _ _☐ _ _

5. _ _ _ _ _ _ _ ☐ _ _ _ _

6. ☐ _ _ _ _ _

7. _ _ _☐ _ _ _ _ _ _

8. _ _ _☐ _ _

Mystery Word ☐☐☐☐☐☐☐☐

Vorstellen des Produkts

Ein Firmenvertreter präsentiert einer Gruppe von potenziellen Kunden eine neue Computersoftware zum Organisieren von Projektunterlagen.

Hello everyone. For those of you who don't know me, I'm Peter Weaver from APS Communications. I'm going to be talking to you about our project management software solution, APS Project, and explaining the potential benefits for your company.
First of all, though, I want to ask you a question. How many of you have worked on a project where you felt frustrated because you didn't have the most up-to-date versions of the project documents? Can you put your hands up? Okay, so that's about half of you. So you know how frustrating that can be. Well, with the help of APS Project, you will never have to experience that feeling again.

With our product, all the project documents are uploaded to a central server. The documents can then be updated by project members directly on the server. That means that every project member always has access to the latest version of each document – so no more confusion over which version is the most recent, no more wasting time trying to get hold of the person with the latest version. You can set the permissions on each document to determine who is allowed to change it – that means only the right people can make changes. It also facilitates work with sub-contractors – you might want to allow them to read documents but not change them.

By storing the documents on our central server, it means you don't have to worry about security or backups – we take care of all of that for you. This saves you time and money. Okay, now let me show you some screenshots of our software, to let you see just how easy it is to use ...

Vokabeln

access	Zugang
confusion	Verwirrung
customised	nach Kundenwunsch (gefertigt)
determine	bestimmen
facilitate	erleichtern
fancy goods	Neuheit
fast-selling	umsatzstark, leicht verkäuflich
fixture	Grundausstattung
frustrating	frustrierend
get hold of	finden
take care of	erledigen
up-to-date version	aktuelle Version
waste	verschwenden
winner	Verkaufsschlager

Infobox

When describing your product, don't just talk about its features. Tell the customer how those features will produce concrete benefits for them.

Übung 10:

Bilden Sie sinnvolle Paare.

1. potential	☐ a feeling
2. put your	☐ care of something
3. experience	☐ time
4. feel	☐ hands up
5. waste	☐ benefits
6. get	☐ you money
7. take	☐ frustrated
8. save	☐ hold of someone

Verhandlungen und Geschäftsabschluss 14

Eine mögliche Definition für „Verhandlung“ ist „miteinander ins Geschäft kommen“. Viele Verhandlungen werden mit dem Ziel geführt, eine „Win-Win-Situation“ herbeizuführen, d. h. eine Situation, in der beide Verhandlungspartner von dem Ergebnis profitieren.

Kostenvoranschläge

Kostenvoranschläge – die Verhandlungsgrundlage für Käufer und Verkäufer.

17 November 2005

Dear Mr Thompson,

Thank you very much for your letter of 14 November 2005, in which you expressed interest in our current range of office furniture.
As you can see from the enclosed brochure, we pride ourselves on a comprehensive range of items which should meet most if not all of your requirements. Deliveries can be made from stock, subject to availability.
The brochure includes an up to date price list. Please note that our prices are quoted FOB Hamburg Incoterms 2004. Special quotations, including substantial discounts, are of course available depending on quantities ordered.
You mention that you plan to be in Berlin next week. I would be pleased to show you our production lines and shipping facilities.
I would also welcome the opportunity to discuss your requirements in more detail.
I look forward to hearing from you.

Yours sincerely

Harald Samson
Managing Director

Enc: Brochure

Vokabeln

availability	Verfügbarkeit
competitive	wettbewerbsfähig
estimate	Kostenvoranschlag
firm offer	festes Angebot
FOB	Free On Board
good for	kreditwürdig
gross	brutto
Incoterms	International Commercial Terms
net	netto
range	Sortiment
value added tax	Mehrwertsteuer
VAT	

14 Verhandlungen und Geschäftsabschluss

Übung 1:

Ordnen Sie den Vokabeln die entsprechenden Übersetzungen zu!

1. range	☐ Rabatt
2. associated	☐ zugehörig
3. availability	☐ wesentlich
4. substantial	☐ Sortiment
5. discount	☐ Verfügbarkeit
6. facilities	☐ umfassend
7. comprehensive	☐ Einrichtungen

Infobox

Buyers and sellers all over the world use Incoterms 2000 to facilitate their trade. These are three letter abbreviations designed to ensure that both sides understand each others obligations, in other words, who pays for what. There are currently 13 terms, each precisely defined by the International Chamber of Commerce (ICC).

Übung 2:

Finden Sie die Wortverbindungen, wie sie im Text vorkommen. Der erste Teil ist vorgegeben:

1. associated ______________
2. subject to ______________
3. substantial ______________
4. up to ______________
5. price ______________
6. production ______________

Infobox

Preparation for any negotiation is key. This includes deciding on your objectives – what is the best you can achieve, and what is the lowest possible acceptable outcome. The result will normally be somewhere between the two.

Zahlungsmodalitäten

Bei einem Geschäftsabschluss ist es wichtig, auch die Zahlungsmodalitäten genau zu klären, damit es im Nachhinein nicht zu Unstimmigkeiten kommt.

There are many ways to pay for goods obtained abroad. With a bank transfer, the buyer simply instructs his bank to transfer money from his account to the seller's account.

A letter of credit is sent from one bank to another, and authorises payment to a person or a company. An irrevocable letter of credit cannot be cancelled unless both parties agree. A documentary letter of credit is one of the safest methods of payment. The buyer instructs his bank to pay the seller's bank as long as certain specified documents are received as proof. Examples of such documents are bills of lading, insurance certificates, and certificates of origin.

A bill of exchange is an order in writing. The seller (the so called drawer) sends the purchaser (the so called drawee) a bill of exchange, which the buyer then accepts by signing and returning it to the seller. The bill promises that the buyer will pay a certain sum by a certain time, or on demand, to a certain person (the so called payee). The accepted bill can then be sold by the drawer to raise cash.

Vokabeln

bank guarantee	Bankgarantie
bank transfer	Banküberweisung
bill of exchange	Wechsel
bill of lading	Konnossement
cash in advance	Vorauskasse
cash on delivery	Nachnahme
default interest	Verzugszinsen
discount	Skonto
documentary letter of credit	Dokumentenakkreditiv
drawee	Bezogene(r)
drawer	Aussteller(in)
international money order	Internationale Zahlungsanweisung
irrevocable	unwiderruflich
on demand	auf Nachfrage
past due	im Rückstand
payee	Zahlungsempfänger(in)
payment	Zahlung
reimburse	rückvergüten
repay	zurückzahlen
settlement date	Zahlungstermin

Übung 3:

Bilden Sie sinnvolle Paare.

1. bank	☐ demand
2. bill of	☐ certificate
3. on	☐ in advance
4. documentary letter	☐ a contract
5. irrevocable	☐ lading
6. certificate of	☐ transfer
7. insurance	☐ letter of credit
8. extensions of	☐ origin
9. payment	☐ of credit

Übung 4:

Sind die Sätze richtig oder falsch? Kreuzen Sie an!

1. A bank transfer is the only secure way to send money overseas.

☐ richtig ☐ falsch

2. The payee gives money to someone else.

☐ richtig ☐ falsch

3. A bill of lading is a shipping document.

☐ richtig ☐ falsch

4. In a bill of exchange the drawer is the person selling the goods.

☐ richtig ☐ falsch

5. A bill of exchange is an order in writing.

☐ richtig ☐ falsch

Bedingungen stellen und Kompromisse finden

Erfolgreich verhandeln bedeutet auch, Alternativvorschläge zu eröffnen, anstatt Streitgespräche zu führen. Im folgenden Gespräch verhandelt ein EDV-Vertreter mit einem Kunden über den Verkauf von 10 PCs.

Seller: So the total cost of the 10 PCs is 23,990 Euros.

Buyer: That's too much.

Seller: Yes, but let's look at what is included in the package.

Buyer: Not the technical specifications. Again.

Seller: No, of course not. But we haven't discussed the other aspects.

Buyer: Like?

Seller: Delivery. We'll deliver these PCs free of charge.

Buyer: When?

Seller: By next Monday?

Buyer: Ok.

Seller: Installation. Our technicians will install them free of charge.

Buyer: Ok. Sounds good.

Seller: And look at the software supplied – word processing packages, spreadsheets, presentations, email, all you need to run a successful office. And we're throwing in a one day training seminar for all your employees.

Buyer: What about if we don't want all this software. We would prefer to work with programs we know.

Seller: Ok. We could knock off 10% of the price if we deliver without programs.

Buyer: And no training?

Seller: Yes, of course.

Buyer: Great. And what about if we picked up the machines and installed them ourselves?

Seller: You mean from the shop?

Buyer: Yes.

Seller: That would be possible, but then we would probably have to change the warranties.

Vokabeln

agreement	Übereinkunft
assume	annehmen
break down (UK), ~ off (US)	scheitern, abbrechen
close of play	Feierabend
compromise	Kompromisse schließen
demand	Forderung
drive	aushandeln
knock off	nachlassen
prefer	bevorzugen
reassure	versichern
stipulate	zur Bedingung machen
throw in	etwas dazugeben
unsettled	ungeklärt
You drive a hard bargain.	Sie führen harte Verhandlungen.

Buyer: In what way?
Seller: Well, at the moment we are providing a warranty for 12 months – on site service. But that assumes that we have done the installation ourselves.
Buyer: Ok. How about if we change the warranty to cover say 6 months only, and you send one of your technicians to supervise the installation.
Seller: Hmm. You drive a hard bargain. But I think it sounds ok. I'll have to check with my boss.
Buyer: Ok, could you send me a new offer, say by close of play tomorrow?
Seller: No problem.

Infobox

Some more ways of setting conditions
We could ... if you agreed to ...
If you accepted ..., we could ...
If you ... we'd be prepared to ...
We will ..., provided that you ...
As long as ..., we would be happy to ...

Übung 5:

Formulieren Sie die Sätze in korrektem Englisch!

1. You drive hard bargains.

____

2. I'll send you the quotation by closing of play tomorrow.

____

3. We give you a discount if you agreed to buy over 500 units.

____

4. As long you pay us in cash, we would be happy to forget the paperwork.

____

5. Let's look to what's included in the package.

____

6. Our warranty assumes we done the installation ourselves.

____

Infobox

Clarifying
Making sure you understand what is being said is clearly important for any negotiation. One way is to repeat what you understood in your own words. Here are some phrases you can use:
So, if I understand you correctly, ...
So what you're saying is, ...
In other words, ...
You mean ...
I'm not sure whether I got that right.
Could you repeat that please?
Are you still with me?
I beg your pardon, but I missed that.
I'm sorry. I'll repeat that.

Übung 6:
Welche Wörter gehören in die Lücken? (prefer, bargain, assumed, throwing, off)

Dear Jack

I am enclosing a revised quotation as requested. As you will note, I have (1.) _____ _____ that you will organise transport yourselves. You will understand, I am sure, that we (2.) ____________ to do business with people we know and trust. But you drive a hard (3.) ___________. As agreed, we are (4.) ___________ in an extra 500 crates. And I am sure you will be happy to note that we have knocked a further 25% (5.) ______ _______ the price of future purchases as a measure of our goodwill.

Ein Geschäft abschließen

Um keine unliebsamen Überraschungen zu erleben, ist es wichtig, die Abschlussphase einer Verhandlung richtig zu gestalten. Beide Verhandlungspartner müssen sich über das Verhandlungsergebnis im Klaren sein. Hilfreich hierbei ist ein schriftliches Protokoll.

Melanie: Right, that just about wraps it up. I've got a plane to catch, so if you don't mind I'd like to end there, Richard. We can finish off the final details on the phone.

Richard: I'd rather we summarised very briefly before you go.

Melanie: What? Ok. But it'll have to be quick.

Richard: Basically you've agreed to transport all the components to the site by October 5th.

Melanie: Correct.

Richard: You will look after all the insurance aspects, and be responsible for loading and unloading.

Vokabeln

all included	alles in allem
deadline	letzter Termin
I'd rather we summarised very briefly.	Es wäre mir lieber, wir würden es kurz zusammenfassen.
I'll be in touch.	Ich werde in Verbindung bleiben.
Is there anything you'd like to add?	Gibt es irgendetwas, das Sie gerne hinzufügen würden?
liaison	Zusammenarbeit
minutes	Protokoll
negotiation	Verhandlung
paperwork	Papierkram
set up a meeting	eine Besprechung organisieren
You'll let me know by ...	Bitte benachrichtigen Sie mich bis ...

Melanie: Well, loading yes. But we haven't discussed unloading yet.
Richard: You'll also deal with all the paperwork at the border crossing?
Melanie: Yes. When will you get the licenses to us?
Richard: Tuesday?
Melanie: That should be ok.
Richard: Ok. Good. Moving on to the question of workers. I'm providing 50 labourers for the site, but you're providing the supervisors.
Melanie: One supervisor.
Richard: Will one be enough? Does he speak Spanish?
Melanie: Hadn't thought of that. I'll ask him.
Richard: Ok, so you'll let me know by email by tomorrow – otherwise I'm going to have to find a translator.
Melanie: Ok.
Richard: What about facilities for the workers?
Melanie: Well, it's your site.
Richard: Well, yes, but we will need to discuss exactly what's needed.
Melanie: Sure.
Richard: And ...
Melanie: Look, I really need to get that plane.
Richard: Ok. There are still a couple of outstanding points on my list. I think we'll need to set up another meeting.
Melanie: Like what?
Richard: The question of what happens if there's bad weather, for example. It's notorious for flash floods around that area.
Melanie: Ok.
Richard: And there's also the liaison thing with the piping contractor. I'm sure there'll be something to clarify there. Is there anything you'd like to add?
Melanie: Yeah. We agreed on a price of $100,000. All included. It looks like we may need to adjust that a little.
Richard: Yeah. Well. Ok. I'll be in touch. Have a good flight, Melanie.

Infobox

Do insist on clarity in all telephone business dealings, and don't allow pressure to lead you into giving the wrong impression. Before making your call make a list on a notepad of all important points you have to discuss. Tackle them one by one, carefully noting the replies for reference. Following the conversation, write an immediate report on the exchange with the other party and if necessary, for complete clarity, formulate it as a business letter.

Übung 7:

Bringen Sie die Wörter in den folgenden Sätzen in die richtige Reihenfolge.

1. summarised I'd rather we very before you briefly go

____

____

2. outstanding are still my a couple of there points on list

____

____

3. touch be I'll in

____

____

4. add is anything there like to you'd

____

____

5. get licenses to when the will you us

____

____

6. we'll meeting need to set I think up another

____

____

7. price we agreed $100,000 on a of

____

____

Infobox

Ending a negotiation

There are good reasons why you should review what you have agreed before you leave a negotiation. Most important is that if you find any problems it is easier to sort them out straightaway, rather than by letter or phone some time after your meeting. If possible produce a written summary, and include precise details about what each party has agreed to do, any agreed dates and deadlines, details of payment provisions and decisions about future discussions. And don't forget to get the other party to sign the document.

Übung 8:

Vervollständigen Sie die Sätze. Benutzen Sie dann die gefundenen Wörter, um das Mystery Word zu bilden.

1. We have a couple of outstanding ☐_ _ _ _ _ .

2. At the end of a meeting it is always useful to make a short _ _ _ _ _ ☐ _ .

3. We can discuss that at the next _ _ _ _ ☐ _ _ .

4. Let's keep in _ _ _ ☐ _ .

5. Can I ask you a simple _ _ ☐ _ _ _ _ _ .

Mystery Word ☐ ☐ ☐ ☐ ☐

Aufträge und Bestellungen 15

Um Aufträge und Bestellungen auf Englisch abzuwickeln, muss man Anfragen, Angebote, die Auftragserteilung selbst, aber auch Mahnungen bei Zahlungsverzug formulieren können.

Anfrage

Die Zeitsekretärin Louisa Harding ruft bei Penkin Ltd an, um einige Büroartikel zu bestellen.

Susan: Penkin Ltd. Susan James speaking. Can I help you?

Louisa: Good morning. Did you say Penkin?

Susan: Yes, that's right.

Louisa: Ah good. My name is Louisa Harding. I'm ringing to ask about ordering some office supplies. Are you the right person to be speaking to?

Susan: You need customer service. One moment please. I'll put you through.

Louisa: Thank you.

...

John: Customer service. John Travers speaking.

Louisa: Hello. My name is Louisa Harding. I'd like to order some office supplies. It's rather urgent.

John: No problem. We can have your order in the post today. What would you like to order?

Louisa: I need several things – 10 boxes of files, 200 pens, 30 printer cartridges; the list is quite long.

John: Excuse me. Do you have a copy of our catalogue? It would speed things up if you could tell me the item numbers.

Louisa: Ah, I'm afraid not. You see I'm a temp. I'm just standing in for the secretary who's off sick.

John: No problem. Do you have internet access?

Louisa: Yes.

John: Good. You can order everything you need online. The address is Penkin.co.uk. Just click on "orders".

Louisa: Oh great. Do I need a customer number or anything?

John: Yes, but that's easy to organise. It's all on the website.

Louisa: Great. You've saved my life.

John: You're welcome. Just give me a call if you need any help filling in the order form.

Louisa: I will. Thanks. Bye.

John: Goodbye.

Vokabeln

customer service	Kundendienst
item number	Artikelnummer
off sick	krank
order	Bestellung
stand in	vertreten
temp	Aushilfe
urgent	dringend

15 Aufträge und Bestellungen

Übung 1:

Bringen Sie den Dialog in die richtige Reihenfolge!

1. Goodbye.
2. Customer service. John Travers speaking.
3. No problem. Do you have internet access?
4. Hello. My name is Louisa Harding. I'd like to order some office supplies. It's rather urgent.
5. No problem. We can have your order in the post today. What would you like to order?
6. Excuse me. Do you have a copy of our catalogue? It would speed things up if you could tell me the item numbers.
7. I will. Thanks. Bye.
8. Ah, I'm afraid not. You see I'm a temp. I'm just standing in for the secretary who's off sick.
9. You're welcome. Just give me a call if you need any help filling in the order form.
10. Great. You've saved my life. Thanks.
11. Yes.
12. Yes, but that's easy to organise. It's all on the website.
13. You can order everything you need online. The address is Penkin.co.uk. Just click on "orders".
14. Oh great. Do I need a customer number or anything?
15. I need several things – 10 boxes of files, 200 pens, 30 cartridges; the list is quite long.

Lösung: _

Übung 2:

Vervollständigen Sie die Sätze!

1. I'm ringing to ask _ _ _ _ _ _ _ ordering some office supplies.
2. Are you the right _ _ _ _ _ _ _ to be speaking to?
3. I'd like to order some office _ _ _ _ _ _ _.
4. What would you _ _ _ _ _ _ _ to order?
5. Do you have a _ _ _ _ _ of our catalogue?
6. You can order everything you _ _ _ _ _ online.
7. Do I need a _ _ _ _ _ number or anything?
8. It's all on the _ _ _ _ _ _ _.
9. Just give me a call if you need any _ _ _ _ _ filling in the order form.

Übung 3:

Schreiben Sie besser:

1. I ring to ask about ordering some office supplies.

_ _

_ _

2. Are you the right people to be speaking to?

_ _

_ _

3. I'd like to order any office supplies.

_ _

_ _

4. What will you like to order?

_ _

_ _

5. Have you a copy of our catalogue?

_ _

_ _

6. You can ordering everything you need online.

_ _

_ _

7. Do I need a customer number or nothing?

_ _

_ _

8. It's all by the website.

_ _

9. Just give me a phone if you need any help filling in the order form.

_ _

_ _

Angebot

Ein Angebot sollte normalerweise alle Preiskonditionen beinhalten, also auch Bedingungen der Bezahlung und Lieferung.

From: Schmidt & Co.
To: Mr Moony, Beauty-Care
Fax Enquiry dated 12 October 2005

Thank you for the above-mentioned enquiry, in which you ask for information regarding our new cosmetics range. I have enclosed a copy of our latest catalogue, together with a wholesale price list. Please note that the prices do not include postage and packing. Our normal terms of payment are 30 days net, subject to availability.
Please do not hesitate to contact me if you have any further questions.

Sincerely yours
Helmut Schmidt, Sales Manager

Vokabeln

above-mentioned	oben angegeben
availability	Verfügbarkeit
banker's draft	Bankwechsel
delay	Verzögerung
enquiry	Anfrage, Nachfrage
net	Netto
packing	Verpackung
postage	Porto
wholesale	Großhandel

Übung 4:

Finden Sie die richtige Wortfolge.

1. please and packing note that the do not include prices postage

_ _

2. we a list and terms copy of our price of enclose payment

_ _

3. we are a first order of 3% discount happy to offer

_ _

4. to me if you please do not further hesitate have any contact questions

_ _

_ _

5. our 30 normal of payment net terms are days

_ _

6. catalogue I a enclosed latest have copy of our

_ _

7. thank enquiry you for mentioned the above

_ _

8. July special terms end are these available until the of

_ _

9. is stock subject to this availability offer

_ _

_ _

Infobox

Some more ways to discuss payment

Payment on receipt of invoice
Payment on receipt of goods
Terms of payment: cash with order
Payment by banker's draft

Terms of delivery

Please allow at least 21 days for delivery.
We can promise delivery within 7 days.
As only limited quantities are available, we would advise you to place your order without delay.
We can ship within 4 days on receipt of your order.

Übung 5:

Finden Sie die Wortverbindungen, wie sie im Text vorkommen. Der erste Teil ist vorgegeben.

1. above _ _ _ _ _ _ _ _ _ _ _ _ _ _ _
2. terms of _ _ _ _ _ _ _ _ _ _ _ _ _ _ _
3. without _ _ _ _ _ _ _ _ _ _ _ _ _ _ _
4. banker's _ _ _ _ _ _ _ _ _ _ _ _ _ _ _
5. price _ _ _ _ _ _ _ _ _ _ _ _ _ _ _
6. postage and _ _ _ _ _ _ _ _ _ _ _ _ _ _ _
7. subject to _ _ _ _ _ _ _ _ _ _ _ _ _ _ _
8. fax _ _ _ _ _ _ _ _ _ _ _ _ _ _ _

Auftrag und Bestellung

Aufträge und Bestellungen enthalten normalerweise die folgenden Punkte: Bezug auf ein Angebot; präzise Details dessen, was bestellt wird; Preis; Bezahlung; Lieferbedingungen und eventuelle Sonderabsprachen. Es folgen zwei Beispiele für Bestellungen in Form von E-Mails.

Dear Mr Hamilton

Thank you for your offer of November 13. Please supply us with 700m of 13 amp cable, item no 2765M, as soon as possible. We note that the total price for the cable is $4670, including delivery to our construction site in Alexandria. Payment will be made on receipt of your invoice. We would appreciate it if you could clearly label the consignment with the words "Section 4B". Could you also confirm delivery date by return.
Many thanks.

Colin Anderson
Purchasing Manager

Vokabeln

by return	umgehend
confirm	bestätigen
consignment	Lieferung
delivery terms	Lieferbedingungen
invoice	Rechnung
label	beschriften
on receipt	nach Eingang

Dear Ms Jameson

Thank you for the copy of your latest catalogue, which you sent us last week. I am pleased to be able to inform you that we would like to place the following order with you:
Item: Seal 23B
Quantity: 30
Price: $37.50
Item: Sealant 456KJ
Quantity: 2 tubes
Price: $2.50
Postage and Packing: $3.50
Delivery Address: 564 Jackson Avenue, Boston, Massachusetts, 05362, USA
I authorise payment of $43.50 from my Visa account number 3456 4678, expiry date 4/07.

Best wishes

Kenneth Clarkson

Infobox

Some phrases for making orders

We would like to/We are pleased to place the following order:
We thank you for your offer of (date) and are pleased to place the following order:
Please enter the following order for immediate delivery:

Übung 6:
Welche Wörter gehören zusammen?

1. label the	☐ delivery date
2. authorise	☐ consignment
3. place an	☐ the price
4. confirm	☐ delivery
5. note	☐ order
6. promise	☐ 21 days for delivery
7. allow	☐ payment

Infobox

Stamps

And don't forget to stamp your letters – but with which stamps?
Letters are sent by two alternative routes:
1. First Class – guaranteeing next-day delivery.
2. Second Class – where delivery can take two or three days.

Übung 7.
Welche Wörter gehören in die Lücken?
(payment, by, confirm, offer, consignment)

Thank you for your (1.) _ _ _ _ _ of 15 January 2006. Please supply us with 30 printers, item no 65Gh, (2.) _ _ _ _ _ March 30. We note that the total price for the (3.) _ _ _ _ _ is $6000, including delivery to our offices in Hamilton. (4.) _ _ _ _ _ will be made on receipt of the goods. Could you also (5.) _ _ _ _ _ delivery date by return.

Übung 8:
Übersetzen Sie!

1. Lieferbedingungen _ _ _ _ _ _ _ _ _ _ _ _ _ _
2. nach Eingang _ _ _ _ _ _ _ _ _ _ _ _ _ _
3. beschriften _ _ _ _ _ _ _ _ _ _ _ _ _ _
4. Verzögerung _ _ _ _ _ _ _ _ _ _ _ _ _ _
5. Bankwechsel _ _ _ _ _ _ _ _ _ _ _ _ _ _
6. versprechen _ _ _ _ _ _ _ _ _ _ _ _ _ _
7. Lieferung _ _ _ _ _ _ _ _ _ _ _ _ _ _

Mahnungen und Zahlungsverzug

Bleibt die Zahlung einer Rechnung aus, ist es nötig, ein Mahnschreiben zu schicken. In diesen Fällen ist es wichtig, den richtigen Ton zu treffen.

First Reminder

Dear Sir

This is a friendly reminder to let you know that, according to our records, we have not yet received payment of $35,000 which was due on March 31.

A copy of our statement of account is enclosed.
As the terms of our agreement included a discount for early payment, we would therefore be grateful if you could settle the amount owing within the next few days.

Yours faithfully
Andrew Richardson

Second Reminder

Dear Sir

We would like to call your attention to our letter of ..., together with the copy of your statement of account which was enclosed with the letter. The balance of $35,000 is now long overdue.
As you will appreciate it will not be possible for us to continue supplying you unless remittance is paid promptly and in full. Please confirm by return that you have done so.

Yours faithfully
Andrew Richardson

Third Reminder

Dear Sir

We regret that the amount of $35,000 is still outstanding, despite two reminders. As you have neither arranged for payment nor sent us an explanation of the delay, we must insist that you arrange for immediate settlement of your account. Failure to do so will leave us with no alternative but to take legal action.

Yours faithfully
Andrew Richardson

Vokabeln

balance	Saldo
confirm	bestätigen
contractual problems	vertragsrechtliche Probleme
discount	Preisnachlass
discount for early payment	Skonto
failure	Versäumnis
insist	bestehen
outstanding obligations	Verbindlichkeiten
overdue	überfällig
reminder	Mahnung
remittance	Geldsendung
settle	bezahlen
settlement	Bezahlung
take legal action	rechtliche Schritte einleiten

Übung 9:

Bilden Sie sinnvolle Paare.

1. friendly	☐ outstanding
2. immediate	☐ overdue
3. still	☐ reminder
4. long	☐ payment
5. first	☐ settlement
6. early	☐ return
7. legal	☐ reminder
8. by	☐ action

Übung 10:

Welche Wörter gehören in die Lücken? (settlement, discount, insist, failure, settle, remittance, overdue)

1. We are able to offer a 7 per cent ___________________.

2. Please transfer the ___________________ in full by the end of the month.

3. We ___________________ that you ___________________ your account immediately.

4. May we remind you that your payment is ___________________.

5. Our contract stipulates ___________________ of any outstanding balance within 14 days of delivery.

6. ___________________ to settle your account will result in legal action.

Infobox

Some possible answers to reminders

We very much regret the inconvenience this has caused.
We would like to take this opportunity to apologise for our late payment.
One of our major customers went into receivership.
We are expecting payment from one of our debtors.
We hope you will understand our position.

Übung 11:

Übersetzen Sie.

1. cash in advance

____

2. cash on delivery

____

3. payment term

____

4. pro forma invoice

____

Angesichts der wachsenden weltweiten Konkurrenz wird die Bindung der Kunden an die Firma immer wichtiger. Dieser Lernschritt betrachtet einige fundamentale Erwägungen des Kundendienstes.

Kundendienst

Die Herangehensweise der Firmen an den Kundendienst hat sich in den letzten Jahren verändert. Es kommt darauf an, auch nach dem Verkauf noch ein gut durchdachtes Konzept für die Kundenbetreuung zu haben.

The business world is becoming more competitive. Globalisation is removing barriers to reaching customers. Many products or services are basically the same. Customer service can therefore be the determining factor to convince people that they are buying from the right provider. The question is: What factors contribute to good customer service? This buzz-word is now the basis of many companies, the factor they claim to have over their competitors. A company-wide policy and commitment to customer service creates this basis. The management must actively participate in the education of staff. The management must provide training. Employees who deal directly with customers will be more confident if they are trained in their interaction with customers. They should also be given the authority to deal with customers and provide solutions which match the customers' demands and the company's philosophy. Employees have to be motivated and supported. It is also essential to understand the customer. Every effort should be made to listen to customers. Only when this is true, can a company seek to fulfil those needs and expectations.

Vokabeln

buzz-word	Modewort
commitment	Selbstverpflichtung
customer service	Kundendienst
expectations	Erwartungen
have over	Vorsprung haben
interaction	Interaktion
needs	Bedürfnisse

Infobox

It is important to consider the intercultural differences of the approach to customer service. In the English speaking world, everyone has heard of the saying: The customer is king. The United States of America has led the customer service revolution in recent years. Many companies now look to the literature and research from the USA to formulate their approach to customer service.

16 Kundenberatung, Reklamation und Kulanz

Übung 1:

Welches ist die beste Übersetzung?

1. Die Geschäftswelt wird zunehmend von Konkurrenz geprägt.

a) Currently, the business world becomes more competitive.

b) Currently, the business world is becoming more competitive.

c) Currently, the business world has become more competitive.

2. Welche Faktoren gehören zu gutem Kundendienst?

a) What factors contribute to good customer service?

b) What factors are contributing to good customer service?

c) What factors had contributed to good customer service?

3. Angestellte, die direkten Kundenkontakt haben, werden selbstbewusster sein, wenn sie in der Interaktion mit Kunden ausgebildet sind.

a) Employees who deal directly with customers were more confident if they are trained in their interaction with customers.

b) Employees who deal directly with customers will be more confident if they are trained in their interaction with customers.

c) Employees who deal directly with customers have been more confident if they are trained in their interaction with customers.

4. Die USA haben in den vergangenen Jahren die Revolution im Kundendienstbereich angeführt.

a) The United States of America leads the customer service revolution in recent years.

b) The United States of America is leading the customer service revolution in recent years.

c) The United States of America has led the customer service revolution in recent years.

Übung 2:

Was passt in die Lücken?
(interaction, formulate, needs, authority, commitment, approach, expectations)

1. We need to _______________ an answer to the problem of fees.

2. Our _______________ so far has been very relaxed.

3. Before we do the training we should do a ______________ analysis.

4. The strikers showed full _______________ to their beliefs.

5. The police have the ________________ to arrest troublemakers.

6. Our customers' ______________ have changed dramatically.

7. Positive ________________ between board members is critical to the company's success.

Übung 3:

Wie lauten die Sätze richtig?

1. Customer is the factor competitors service which to companies claim over their have.

____

2. The provide management training must.

____

3. It customer is to understand the essential.

____

4. Every made customers should effort be listen to to.

____

5. It important to differences the service is intercultural of the consider approach to customer.

____

6. The king is customer.

____

Kundenzufriedenheit und Kulanz

Die Voraussetzung für guten Kundendienst ist, dem Kunden richtig zuzuhören. Allerdings müssen die Wünsche des Kunden mit den Möglichkeiten des Verkäufers abgestimmt werden.

Companies look at what factors make a customer satisfied. At the first stage, the customer expects to receive at least what he or she paid for. This is, however, the very basic necessity and does not lead to customer satisfaction. Nowadays, customers take for granted basic after sales service from suppliers. This may not be enough to distinguish one supplier from another. It is the unexpected service which will bring customers back again and again. If you can surprise your customer, this will leave a lasting impression. Customers are human, and will remember the way they are treated when they give over their hard earned cash. How can companies find out what their customers expect? Consider the following:

16 Kundenberatung, Reklamation und Kulanz

A personal contact to the customer can lead to a build up of trust and respect. A long term relationship can be established. This leads to the feeling that my supplier really cares about me.

Stay in contact with the customer. This may involve meetings, discussions or written correspondence which discloses the needs or expectations of the customer.

Give a readily accessible point of contact. This may be one employee of the company or perhaps through the use of a customer hot-line.

Genuine attempts to satisfy the customer, and to go beyond what is normal, will be noticed and appreciated. The company that is prepared to go out of its way to meet customer expectations has the best chance of success.

Vokabeln

appreciated	anerkannt
distinguish	unterscheiden
enhance	verbessern
hard earned cash	sauer verdientes Geld
mention	erwähnen
necessity	Notwendigkeit
notice	bemerken
overview	Überblick
survey	Umfrage
take for granted	sich auf etwas verlassen

Infobox

The text above mentions some ways in which companies can maintain contact with their customers. Another common way is to conduct customer surveys. This gives the customer a chance to measure the performance of their supplier. Surveys however are not customer specific. They may give a general overview of a company's performance, but individual cases can not be examined in detail. As always, it is not enough to only collect information. The company must analyse and use the information gathered to enhance customer satisfaction.

Übung 4:

Bilden Sie sinnvolle Paare!

1. look	☐ cash
2. take for	☐ at
3. go	☐ line
4. hard earned	☐ out
5. find	☐ about
6. care	☐ beyond
7. hot	☐ granted

Übung 5:

Ordnen Sie diese Verben ihren entsprechenden Übersetzungen zu!

1. to mention	☐ untersuchen
2. to appreciate	☐ offenlegen
3. to survey	☐ bemerken

4. to distinguish ☐ erwähnen
5. to disclose ☐ unterscheiden
6. to notice ☐ verbessern
7. to enhance ☐ anerkennen

Übung 6:

Vervollständigen Sie die Sätze!

1. This may not be enough to distinguish one supplier _ _ _ _ _ another.
2. If you can surprise your customer, this _ _ _ _ _ leave a lasting impression.
3. A personal contact _ _ _ _ _ the customer can lead to a build up of trust and respect.
4. This leads to the feeling that my supplier really cares _ _ _ _ _ me.
5. Give a readily accessible _ _ _ _ _ of contact.

Kundengespräch und Kundenberatung

Die Beziehung zwischen Käufer und Verkäufer ist ein wichtiger Faktor, wenn es darum geht, Kundenzufriedenheit herzustellen. Ein junger Autoverkäufer versucht, einem erfahrenen Käufer ein gebrauchtes Auto zu verkaufen.

Mr Arnold: Look. You want to sell me the car. I want to buy the car. All I want is a fair price. Let's forget about all the tricks of the trade which they taught you on your "how to be a salesman" courses. All that stuff you have to learn by heart. Like how to deal with behavioural traits. Just give me the facts.

Mobile dealer: Ok. Ok. I was just trying to tell you about the benefits to you if you buy the car.

Mr Arnold: I know the benefits. I am a driver. I have probably owned more cars than you have had hot breakfasts. Got it?

Mobile dealer: Got it.

Mr Arnold: Let's start again. Tell me about the car.

Mobile dealer: The car is 6 years old.

Mr Arnold: Right.

Mobile dealer: And has had three careful owners.

Mr Arnold: Three owners. Right. Do you have the log book?

Mobile dealer: Yes, of course. It's in the office.

Mr Arnold: We'll have a look at it later.

Vokabeln

behavioural traits	Verhaltensmerkmale
benefit	Vorteil
dealer	Händler
tricks of the trade	Kniffe

Mobile dealer: It's done 150,000 km.
Mr Arnold: Ok.
Mobile dealer: And it's never been in a crash.
Mr Arnold: As far as you know.
Mobile dealer: As far as I know.
Mr Arnold: What about the engine?
Mobile dealer: Almost new.
Mr Arnold: What is almost new? Don't start me off again!
Mobile dealer: Sorry. I mean quite new: I mean I'll go and check exactly what I mean.
Mr Arnold: That's better. The facts are slowly emerging. You're beginning to listen to what I'm saying at last.

Infobox

It is not enough to hear customers. To hear does not mean to listen. Active listening is a skill which must be trained and practised. However, merely listening does not automatically lead to understanding. In many conversations, the two parties leave with very different ideas as to what was discussed or agreed. Imagine the difficulty in a non-native language. It is therefore very important to ask questions. This shows interest, and will clear up any possible misunderstandings. After the customer has finished, summarise his complaint. That will show him that you take it seriously. And never forget: Every complaint is a chance to improve your product or services.

Übung 7:

Enträtseln Sie das Geheimwort!

1. aufklären, 2. vorstellen, 3. überreden, 4. auswendig, 5. hören, 6. verstehen

1. _ _ ☐ _ _

2. ☐ _ _ _ _ _ _

3. _ _ _ ☐ _ _ _ _

4. _ _ _ _ _ _ ☐

5. _ ☐ _ _

6. _ _ _ _ _ _ _ _ ☐ _

Mystery Word ☐ ☐ ☐ ☐ ☐ ☐

Übung 8:

Schreiben Sie besser:

1. Now that I have the customer, how I keep them?

_ _

2. These consultants have now taught to listen to their customers.

_ _

3. Imagining the difficulty in a non-native language.

_ _

4. It is therefore very important for asking questions.

_ _

Reklamation

Eine der schwierigsten Aufgaben für Firmen ist der Umgang mit Kundenreklamationen. Im folgenden Brief beschwert sich ein Geschäftsmann bei einem Reisebüro, das für ihn eine Geschäftsreise in die Türkei organisiert hat.

Dear Sir

I am writing to complain about the travel arrangements which your company organised for my recent trip to Turkey, and to claim compensation for unexpected expenses incurred.

The problems started before I had even left the UK, when my secretary noticed that you had booked economy class tickets instead of first class, as her email of 12 December clearly requested. However this problem was resolved in time, and I am happy to say that the airline in question lived up to all its claims.

However, it was once I arrived in Turkey that disruptions caused by the incompetence of your staff began to seriously interfere with my business plans. First of all the hotel you booked for me was still under construction, which caused considerable inconvenience as the replacement offered by your representatives was certainly not adequate for my needs. It had no air conditioning, and the room I was offered did not even have a bathroom. I was forced to find a hotel in Istanbul for myself, at a price significantly higher than that I had been expecting. I have enclosed a copy of the hotel bill, and expect a refund of the difference in prices.

Unfortunately the new hotel was not within walking distance of my client's offices – indeed I had to take taxis every day as the distances involved made this the only possible form of transport available to me. I was unable to obtain legible receipts for these costs, but I can assure you that the total cost was in the region of £250. My lawyer informs me that I can reasonably expect these costs to be covered by you.

You will understand that I was extremely disappointed to receive such service from your company, and I can only hope that you will arrange for speedy compensation.

I look forward to hearing from you

Yours faithfully Henry Williams

Vokabeln

claims	Ansprüche
compensation	Entschädigung, Ausgleich
inconvenience	Unannehmlichkeit
refund	Geld zurück

16 Kundenberatung, Reklamation und Kulanz

Übung 9:

Finden Sie die Wortverbindungen, wie sie im Text vorkommen. Der erste Teil ist vorgegeben:

1. considerable ____________
2. hotel ____________
3. walking ____________
4. claim ____________
5. air ____________
6. first ____________
7. yours ____________

Übung 10:

Bringen Sie folgende Sätze in Ordnung. Sie sind einem Beschwerdebrief entnommen.

1. I complain am writing accommodation to about my hotel.

____

2. My was dirty room,

____

3. conditioning was air broken the,

____

4. cold and the only restaurant served meals.

____

5. addition, the staff unfriendly were In extremely.

____

6. Worst, the was of all located hotel

____

7. the rubbish near town dump,

____

8. unbearable which the smell made.

____

9. like I would know to how

____

10. compensate you plan to me

____

11. this for situation unacceptable.

____

12. lawyers Otherwise hearing from you will be my.

____

Übung 11:

Ordnen Sie folgende Vokabeln den entsprechenden Übersetzungen zu!

1. versichern	☐ compensation
2. Unannehmlichkeit	☐ refund
3. Ansprüche	☐ legible
4. leserlich	☐ considerable
5. Entschädigung	☐ claims
6. Geld zurück	☐ inconvenience
7. groß	☐ assure

Innovationen wie Videokonferenzen und das Internet haben Geschäftsreisen nicht abgeschafft. Ob auf Flughäfen oder an Bahnhöfen – überall sieht man reisende Geschäftsleute.

Reisevorbereitungen

Eine erfolgreiche Geschäftsreise muss sorgfältig geplant sein. Sandra Jones schreibt vier E-Mails, um Reiseinformationen einzuholen und Buchungen für eine bevorstehende Reise vorzunehmen.

Dear Sir
I am planning a visit to Orlando from 3 - 7 July, and would like information about your rates and facilities.
Many thanks

Dear Sir
Could you please reserve a non-smoker single room for 2 nights from 16 – 18 July, in the name of Henry Hamilton.

I would appreciate if you could confirm this reservation by return.

Dear Sir
I recently booked a single room for Mr Peters, for 6 nights from 17 – 23 July, (reservation number 15628Jkl). Unfortunately he has had to make some last minute changes to his travel itinerary, and now plans to be in New York from 18 – 24 July. Could you confirm that you will be able to provide accommodation for these dates.

Dear Ms Windward
Please could you reserve a car (preferably a BMW 7 series) for my managing director, Mr Tony Larsson. He will need the car from 12 – 16 July, and would like to collect it at around 10 am from your South Street garage. He would like comprehensive insurance and unlimited mileage. Our company booking number is 2381 8963.

Vokabeln

booking	Buchung
comprehensive insurance	Vollkaskoversicherung
facilities	Ausstattung
itinerary	Reiseroute
last minute changes	Änderungen in letzter Minute
rates	Preise
reserve	reservieren
travel agency	Reisebüro
unlimited mileage	unbegrenzte Kilometerzahl
visa	Visum

17 Geschäftsreisen, Terminvereinbarung und Unterkunft

Übung 1:

Bilden Sie die richtige Verbform.

1. I am plan a visit to London next month.

____

2. Could you reserving a single, with bath, from 2 – 6 December.

____

3. I would liking information about your hotel.

____

4. Please confirmed my reservation.

____

5. I have change my plans, and will now arriving on Sunday.

____

6. Have you stay here before?

____

7. Will you be pay by credit card?

____

8. Like you a non-smoker?

____

Übung 2:

Welche Wörter gehören zusammen?

1. reserve	☐ mileage
2. comprehensive	☐ thanks
3. last minute	☐ return
4. single	☐ changes
5. unlimited	☐ room
6. many	☐ insurance
7. by	☐ a car

Anreise

Zwei Kollegen sprechen über ihre bevorstehende Geschäftsreise.

Jack: You've never flown before?
Judy: That's right.
Jack: No problem. I'll tell you what to do. You get to the airport right? First thing you do is check-in.
Judy: Ok. What does that mean?
Jack: You take your luggage and your ticket over to the check-in counter. Someone from the airline will check your travel documents – basically your

Vokabeln

aisle	Gang
announcement	Durchsage
car rental	Autovermietung
delay	Verspätung
depart	abfahren
departure lounge	Abflughalle
emergency exit	Notausgang
last call	letzter Aufruf
leg room	Beinfreiheit
lost property office	Fundbüro
luggage	Gepäck
metal detector	Metalldetektor
platform	Gleis
x-rayed	durchleuchtet, geröntgt

ticket and maybe your passport, and take your luggage from you.

Judy: I thought I could take stuff with me on the plane.

Jack: Yes. Hand luggage. One small bag.

Judy: Oh right.

Jack: After checking-in you'll normally have a bit of time – you can wander round the airport or go through to the departure lounge.

Judy: What's that?

Jack: Basically where you wait for the aeroplane to be ready.

Judy: And no more checks?

Jack: Wait a minute. To get to the departure lounge you'll need to go through a passport and ticket check as well as a security check.

Judy: Ok. Will they search me?

Jack: Well, they'll do a body search with a metal detector, and your hand luggage and jacket will be x-rayed.

Judy: Is it a strict search?

Jack: Ideally yes, but normally it's pretty cursory – they don't really have time to do everyone thoroughly.

Judy: Ok.

Jack: Once you're past the checks you can go to duty free, at least if you're travelling to certain countries.

Judy: Great. I've got a long list of things to buy ...

Jack: Hang on. There are limits you know. You can't buy as much as you want.

Judy: Oh.

Jack: Anyway, after a while you'll be called forward to your gate.

Judy: Gate?

Jack: That's where the aircraft is. They'll probably check your documents again before you actually get on the plane.

Judy: Can you sit anywhere?

Jack: No. When you check-in you get your seat number.

Judy: All right.

Jack: I always ask for a window seat because I can see everything, but you'll probably want an aisle seat because of your long legs. Or better still, ask for a seat by the emergency exit – there's normally more leg room there.

Infobox

Pronunciation

There are two other constructions in English which are pronounced the same way as aisle. "I'll" is short for "I will", and "isle" is another word for island (as in the British Isles).

Übung 3:
Welche Wörter gehören zusammen?

1. aisle	☐ on
2. after	☐ search
3. hang	☐ exit
4. cursory	☐ seat
5. security	☐ a while
6. emergency	☐ check

Übung 4:
Sind die Sätze inhaltlich richtig oder falsch?

1. Leg room is a problem for short people, but not for tall.

☐ richtig ☐ falsch

2. You find "aisles" in churches all over the world.

☐ richtig ☐ falsch

3. In an ideal world security checks at airports would be thorough.

☐ richtig ☐ falsch

4. Cursory checks take longer than thorough checks.

☐ richtig ☐ falsch

5. You can say "hang on" when you want someone to wait for you.

☐ richtig ☐ falsch

6. You normally need a passport to fly from one continent to another.

☐ richtig ☐ falsch

7. You don't need a ticket to go into a departure lounge.

☐ richtig ☐ falsch

Besuch bei Geschäftspartnern

Einem japanischen Besucher wird eine Whisky-Destillerie in Schottland gezeigt. Er denkt darüber nach, eventuell in diese Firma zu investieren.

Guide: Well, here you are, the entrance to the distillery, built in 1878, two years after the company was founded.
Visitor: Very impressive.
Guide: Yes, indeed. Over there you can see the main reason for this location, the spring which gives us the water so essential to our product.
Visitor: How reliable is the source?
Guide: Very good. We've never had any problems with it in over 130 years of production. Now, you already know something about the process of making whisky from the audiovisual presentation earlier.

Visitor: Yes, of course. When did you build the visitors centre?

Guide: Well, it's only ten years old – but we cater for up to 400 visitors a day now, in peak season anyway.

Visitor: What about the shop? Do you sell much there?

Guide: Well, most people like to buy a souvenir of their visit, and some of the merchandise is simply aimed at marketing Scotland, as opposed to this distillery.

Visitor: What about whisky? Don't you sell much here?

Guide: No, not really. Two reasons for that. Our main markets are in Asia and mainland Europe, so we export something like 98 per cent of our whisky. And of course the tax on whisky in this country makes buying whisky a very expensive luxury for many people. We spend a lot of time lobbying the government, but it's a good source of income for them. Now this is the employees' canteen. We employ around 50 people on this site, all locals. Most of them grew up in the village just down the road. This makes our workforce unique – most of their families have been supplying us with labour since we started, and there is certainly a special bond between the company and the village. I'd like to introduce you to one or two of the key staff, if I may. This is Hamish McDougal, who's just taken over marketing.

Hamish: Pleased to meet you.

Guide: And this is Hamish MacDonald. He's responsible for the maintenance of the warehouses where we hold the whisky in bond until it leaves us.

Second Hamish: Hello.

Guide: And this is Hamish McCallum. He's in charge of the barley supply, as well as one or two other things. As you know barley is one of key raw materials we use. Ours comes from farms near Aberdeen, on the East coast.

Third Hamish: Hi.

Visitor: A lot of Hamishes.

Guide: Yes. We have three more, in fact, but they're working in another part of the distillery at the moment.

Vokabeln

cater for	versorgen
employee	Angestellter
in bond	Zollverschluss
location	Ort
market	vertreiben
merchandise	Waren
raw material	Rohstoff
sell	verkaufen
source	Quelle (hier: Geld)
spring	Quelle (hier: Wasser)
workforce	Arbeitskräfte

Übung 5:

Ersetzen Sie die Klammern durch Wörter aus dem Text:

1. Our main (place where things come from) is a mine in the Western Sahara.

_ _

2. We (supply goods to) customers from all over Europe.

_ _

3. We have three (places) in the UK: London, Manchester and Liverpool.

_ _

4. We recently had to increase our (people who work for the company) to cope with new orders.

_ _

5. Our (things we make and sell) stays in bond in this warehouse until it is ready for shipping.

_ _

6. We were (started) 300 years ago.

_ _

Übung 6:

Füllen Sie die Lücken mit Wörtern aus dem Text.

1. We need to keep these goods in a special temperature controlled _ _ _ _ _ _ _ _ _ _ _ _ _.
2. We have an excellent _ _ _ _ _ _ _ _ _ _ _ _ _ _ _ _ _ _ just next to the main source of our raw materials.
3. We _ _ _ _ _ _ _ _ _ _ _ _ _ _ _ _ _ _ _for a wide variety of customers.
4. Most visitors like to buy a _ _ _ _ _ _ _ _ _ _ _ _ _ _ _ _ _ _ of their visit.
5. Our _ _ _ _ _ _ _ _ _ _ _ _ _ _ are all people from the local village.
6. The spring is a very _ _ _ _ _ _ _ _ _ _ _ _ _ _ source of water.
7. He's responsible _ _ _ _ _ _ _ _ _ _ _ _ _ _ _ _ _ sales and marketing.

Unterbringung

Zwei Kollegen sprechen über ein Hotel, das sie gebucht hatten, um eine Kundengruppe unterzubringen.

Sarah: And how was the hotel?
Robin: How much time have you got?
Sarah: That bad, huh?
Robin: Well, it all started very well. We'd booked the hotel because of its conference facilities, as you know. Meeting rooms, that sort of thing.

Sarah: Go on.
Robin: Well. The hotel was certainly easily accessible from the airport. What they forgot to tell us is that the planes take off and land about half a mile away. Every ten minutes.
Sarah: Ah. What about the amenities?
Robin: They were pretty good. Lots of places to go and things to do. There was a shuttle bus into town, so people could go shopping or sightseeing if they wished.
Sarah: Sounds ok.
Robin: Yeah. But the real problems were inside the hotel, mostly with the catering. We'd ordered a package deal with set meals you see – choice of two menus, plus vegetarian.
Sarah: Ok.
Robin: Well, the hotel management forgot to tell the hotel staff. So they gave everyone the à la carte menu. Everybody ate very well on the first day, but of course the prices were a little different. And then they charged all our guests separately, instead of putting everything on our bill.
Sarah: Whoops.
Robin: Precisely.
Sarah: What about the food after that? Was it good?
Robin: After that we had our set meals – buffet service for the evenings, which was very nice, and reasonable choice. A little spicy perhaps for most Europeans' tastes. But certainly not to the first day's standard, that's for sure. Quite a let down, in fact.
Sarah: Oh dear.
Robin: There were also some other small problems – nothing serious, but niggling.
Sarah: Like?
Robin: Like the laundry. Half our guests put stuff in for cleaning, but there was some sort of mix-up, and they didn't get their own stuff back. They all had to go down to the manager's office and identify their own shirts.
Sarah: Hmm.
Robin: Yes. People got quite annoyed. But the worst problems were at the end, when people were trying to book out.

Vokabeln

accessible	zugänglich
amenity	Einrichtung
awkward	peinlich
catering	Gastronomie
maintenance	Instandhaltung
management	Unternehmensführung
package	pauschal
service charge	Bedienungsgeld
staff	Personal, Mitarbeiterstab
You're kidding?	Sie machen wohl Witze?

Sarah: What happened?
Robin: They got all the bills wrong. People were asked to pay for all sorts of things they hadn't had, like stuff from the mini bars in the rooms, visits to the local golf club, newspapers, you name it. And then they asked for a 10 per cent service charge!
Sarah: You're kidding?
Robin: No.
Sarah: Ah.
Robin: So it didn't work out as well as we had hoped. But at least the presentations went ok, and I think we'll get some orders.
Sarah: Thank goodness for that.

Übung 7:

Übersetzen Sie die folgenden Sätze!

1. Die Gastronomie war super.

____

2. Ich habe für das Zimmermädchen ein Trinkgeld hinterlassen.

____

____

3. Es waren zwei Wäschesäcke in meinem Schrank.

____

4. Bedienungsgeld ist nicht inklusive.

____

5. Es war ein Fünf-Sterne-Hotel, daher waren die Einrichtungen exzellent.

____

6. Der Strand war vom Hotel leicht zugänglich.

____

7. Wir haben eine Pauschalreise gebucht.

____

Übung 8:

Benutzen Sie die folgenden Wörter, um die Lücken zu füllen:
(was, forgot, turned out, believe, weren't, work out, wished)

1. What they _____________ to tell us is that the restaurant was closed for repairs.

2. It didn't _____________ as we had hoped.

3. You won't _____________ this.

4. It _____________ that most of the staff had the day off.

5. There _____________ some sort of mix-up.

6. There _____________ many things to do or places to go.

7. People could go swimming if they _____.

Auf internationalen Messen ist Englisch als die Business-Sprache Nr. 1 nicht mehr wegzudenken. Ob beim Kundengespräch, bei der Präsentation der Produkte oder bei der Messevorbereitung – es gilt, in jeder Situation die passenden Worte zu finden.

Messestandgestaltung

Zwei Kollegen diskutieren die Vorbereitungen für die nächste Messe.

Ashley: Alright, let's start. We need to send in the order for our stand by the end of the day. I have brought the offers I've gathered and I'd like to run my conclusions by you. If you'd just take a look at the numerous brochures filled with the plethora of stands available on the market. First, we have to decide if we want to invest in a custom designed display stand or simply rent a prefabricated one. I prefer prefabricated; we won't have to spend the entire day deciding between bespoke, modular, pop-up or banner stands. They would show us a few samples.

Francis: If I could just cut in here?

Ashley: Sure.

Francis: I sense that you're not impressed by the multitude of stands out there.

Ashley: You're right. It's not simple to choose.

Francis: Well, I've been to lots of exhibitions and I think I understand the importance of, say, choosing wall mounting only literature stands or revolving carousels. If we make a poor decision today, the hospitality area might not have enough space for the potential customers to move between the graphic panels and the literature stands. I think we have to invest the time and energy to create a design which will be versatile enough for us to purchase and reuse in the future. And don't forget the transportation and set up stages. It's imperative that the stand be portable, lightweight, and flexible.

Ashley: I guess you've got a point.

Vokabeln

application form	Anmeldeformular
banner	Fahne
bespoke	maßgeschneidert
custom designed	spezialangefertigt
exhibition	Ausstellung
graphic panel	Bildtafel
hospitality area	Begegnungsfläche
lightweight	leicht
literature stand	Prospektstand
modular	zusammensetzbar
plethora	Fülle
pop-up	aufklappbar
portable	tragbar
prefabricated	vorgefertigt
rent	mieten
versatile	vielseitig
wall mounting	Wandaufhängung

18 Messevorbereitungen, Produktinformation und Verkaufsgespräche

Infobox

The term "rent" is used in The United States and "hire" is the equivalent in British English. Hire in US American English describes the process of acquiring new employees. As in the following sentence: John was hired as manager of the new video rental shop.

Übung 1:

Welche Wörter gehören zusammen?

1. custom	☐ area
2. revolving	☐ decision
3. hospitality	☐ rental
4. poor	☐ designed
5. potential	☐ mounting
6. video	☐ customers
7. wall	☐ carousel

Übung 2:

Bringen Sie die Wörter in die richtige Reihenfolge.

1. we in the order for our end of the need to send stand by the day

_ _

2. to run my conclusions I'd like by you

_ _

3. if I in here could just cut Ashley

_ _

4. simple it's not choose to

_ _

5. stages and the transportation and don't forget set up

_ _

_ _

6. I a guess got you've point

_ _

Übung 3:

Welche Präpositionen gehören zu den folgenden Wörtern?

1. send

_ _

2. not impressed

_ _

3. set

_ _

4. deciding

_ _

5. invest

_ _

6. plethora

_ _

7. filled

_ _

Informationsmaterialien anfordern und zusammenstellen

Die Vorbereitungen für die Messe laufen auf Hochtouren. In einer E-Mail an seine Kollegin klärt der Marketing Manager Elliot Smith wichtige Punkte, die vor Messebeginn noch zu erledigen sind.

Hello Sofia

Thank you for your quick reply. In my last email, I informed you that we need to complete the pamphlets for the upcoming trade show. Unfortunately, I forgot to mention the deadline. The trade show begins on 12 July. This means that we must have all of the arrangements completed by Thursday. I suggest we divide the tasks and conquer them in the next two days! First and foremost, the train tickets must be reserved and two rooms at the conference hotel booked. Jackson will inquire about the rates for a corner stand in the main hall.
As far as the literature, I am going to contact the graphic designers to give them our logo and the colour scheme. I have an appointment with the photographer on Wednesday to take pictures of all components to be included this year. She will also make a small photo shoot tour of the factory so we can update the current pictures. I still have the telephone number of the catering company and the electrician we used two years ago.
I hope they can fit us in this year, they were both excellent.
So, that just leaves the coordination between the graphic designers with the printers, I would appreciate it if you could manage that. How many business cards are we going to have printed this year? You could call Jackson, he would know. I almost forgot the carpenter! She has designed a unique system of shelves for us which are really sturdy – so there shouldn't be any accidents this year. Once you reach her, please ask for an invoice. I'm a little concerned about how much she will charge! Let me know if I can help in any way.

Regards
Elliot

Vokabeln

caterer	Lieferfirma
charge	berechnen
deadline	letzter Termin
electrician	Elektriker
invoice	Rechnung
pamphlet	Broschüre
printer	Drucker

18 Messevorbereitungen, Produktinformation und Verkaufsgespräche

Übung 4:

Was gehört in die Lücke? "Much" oder "many"?

1. How _ _ _ _ _ money will we need for the start up?
2. Have you decided how _ _ _ _ _ to charge for the installation?
3. We ordered too _ _ _ _ _ banners!
4. There is too _ _ _ _ _ work to be done.
5. How _ _ _ _ _ overtime can you manage?
6. Why so _ _ _ _ _ crates of champagne?
7. How _ _ _ _ _ time did you save by taking a taxi?

Übung 5:

Ergänzen Sie mit Wörtern aus dem Text.

1. The _ _ _ _ _ is responsible for laying the cables.
2. Call the _ _ _ _ _ and tell them we need 1000 more copies.
3. We have a new stand and new _ _ _ _ _ on which to display our products.
4. The _ _ _ _ _ had to cancel. Go to the supermarket, quick!
5. It's important to give a _ _ _ _ _ to any new contacts so that they can get in touch with you.
6. Take our _ _ _ _ _ and you will find all of the details about our product.
7. I am not able to pay the bill until they send us the itemized _ _ _ _ _.

Übung 6:

Bringen Sie den Dialog in die richtige Reihenfolge!

1. Susan Peters, but don't worry. The same thing happened to me a few months ago. I wasn't sure what to say to them and they just continued talking!
2. I just asked him about his job and then I managed to remember which trade fair I dealt with that company.
3. I thought to ask him for his business card!
4. Hi, Jasmine it is so good to see you again!
5. We had dinner and then came up with an idea for a joint venture.
6. How did you find out who it was?
7. And then?
8. Hello, umm, I seem to have forgotten your name. I'm sorry. You know how it is with these conventions. So many people.
9. I hope you took him out for a drink after that.

Lösung: _

Messestand aufstellen

Zwei Kollegen bauen gemeinsam ihren Messestand auf.

Milton: Finally here! After such an exhausting trip, I'm ready for the live entertainment!
Louise: Milton, even though this modular stand has been erected, the electricity installed and the carpet laid, you know we have a great deal of work to do before we can relax. Look at all of these cardboard boxes! Where will we put it all?
Milton: Where is the list? Caroline, who was here last year, faxed me some tips. Where is it?
Louise: I have it in my briefcase. Here it is. It is quite long. Let's get started. First, decide where the light boxes will be and then arrange the demos.
Milton: Put the light boxes to the right of the multimedia station. No, reposition it a bit more to the right. Good. Next, position the demos in front of the lights ... perfect.
Louise: Now on to the literature racks.
Milton: Right, open the box beside the projection screen. Separate the certificates from the post cards. The bound versions are heavier, they should be arranged on the shelf above the counter top on which we will display the novelties. ... Ok.
Louise: We are almost finished. Do you want a drink? Where is the refrigerator anyway?
Milton: Check to the left of you, below the banner.
Louise: Hum, Milton, it's not there!

Vokabeln

arrange	aufstellen
bound	gebunden
cardboard box	Pappkarton
demo	Demo
erect	aufstellen
fax	faxen
light box	Leuchtkasten
novelties	Neuheiten
position	Stelle
projection screen	Bildschirm
rack	Gestell
version	Fassung

Übung 7:

Ergänzen Sie die fehlenden Präpositionen:

1. We need to arrange transport _ _ _ _ _ _ _ _ six o'clock.

2. The stands still need _ _ _ _ _ _ _ _ be erected.

3. Don't forget to put _ _ _ _ _ _ _ _ the racks.

4. We switched ____________ the refrigerator yesterday evening.

5. Separate the brochures ____________ the novelties.

6. The carpet needs to be cleaned ________ ____ we can relax.

7. Put the posters ____________ the left hand side.

Übung 8:

Schreiben Sie folgende Sätze als Aufforderung. Finden Sie Beispiele im Text.

1. Jake places the snacks on the counter.

____

2. She separated the damaged posters from those intact.

____

____

3. My team leader checks on the progress daily.

____

4. Our department head opens each meeting with a joke.

____

5. The staff erected the stand.

____

6. They will reposition the light boxes.

____

7. Winston looked at the refrigerator.

____

8. They are to share the work.

____

Infobox

If you must travel to your next trade fair and want only a small stand, try a desk top version with a travel case.

Übung 9:

Vervollständigen Sie die Sätze!

1. The projection screen must be fixed to the wall 1 metre _____ the floor.

2. The man to the _____ you is our new associate.

3. Put the cardboard box to the _____ the interactive display.

4. The pop up stand _____ which the logo is printed is faulty.

5. The decision to reserve our stand location _____ was a wise one.

6. You will find all of the details _____ the report.

7. The costs were _____ our allotted budget.

Auf der Messe

Ein potenzieller Kunde besucht einen Messestand.

Customer: Hello, what a becoming stand. Well done. I'm from Hong Kong International.
Claudia: Oh, why thank you. We're also pleased with the stand. Hong Kong International ... you requested information about the location of our stand in an email, didn't you?
Customer: Why yes, "Around the corner from the refreshment stand in Hall 2." Your directions were very clear.
Claudia: Yes, I see you made it. Can I tempt you with a glass of champagne or orange juice while you browse?
Customer: That would be lovely. Thank you, mmm.
Claudia: I have a feeling you might enjoy this display.

Vokabeln

becoming	vorteilhaft
boost	Auftrieb geben
browse	sich umsehen
business card	Visitenkarte
draft	entwerfen
exchange	tauschen
facilitate	erleichtern
forerunner	Marktführer
impression	Eindruck
request	bitten, ersuchen
specifications	genaue Angaben

Customer: Yes, this I just what I need! I have heard that your firm is the forerunner in this technology. I would like to see at first hand how your product might boost our sales.
Claudia: Sure, try the hors-d'oeuvre, won't you?
Customer: Don't mind if I do. It has been a trying day.
Claudia: Here let me refill your glass. Feel free to relax and glance through the case study done of a company quite similar to yours. I will prepare the virtual reality demonstration. Oh, this is the brochure with the specifications and the quality management details.
Customer: Take your time ...
(Later)
Claudia: Well, sir, what is your impression?
Customer: I will have to draft a report to the CEO before I disclose too much, but I believe it is ideal for us at this point.
Claudia: Excellent! After having looked at your website, I thought this version might just suit your needs. Would you like to exchange business cards to facilitate further contact?
Customer: Absolutely. Here you are.

Übung 10:

Füllen Sie die Lücken mit Wörtern aus dem Text.

We have (1.) _ _ _ _ _ the leaflet with the new (2.) _ _ _ _ _. Now, we can come to HK international. They are (3.) _ _ _ _ _ prospective suppliers. I met with them at the reception and we (4.)_ _ _ _ _ business cards. I (5.)_ _ _ _ _ we will stay in contact. Email really (6.)_ _ _ _ _ such tasks as maintaining a relationship! It (7.)_ _ _ _ _ much better than snail mail did.

Übung 11:

Bilden Sie sinnvolle Paare.

1. exchange	☐ letter
2. stay in	☐ relationships
3. draft a	☐ impression
4. maintain	☐ sales
5. make an	☐ business cards
6. boost	☐ contact

Übung 12:

Wählen Sie eine Phrase aus dem Text, die dieselbe Bedeutung hat.

1. to experience in person

_ _

2. Yes, thank you.

_ _

3. have some

_ _

4. look around

_ _

5. technical details

_ _

6. Do you want something to drink?

_ _

7. Good job.

_ _

8. go to the corner and turn

_ _

9. You have arrived successfully.

_ _

Werben und Vermarkten sind Schlüsselelemente in jeder Firma. Das Ziel ist, das richtige Produkt zum Kunden zu bringen – am richtigen Ort, zur richtigen Zeit und zum richtigen Preis.

Werbestrategien und Methoden

Wer seine Produkte erfolgreich vermarkten will, muss sich vorher die richtige Strategie zurechtlegen. Im folgenden Dialog diskutieren zwei Verlagsangestellte die Vermarktung eines neuen Buches.

John: Morning Thomas. Emily said you wanted to see me.
Thomas: Hi John, good to see you. There are a couple of things I want to talk to you about.
John: Ok. About the new book?
Thomas: Yeah, that's right. Can you just go over our promotion strategy again?
John: Sure. Basically we'll be running a two day advertising campaign in the national press, followed by presentations to clubs and associations all over Germany. We'll also be giving away 500 copies via local radio stations as prizes, and it'll be available from our stand at all the major book fairs.
And of course in all the normal bookshops.
Thomas: Ok. What about the catalogue?
John: It'll be in the next edition.
Thomas: Internet presence?
John: It's on our website and in major bookstores. And we'll get reviews in as many online journals as we can. I'm sending around 300 copies out next week.
Thomas: That sounds fine. What about people? Who's doing the presentations?
John: Both the authors, backed up by someone from the marketing department.
Thomas: Ok. Price? 19.99, I suppose.
John: Yes, that's right.
Thomas: Ok good. Thanks. Oh, there is one other thing. Competitors?
John: Well, as you know our biggest competitors on this project are Boggs and Co, and Hearn brothers. It seems Boggs have had a major fire in their warehouse, so all their products are delayed.

Vokabeln

advertiser	Inserent
advertisement	Anzeige
available	verfügbar
competitor	Konkurrent(in)
edition	Ausgabe
presence	Präsenz
promotion strategy	Werbestrategie
review	Rezension

19 Werben und Vermarkten

Infobox

Marketing is often discussed in terms of the following factors:
product – what you are selling
promotion – ensuring that people know about what you are selling
place – making sure that the product is available and accessible
price – how much the customer pays for the product
people – your own staff as well as the customer
process – how you operate
physical evidence – what the customer actually sees and gets

Übung 1:

Bringen Sie die Wörter in den folgenden Sätzen in die richtige Reihenfolge.

1. There want to you are a of things I to couple talk about.

_ _

2. They're department up by marketing someone from backed the.

_ _

3. Can strategy the promotion you just go over again?

_ _

4. Basically national we'll running a in the two day be campaign press.

_ _

5. wanted to Emily said you see me.

_ _

6. catalogue What the about?

_ _

7. doing Who's presentations the?

_ _

Übung 2:

Vervollständigen Sie die Wortverbindungen aus dem Text.

1. national

_ _

2. advertising

_ _

3. promotion

_ _

4. biggest

_ _

5. internet

_ _

Übung 3:

Übersetzen Sie!

1. competitor

_ _

2. delay

_ _

3. advertising campaign

_ _

4. review

_ _

5. copy

_ _

Übung 4:

Hier finden sich einige Fehler. Verbessern Sie die folgenden Sätze:

1. Hi John, good to you see.

_ _

2. It'll be available out of our stand at all the major book fairs.

_ _

_ _

3. I send around 300 copies out next week.

_ _

4. Oh, there is one another thing.

_ _

Marktforschung

Marktforschung ist nötig, um herauszufinden, was die Kunden wünschen, wie viel sie ausgeben würden und wie man sie zum Kauf anregen könnte. Dieser Artikel beschreibt den Unterschied zwischen der Marktforschung im quantitativen und im qualitativen Bereich.

There are basically two types of market research – quantitative and qualitative. The former deals with numbers, the latter with trying to understand what is happening. Here are some examples of quantitative research:
A man sitting in a restaurant kitchen and making a list of what each customer orders from the menu.
A questionnaire which asks respondents to write down how many telephone calls they make every day.
A car manufacturer who asks customers to choose their favourite car colour.
All the data collected can be sorted numerically, and can be used to find out exactly what people do or like, for example.
Qualitative research is very different. Here the aim is to discover subjective meaning, to find out how people feel about something. The following list

Vokabeln

forecast	Prognose
market research	Marktforschung
qualitative	qualitativ
quantitative	quantitativ
questionnaire	Fragebogen
representative	repräsentativ
respondent	Befragter, Proband
sales research	Verkaufsforschung
sample	Stichprobe
survey	Umfrage

gives some examples: A survey asking people to explain why they like a particular type of bread.
An interview with shoppers to assess their feelings about a new store layout.
A group discussion about a new version of a computer program.
Of course with both types of research the key is to ask the right number of people the right questions, and analyse their responses correctly.

Infobox

Competitive intelligence
Finding out about competitors can be a very important part of your market research. Typical questions to ask include:
Who are the competitors in my geographical area?
What do my customers think?
What can industry experts tell me?
How do my competitors market their products or services?

Übung 5:

Finden Sie für die gegebenen Wörter die Entsprechungen im Text.

1. client

____

2. pay out

____

3. quantity

____

4. note

____

5. answers

____

6. find out

____

Übung 6:

Finden Sie die richtige Definition für diese Begriffe:

1. qualitative

a) to do with numbers

b) to do with understanding

c) to do with quantity

2. questionnaire

a) a list of questions

b) a list of questions with answers

c) a list of answers

3. persuade

a) convince b) ignore c) pay

4. respondents

a) people who ask questions

b) people who are asked

c) people who answer

Infobox

Another possible reason for market research is to build up a customer profile. Here are some typical areas to look at:
Who are the customers? (children, business people, old age pensioners)
When do customers buy? (seasons, time of day, which day)
How do customers buy? (cash, credit, barter)
Where do customers buy? (online, department store, catalogue)
Why do customers buy? (brand name, convenience, impulse)

Übung 7:

Welche der folgenden sechs Beispiele gehören zur Gruppe des "quantitative research"?

1. Counting how many people pass through the railway station.
2. Asking potential customers to select the actor they like most from a list of five famous actors.
3. Interviewing a bank's customers to find out why they use that bank.
4. Watching children at a playground to see how many are wearing light coloured clothes.
5. Using the internet to examine website designs.
6. Asking respondents to write down how many telephone calls they make every day.

Werbemedien

Werbung versucht, zwischen Konsument und Produkt eine Beziehung herzustellen. Werbemedien wie Postwurfsendungen oder Fernsehspots werden dazu benutzt, um das Unternehmen und seine Dienstleistungen oder Produkte bekannt zu machen.

Successful advertising generates sales. There are lots of ways to advertise a product. Let's look at traditional media first, which is often divided into national, local and specialist. Television commercials are expensive, but can be very effective at reaching a wide audience. The same goes for cinema; although less people may see the ad, the audience is probably more focussed.
Radio stations can also be very powerful, particularly if you have a catchy jingle. Outdoor advertising is another mass-market medium, and includes bill

Vokabeln

artwork	Grafik
billboard	Reklametafel
copy	Text
direct mail advertising	Postwurfsendung
jingle	Spruch
leaflet	Prospekt
media advertising	Werbung in Medien
outdoor advertising	Außenwerbung

boards, transport such as buses, and the use of street furniture such as public toilets and bus stops; recent innovations allow movement on such advertising. Print media such as newspapers and magazines can target a wide variety of audiences, and then there are leaflets and mail shots, posters, exhibitions and of course point of sale. Word-of-mouth can also be very useful – it really depends on your product and its market. Online media has become very popular in recent years. Websites are a useful way to reach a potential customer; other methods include emails and banner advertising. However the jury is still out on exactly how useful the internet is for advertisers.

Übung 8:

Sind die Sätze richtig oder falsch?

1. Street furniture includes lamp posts.

☐ richtig ☐ falsch

2. Leaflets can be easily produced on a PC.

☐ richtig ☐ falsch

3. Billboard advertising is common inside offices.

☐ richtig ☐ falsch

4. It costs about the same to send 10 emails and 1000 emails.

☐ richtig ☐ falsch

5. Internet advertising is relatively cheap.

☐ richtig ☐ falsch

Infobox

Not all advertising tries to sell a particular product. Corporate advertising often aims to convey a good image of a company. Generic advertising promotes a product as a whole, rather than a specific brand. Classified ads are common in newspapers, and are arranged according to various categories such as houses, second hand goods and staff recruitment.

Übung 9:

Ordnen Sie folgende Vokabeln den entsprechenden Übersetzungen zu!

1. relationship	☐ sich zum Ziel setzen
2. commercials	☐ Kleinanzeige
3. audience	☐ abhängig sein von
4. to target	☐ Verhältnis
5. depend on	☐ Zuschauer
6. classified ads	☐ Werbespots

Infobox

SPAM is unsolicited email, and is the online equivalent to junk mail.

Übung 10:
Welcher Begriff gehört nicht dazu? Kreuzen Sie an.

1. a) newspaper b) mail shot c) poster d) cinema e) leaflet
2. a) press b) TV c) radio d) cinema e) word-of-mouth
3. a) website b) banner c) street furniture d) search engine e) email
4. a) radio b) TV c) newspaper d) leaflet e) magazine

Eine Verkaufspräsentation

Ein Verkaufsleiter präsentiert einer Gruppe von potenziellen Kunden ein neues Produkt.

Good evening everybody, and thank you for coming. I'd like to start this presentation with a question. Is there anyone in this room who would like to be able to communicate with foreigners in their own language? With ease and accuracy? Of course we would. The problem is that learning a foreign language takes a lot of time and effort, and it's normally quite expensive.
What I want to do today is to show you a product which will help you solve this problem. It won't help you learn any languages, but what it will do is allow you to get your message across to anyone in the world.
Easylang meets this challenge. The concept is simple - look at the slide. You speak into a microphone here, and the listener listens to a speaker, here. Both speaker and listener work in their own language – there is no need to speak or understand the other tongue. Inside the box here is a clever little processing device which translates from one language to the other. The whole thing weighs about 500g, and costs less than a meal in a fast food restaurant.
Easylang will allow you to communicate with anyone in the world, anyplace, anytime.
All you have to do is fill in the form in front of you, fax it to the number at the top of the page, and you will be the proud owner of an Easylang set within two weeks.

Vokabeln

accuracy	Genauigkeit
challenge	Herausforderung
device	Gerät, Vorrichtung
ease	Leichtigkeit
effort	Anstrengung
form	Formular
slide	Dia
tongue	(hier) Sprache

Übung 11:
Enträtseln Sie das Geheimwort!

1. Nachricht, 2. Sprache, 3. Herausforderung,

4. Frage, 5. teuer

1. _ _☐_ _ _ _

2. _☐_ _ _ _ _ _

3. _ _ _ _☐_ _ _ _

4. _ _☐_ _ _ _ _

5. _ _ _ _ _☐_ _ _

Mystery Word ☐ ☐ ☐ ☐ ☐

Infobox

Many sales presentations in English use a five part structure:
1. get the listeners' attention
2. outline the problem
3. offer the solution
4. summarise the benefits
5. explain what the listener needs to do in order to get hold of the product or service.

Übung 12:
Bilden Sie sinnvolle Paare.

1. meet the	☐ form
2. fill in the	☐ the number
3. top of the	☐ you
4. solve the	☐ challenge
5. in front of	☐ page
6. fax to	☐ presentation

Übung 13:
Benutzen Sie nun die Phrasen der Übung 12, um die Lücken in der folgenden Übung zu füllen.

Look at the sheet of paper (1.) _ _ _ _ _ _.

The first task is to write your name in the space at the (2.) _ _ _ _ _. Once you have done this you are ready to (3.) _ _ _ _ _. Your aim is to (4.) _ _ _ _ _ in twenty minutes. If you are successful I will (5.) _ _ _ _ _ which will allow you to apply for the next course.

Good luck.

Übung 14:
Füllen Sie die Lücken mit Wörtern aus dem Text.

1. I'd like to start this presentation _ _ _ _ _ a question.

2. All you have to _ _ _ _ _ is send us a form.

3. The problem is _ _ _ _ _ learning a foreign language is expensive.

4. What I _ _ _ _ _ to do today is help you solve this problem.

5. Easylang will _ _ _ _ _ you to communicate with anyone in the world, anyplace, anytime.

6. Good evening everybody, and thank you _ _ _ _ _ coming.

Viele Firmen haben eine eigene Abteilung für Öffentlichkeitsarbeit, die dafür verantwortlich ist, das Image ihrer Firma in den Medien zu formen. Öffentlichkeitsarbeit ist nicht direkt am Verkauf von Produkten beteiligt. Sie sorgt vielmehr für ein positives Ansehen in der Öffentlichkeit, um damit die Kaufentscheidung der Abnehmer zu beeinflussen.

Medien

Im folgenden Dialog werden die Maßnahmen und Medien besprochen, die die Firma einsetzen möchte, um die Abnehmer über ihr Produkt zu informieren.

Frank: Afternoon, Ralf. Are you ready for our meeting?

Ralf: Hi Frank, you're early! Er, just give me a second. Here, look at this magazine and tell me what you think about the advertisement on the inside cover.

Frank: Ok ... Wow! That's good! Did we come up with that?

Ralf: Yeah, we sure did! It was the PR director's idea, but I did most of the creative work.

Frank: Great work, Ralf. Will we be placing it in any other media?

Ralf: Yeah. We're going to take the slogan from the print ad and adapt it to a broadcast campaign. The plan is to air both radio and television spots beginning next month. We thought that the print campaign would plant the seeds, and then we'll really have a strong broadcast presence until we go public with our stock next year.

Frank: Good idea. What kind of image are we looking to present?

Ralf: Well, from the ad we're running, we want to imply that we're a forward-thinking company. What we want to do in the broadcast bit is to tell the public that we have great growth potential, and that we're going to be around for a very long time.

Frank: And that's what you wanted to speak to me about, isn't it?

Ralf: That's right. I want you to handle the television campaign. You'll be in charge of the whole show, from producing to placing the ad. I have a budget set out, and I want you to find the most effective mix of time spots for airing it. We can set up a meeting next week

Vokabeln

campaign	Kampagne
go public	an die Börse gehen
image	Image
inside cover	innere Umschlagseite
place (in)	platzieren
run	leiten
slogan	Slogan
time spots	Zeitpunkte

with the producer to get the ball rolling. We have to have the spot in three weeks. Do you think you can handle it?
Frank: Count me in! It sounds like a great project! I'll need a bit more information about the image we're looking to present, though.
Ralf: I thought you'd have more questions, so I've asked Inga, who will run the radio campaign, to come by soon. I'd like you to stick around, and then maybe all three of us can coordinate the message that you'll be presenting ...
Frank: You are the man, Ralf! Before she comes, do I have time to get some coffee?
Ralf: Sure. Maybe we should get some for all of us. I'll walk down with you ...

Übung 1:

Vervollständigen Sie die Sätze!

1. Look at this _____ and tell me what you think of the advertisement on the inside cover.
2. Did we _____ with that?
3. Will we be _____ it in any other ____ ?
4. That's what you wanted to speak to me about, _____?
5. I want you to _____ the television campaign.
6. I thought you _____ have more questions.
7. I'd like you to _____ around.

Übung 2:

Bringen Sie die Wörter in den folgenden Sätzen in die richtige Reihenfolge.

1. you meeting ready are for our?

____

2. a second me give just.

____

3. placing we be will it in media any other?

____

4. The beginning air and television spots plan is to both radio next month.

____

____

5. kind of we looking image are to What present?

____

6. I to handle want you the campaign television.

____

____

7. Do you handle you think can it?

____

Infobox

The term "media" is actually the plural of the word "medium", and refers to modes of mass communication such as newspapers, magazines, television or radio. The goal of PR is to send a message through one or more of the media so that a specific audience (often referred to as a "target audience") receives that message. The audiences which PR targets normally have similar characteristics such as being single or married, belonging to a specific political party, or even belonging to a particular social class. Media campaigns employ messages that attempt to attract the attention of target audiences.

Übung 3:

Welches Wort kann auf das gegebene folgen?

1. mass

____

2. target

____

3. similar

____

4. political

____

5. media

____

6. social

____

7. public

____

Übung 4:

Verbessern Sie die folgenden Sätze:

1. Just give to me a second.

____

____

2. Did we to come up with that?

____

____

3. That's what you wanted to speak to me about, didn't you?

____

____

4. Do you can handle it?

____

5. We thought that the print campaign would to plant the seeds.

____

____

6. You'll be in charge of the whole movie.

____

____

7. It hears like a great project.

____

20 Öffentlichkeitsarbeit

Pressekonferenz

Zwei PR-Berater bereiten eine Pressekonferenz vor und diskutieren über die optimale Darstellungsform in der Öffentlichkeit.

Alison: Good morning, Tony. Have you got a minute?

Tony: Oh, hi Alison. Yeah, I have a minute. What can I do for you?

Alison: Well, I've been thinking about this new media campaign, and want to run a couple of ideas by you.

Tony: Ok, shoot.

Alison: All right. So, we're going to have both a television and radio campaign, right? Well, I'd like to propose some softer initiatives as well. First, how about we run a press conference for some trade publications?

Vokabeln

grill	in die Zange nehmen
handle	behandeln
hoax	Presseente
keep at it	nicht lockerlassen
notepad	Notizblock
press kit	Pressemappe
press conference	Pressekonferenz
press release	Presseerklärung
press spokesman	Pressesprecher
questioner	Fragesteller
reporter	Reporter
take notes	sich Notizen machen

Tony: Er, didn't I already tell you about the press conference?

Alison: Er, no.

Tony: Oh, don't worry, you'll do fine. It should only run for an hour or so ...

Alison: What do you mean, I'll do fine?

Tony: Well, I want you to be the point man, er, woman, for the campaign. And you have experience in holding press conferences as well, so it shouldn't be hard for you, should it?

Alison: Yeah, but an hour is quite a long time! And the press can be quite brutal.

Tony: That's why the whole team will be there to back you up. But you'll be out front and handling all the questions.

Alison: Well ...

Tony: Really, Alison, don't worry about it. It'll be fine. Probably only twenty people will show up and half of them will come for the free doughnuts.

Alison: Oh, sure! Like the last time when the reporters all grilled me about Frank's campaign with the dolphins. Great idea to put shirts on dolphins, wasn't it?

Tony: Uh ... yeah. But come on, Alison. There's no use in colleague-bashing. We can only learn from our mistakes.

Infobox

Press conferences are held when a company or private person (many times a celebrity) would like to share information with the public. The company or person plans a time and date to invite the media round, and then a spokesperson will present a short message with the important information that they wish to convey. This short presentation is generally followed by a question-and-answer session when the press will ask the spokesperson questions in order to get a fuller understanding of the purpose and importance of the message.
Press conferences are an effective way to get information to the media in a direct manner, as nowadays when a company holds a press conference, television cameras, radio microphones and journalists are all likely to be on hand.

Übung 5:

Verbessern Sie:

1. What would I do for you?

____

2. I'd want to propose some better initiatives as well.

____

3. Didn't I already say you about the press conference?

____

4. We can already learn from our mistakes.

____

5. Worry not about it.

____

6. You'll make fine.

____

7. The team will be there to back up you.

____

Übung 6:

Bringen Sie den Dialog in die richtige Reihenfolge!

1. Ok, shoot.
2. Well, I've been thinking about this new media campaign, and want to run a couple of ideas by you.
3. Good morning, Ralf. Have you got a minute?
4. All right. So, we're going to have both a television and radio campaign, right?
5. Yes, that's right.
6. Well, I'd like to propose some softer initiatives as well. First, how about we run a press conference for some trade publications?
7. Oh, hi Inga. Yeah, I have a minute. What can I do for you?

Lösung: ____________________

Übung 7:

Füllen Sie die Lücken mit den korrekten Wörtern:

Press conferences are (1.) _ _ _ _ _ when a company or private person (many times a celebrity) would like to share information with the public.

Press conferences are an effective way to get information to the (2.) _ _ _ _ _ in a (3.) _ _ _ _ _ manner.

The press will sometimes ask the spokesperson questions in order to get a fuller understanding of the (4.)_ _ _ _ _ and (5.) _ _ _ _ _ of the message.

(6.) _ _ _ _ _ magazines are specialized publications that deal with certain topics, for example, plumbing, construction, or the airline industry.

A (7.) _ _ _ _ _ and (8.) _ _ _ _ _ session comes after the spokeswoman's presentation.

Organisation von Betriebsbesichtigungen

Auch das Organisieren von Betriebsbesichtigungen gehört zu den Aufgaben einer PR-Abteilung. Diese Veranstaltungen sollen das Ansehen der Firma in der Öffentlichkeit positiv prägen ...

When a company has a successful year and wants to reward their employees, a company trip might be held. These can take the form of a boat trip, a hiking trip, or even an evening at the opera. Food and drink are normally provided free of charge, and the function can even be held on a workday to give employees an extra day off.

Other excursions are used to promote teamwork. This is especially the case in high-stress positions where teamwork is a job requirement. The department or team is taken to special camps or resorts, and there they are led through a program by a motivational leader. This leader designs a program of activities that helps the team learn things about each other and how to rely upon each other in difficult situations. Frequently, outdoor activities are used.

Lastly are job-related excursions such as trips to factories or production sites. Most of the time the public is not

Vokabeln

excursion	Ausflug
group dynamics	Gruppendynamik
promote	fördern
rely upon	sich aufeinander
each other	verlassen
resort	Ferienort
reward	belohnen
teamwork	Zusammenarbeit
trip	Ausflug
visit	Besichtigung

allowed behind the closed doors of a factory. But frequently, valued customers, clients or suppliers are invited to tour a plant or facility in order to learn more about the company. Some examples are tours of steel factories, agriculture processing plants, and even breweries. Most of these tours are handled by the internal public relations department, but can also include key people from the involved departments.

Übung 8:

Bilden Sie Fragen!

1. Why / companies / excursions / employees?

____

2. Where / excursions / held?

____

3. Why / companies / motivational excursions?

____

4. you / ever / a motivational excursion?

____

5. Which / you like / to tour?

____

6. When / begin / career / here?

____

Sonderveranstaltungen

Zwei Angestellte einer Firma wollen zu einer Ausstellung nach Chicago fahren, um die eigenen Produkte angemessen zu präsentieren – und die Konkurrenz auszustechen.

Jim: Good morning, Simon. Have you got a minute?

Simon: Sure, Jim. What can I do for you?

Jim: Well, I've been thinking that we should put a booth in the national stockholders exhibition in Chicago. What do you think?

Simon: I was thinking about it, too. But I'm not quite sure it will be cost-effective. I mean, most prospective shareholders won't be at such a trade fair.

Jim: You have a point there. I don't think they're the best idea for reaching potential investors. I mean, for cars and boats and other consumer goods, they can't be beat. But for our purposes, it's questionable.

Simon: We're on the same page, then. So why do you think we should send someone to Chicago?

Vokabeln

booth	Stand
consumer goods	Konsumgüter
cost-effective	kostenwirksam
hospitality	Gastfreundschaft
logo	Firmenzeichen, Logo

Jim: Well, I just got off the phone with an old colleague at Parker and Associates, and he told me that our biggest rival, Ennerve, is going to have a booth there. So I thought it might be good at least to keep an eye on what they're up to.

Simon: You're absolutely right. Would you like to go, or do you have someone else in mind?

Jim: If it's all the same to you, I'd like to do it myself.

Simon: Sounds good. What kind of booth do you think we should have? Big but understated would be my first choice.

Jim: Yeah, Ennerve will be large, glitzy and loud, I'm sure. So we'll set up nearby and beat them with logic and discussion, not free balloons.

Simon: Wait a minute, we have to provide something. How about a nice hospitality pack including pens and paper with our logo, and so on...

Jim: Like what we had last year, right?

Simon: Exactly. I really liked the desktop mobile phone stand. Can we give those again?

Jim: I'll see what I can do, Simon.

Simon: Great. And ask Inga if she wants to go, too. She's great with people, and I know she has family in Chicago.

Jim: Sounds good.

Übung 9:

Finden Sie die passenden Wortverbindungen im Text.

1. potential ____________________________

2. biggest ____________________________

3. hospitality ____________________________

4. cost ____________________________

5. old ____________________________

6. consumer ____________________________

7. trade ____________________________

Finanzierung und Bilanzierung sind wesentliche Bestandteile der Unternehmensführung. Sie sorgen für den reibungslosen Ablauf der Geschäfte und sichern den Bestand des Unternehmens. Dieser Lernschritt bietet das wichtigste Vokabular zu diesen Bereichen.

Geschäftsbericht und Jahresabschluss

Jede ins Handelsregister eingetragene Gesellschaft unterliegt der Verpflichtung, am Ende eines Geschäftsjahres einen Finanzbericht abzugeben. Die Aussagen zu den Finanzen müssen verschiedenen Gesetzen und Prinzipien folgen.

At the end of every fiscal year, every public listed company is required to prepare an Annual Report, together with the Balance Sheet and Profit and Loss (or Income) Statement. These reports must be presented to the shareholders of the company at the Annual General Meeting.
Annual Report: The text of this statement normally includes comments on the operations of the company for the year, a comparison of results with previous years, and an outlook for the future of the company.
Balance Sheet: This statement is dated as of the last day of the year. It shows the financial position of the company on that date. The assets of the company are normally shown on the left hand side of the Balance Sheet, and the liabilities and shareholders' equity on the right. The two sides must always be in

Vokabeln

accounts payable	Verbindlichkeiten
accounts receivable	Forderungen
allowance	Steuerfreibetrag
Annual General Meeting	Jahreshauptversammlung
Annual Report	Jahresbericht
assets	Vermögenswerte
Balance Sheet	Bilanz
deduct	abziehen
equipment	Ausstattung
fiscal year	Geschäftsjahr
fixed assets	Anlagevermögen
goodwill	Geschäftswert, Firmenwert
income tax	Einkommensteuer
incurred	aufgelaufen
intangible (assets)	immaterielle Vermögenswerte
inventories	Warenbestandswert
liabilities	Schuldposten
operation	Arbeitsweise
outlook	Vorhersage
Profit and Loss (or Income) Statement	Gewinn- und Verlustrechnung
shareholders equity	Eigenkapital
stake	Beteiligung

21 Finanzierung und Bilanzierung

balance. The assets are split into current assets, such as cash, accounts receivable and inventories, and fixed assets which may include property, plant and equipment, and intangibles such as goodwill. The liabilities will also be separated into current liabilities which are due within one year (for example, accounts payable), and long term liabilities. Lastly the shareholders equity, which is the total equity interest of the shareholders will be shown.
Profit and Loss Statement: This statement shows whether the company made or lost income during the year. The income often comes from Net Sales, from which expenses such as the Cost of Sales, Administrative Expenses, and Interest Charges incurred are deducted.

Infobox

The theory behind financial statement reporting requirements is the same in most countries. However, the method of reporting and the terminology used, for example between Britain and the United States of America, might be different. With the increase in globalisation, there have been recent moves to standardise the reporting methods between countries. This will help people to analyse and compare reports from all over the world.

Übung 1:

Welches Wort kann auf das gegebene folgen? Vergleichen Sie mit dem Text.

1. Balance ____________
2. Profit and Loss ____________
3. Annual General ____________
4. shareholders ____________
5. property, plant and ____________
6. accounts ____________
7. fiscal ____________

Übung 2:

Übersetzen Sie!

1. incurred ____________
2. outlook ____________
3. goodwill ____________
4. intangibles ____________
5. inventories ____________
6. fiscal year ____________
7. operations ____________

Übung 3:

Welcher Begriff gehört nicht dazu? Erklären Sie warum.

1. a) net sales b) goodwill c) administrative expenses d) cost of sales e) interest charges

2. a) accounts receivable b) fixed assets

c) property plant and equipment d) cash

e) accounts payable

3. a) Balance Sheet b) Profit and Loss Statement c) Shareholders Equity d) Annual Report

4. a) interest charges b) cost of sales

c) administrative charges d) inventories

Bankgeschäfte

Das Bankgewerbe hat sich in den letzten Jahren dramatisch verändert. Banken sind nicht mehr nur Hüter unseres Geldes, sondern vielmehr mit zahlreichen Finanzgeschäften für ihre Kunden befasst. Besonders Investmentbanken agieren globaler und diversifizierter.

Instead of keeping our money under the bed, we are all used to asking a bank to look after our money for us. Many of us have also asked a bank to lend us money to buy a house or a car. This bank business continues today and can be regarded as the basis of banking. In the corporate world, however, the face of banking changed enormously in the twentieth century. Clients of banks became more and more demanding. Banks were required to meet these demands and provide services to match.

The latter part of the twentieth century saw the rapid expansion of investment banks. These banks do not normally lend money to clients; this part of banking is still covered by the commercial banks. An investment bank is more concerned with raising finance on behalf of their clients. This business has become more sophisticated in the last twenty years. New banking products are invented almost every week, as banks strive to

Vokabeln

blue chip	erstklassige Standardaktie
emergence	Hervortreten
interest	Zins(en)
invest	anlegen
investment bank	Investmentbank
investment income	Kapitalerträge
lend	leihen
mature	fällig werden
merger	Fusion
raise finance	einen Finanzierungsplan erstellen
repeal	aufheben
return	Rendite
savings bank	Sparkasse
sight deposit	Sichteinlagen
sophisticated	anspruchsvoll
stockbroking	Wertpapierhandel
strive	sich bemühen
tax-free benefit	steuerfreie Vergünstigung
term deposit	Termineinlagen
waive charges	auf Gebühren verzichten

keep up with the demands of their clients. Globalisation has also led to the emergence of major finance centres, in New York, London, Frankfurt and Tokyo for example. Today, banks are required to serve international clients with products and services that were not thought of 50 years ago.

Infobox

For many years in the United States of America commercial and investment banks were separated by law. The repeal of this law will probably mean that more mergers in the banking world will take place, including across borders. The trick is to find the appropriate partner. Mergers will allow single banks to offer complete packages to clients in their world-wide operations.

Übung 4:

Verbessern Sie die folgenden Sätze:

1. In the corporate world however, the face of banking has changed enormously in the twentieth century.

_ _

_ _

2. Instead to keep our money under the bed, we are all used to asking a bank to look after our money for us.

_ _

_ _

_ _

3. The latter part of the twentieth century has seen the rapid expansion of investment banks.

_ _

_ _

4. This business is becoming more sophisticated in the last twenty years.

_ _

_ _

5. New banking products have invented almost every week.

_ _

_ _

6. Today, banks are be required to serve international clients.

_ _

_ _

7. For many years in the United States of America commercial and investment banks are separated by law.

_ _

_ _

_ _

Übung 5:

Füllen Sie die Lücken mit Wörtern aus dem Text.

1. Instead of keeping our money _ _ _ _ _ _ _ _ _ _ _ the bed, we are all used to asking a bank to _ _ _ _ _ _ _ _ _ _ _ _ after our money for us.
2. Many of us have also asked a bank to _ _ _ _ _ _ _ _ _ _ _ us money to buy a house or a car.
3. An investment bank is more concerned with raising finance on _ _ _ _ _ _ _ _ _ _ _ _ of their clients.
4. The United States of America will _ _ _ _ _ _ _ _ _ _ _ the law which separates commercial from investment banking.
5. When two companies join, it is called a _ _ _ _ _ _ _ _ _ _ _.
6. The banking business is becoming more and more _ _ _ _ _ _ _ _ _ _ _ _ every day.

Übung 6:

Welche der folgenden fünf Beispiele gehören zum Thema „Investment Banking"?

1. Raising finance on behalf of clients.
2. World-wide operations.
3. Asking a bank to lend you money to buy a house.
4. The emergence of financial centres across the world.
5. The introduction of more and more sophisticated products.

Investment und Börse

Die Möglichkeiten zu investieren wachsen von Tag zu Tag. Die Börse bietet Investoren zahlreiche Optionen, ihr Geld anzulegen.

Many companies wish to raise public capital by having their shares traded on a stock exchange. The main centres for share trading are New York, London, Frankfurt and Tokyo. On these and other exchanges, shares and other products such as bonds and derivatives can be traded.

In order to be listed on one of the stock exchanges, the company has to issue a prospectus and a listing application. The company is then bound to follow the rules of the exchange, which may include the filing of reports and the provision of information to the exchange. Once a company is listed, the public, including private people and institutions, are free to buy and sell the product. The products available on

exchanges now include various derivatives of the main products, shares and bonds.
The reasons why people invest on the exchanges are varied. Some seek a short term gain, by speculating that the share price of a particular company will increase. Others look for longer term capital growth, perhaps with the chance of receiving dividends. Share prices are of course subject to fluctuation. The current world business climate is dependent on many factors. Investing on the stock exchanges is never a sure thing, and investors must carefully consider all the implications before committing money to one company or another.

Vokabeln

bond	Obligation
capital growth	Kapitalzuwachs
derivative	Derivat
dividend	Dividende
file	einreichen
fluctuation	Fluktuation
implication	Implikation
investment scheme	Anlageplan
outward investment	Auslands-investition
Personal Equity Plan (PEP)	persönlicher Aktiensparplan
provision	Bereitstellung
share	Aktie
speculate	spekulieren
stock exchange	Börse

Infobox

For large investors, such as institutions and investment banks, the rating agencies are invaluable tools to be used when analysing the creditworthiness of some products listed on exchanges, particularly bonds. Moody's and Standard & Poor's are the two largest rating agencies.

Übung 7:

Enträtseln Sie das Lösungswort!

1. Dividende, 2. Obligation, 3. Derivat,

4. Aktie, 5. Börse, 6. Kapitalzuwachs

1. _☐______

2. __☐_

3. ____☐_____

4. ____☐

5. ☐____ ________

6. ____☐__ ______

Mystery Word ☐☐☐☐☐☐

Übung 8:

Sind die Sätze richtig oder falsch?

1. Investing on the stock exchange is a sure thing.

☐ richtig ☐ falsch

2. There are many reasons to invest on the stock exchange.

☐ richtig ☐ falsch

3. Share prices do not fluctuate.

☐ richtig ☐ falsch

4. Only shares are listed on stock exchanges.

☐ richtig ☐ falsch

5. There are two main rating agencies today.

☐ richtig ☐ falsch

Währungen und Devisen

Wir sind es gewöhnt, Währungen zu tauschen, wenn wir ins Ausland fahren. Auch Firmen müssen bei internationalen Transaktionen die Währung wechseln. Durch die Einführung des Euros ist dies für die teilnehmenden Länder einfacher geworden.

Everybody who has travelled to another country knows of the problems associated with changing currencies. Not only do you have to get used to the physical qualities of the new notes and coins, but also what they are worth in relation to the currency at home.
This is especially difficult when you travel to various countries on the same holiday, and need to convert numerous currencies. Luckily, for those living in Europe, many of these problems have been solved by the introduction of the euro.

For companies with operations in other countries, the story is far more complicated. For the purpose of financial reporting, careful consideration must be given to how these transactions are to be dealt with in the accounts. The translation of foreign currencies into the home currency is dependent on the type of transaction. The whole accounts of a foreign subsidiary must also be translated into the currency of the parent. Companies should also take into consideration the currency exposure they have. Currency rates also fluctuate, which can leave companies with large losses.

Vokabeln

appreciate	im Wert steigen
coin	Münze
convert	umtauschen
currency fluctuation	Kursschwankung
currency	Währung
depreciate	an Wert einbüßen
exchange rate	Wechselkurs
exposure	Aussetzung
hedge against	absichern gegen
legal tender	gesetzliches Zahlungsmittel
note	Schein
revalue	aufwerten, neu bewerten
run	Ansturm, erhöhte Nachfrage
slum	im Wert stark fallen
transaction	Transaktion

Infobox

The introduction of the euro means that people in the participating countries can easily compare prices. Also foreign travelling in the euro-zone has been made easier, as travellers no longer have to keep changing currencies as they move from one country to the next. However, some people were very reluctant to accept the euro, as they felt that the replacement of their own currency with the euro would affect their national identity. Many people relate very strongly to their currency. Time will tell how the peoples of Europe adapt to their new currency.

Übung 9:

Schreiben Sie besser!

1. Everybody who is travelling to another country knows of the problems associated with changing currencies.

_ _

2. The introduction of the euro is solving many of these problems.

_ _

3. The whole accounts of a foreign subsidiary must also been translated into the currency of the parent.

_ _

4. Companies should also bring into consideration the currency exposure they have.

_ _

5. Also foreign travelling in the euro-zone is being made easier.

_ _

6. Time tells how the peoples of Europe adapt to their new currency.

_ _

Übung 10:

Formulieren Sie die Sätze im Passiv!

1. The introduction of the euro has solved many of these problems.

_ _

2. You must give careful consideration to how these transactions are to be dealt with in the accounts.

_ _

_ _

3. We must convert foreign currencies into our own currency.

_ _

4. Parent companies translate the accounts of subsidiaries into the home currency.

_ _

_ _

5. The euro has made foreign travelling easier.

_ _

Sowohl Einzelpersonen als auch Firmen müssen bestimmte Auflagen hinsichtlich Steuererklärungen und der Erstellung von Bilanzen erfüllen. Meist ist man abhängig vom Fachwissen der Buchhalter, Steuerberater und Wirtschaftsprüfer, um sicherzugehen, dass man allen Verpflichtungen nachkommt.

Buchhaltung

Buchhalter sind für verschiedene Aufgaben im finanziellen Bereich verantwortlich. Sie kontrollieren den Geldfluss und stellen sicher, dass Rechnungen bezahlt bzw. pünktlich eingefordert werden. Weiterhin gehört die Lohn- und Gehaltsabrechung und die Erstellung der Bilanzen in den Aufgabenbereich der Buchhaltung.

For hundreds of years people have looked after the finances of larger institutions. Nowadays, the person who is responsible for keeping the financial records of an enterprise is called the bookkeeper. Consider some of the responsibilities of bookkeepers:

1. The collection and payment of invoices:
The bookkeeper ensures that all invoices are either collected or paid on time. This is essential to maintain a good cash flow for the enterprise. Every enterprise relies on its bookkeepers to make sure that all debts can be paid by the due date, to avoid problems with the bank.

2. The payment of wages and salaries:
All payments to employees, including any benefits, must be paid on time.

3. The payment of overheads:
The bookkeeper must ensure that all expenses which occur on a regular basis, such as rent and telephone, are paid on time.

4. Cash flow forecasting:
The bookkeeper may be involved in forecasting the future income and expenses of an enterprise, because of his/her detailed knowledge of the money flow within the enterprise. This helps the management of the enterprise predict future problems, and make plans against such problems.

5. The preparation of financial reports:
The bookkeeper may assist the Finance Director in the preparation of accounts, or management reports, which provide information on the profitability or otherwise of the operations of the enterprise.

22 Abrechnung, Buchhaltung und Steuern

Vokabeln

bookkeeper	Buchhalter
cash flow	Cashflow
computer literacy	Computerwissen
cross reference	Gegenbuchung
double-entry bookkeeping	doppelte Buchführung
due date	Fälligkeitsdatum
enterprise	Unternehmen
extensive	viel
financial records	Rechnungsunterlagen
forecasting	Planung
formal qualification	offiziell anerkannte Qualifikation
invoices	Rechnungen
liabilities	Verbindlichkeiten
liquidity	Liquidität
overheads	Gemeinkosten
predict	voraussagen
profitability	Rentabilität
receipts	Belege
revenue	Einnahmen
salary	Gehalt
source of funds	Kapitalquelle
subtotal	Zwischensumme
wage	Lohn
year under review	Berichtsjahr

Infobox

The position of bookkeeper in many English speaking countries can be attained without extensive formal qualifications. However, knowledge of finance in general and computer literacy are essential skills. In many smaller enterprises, the bookkeeper has an extremely important task, which is to maintain the liquidity of the enterprise and thus keep it in operations.

Übung 1:

Welche Wörter gehören in die Lücken?

Many (1.) ____________ reach their position without extensive (2.) ____________. However, they have important functions in any (3.) ____________. They must ensure that all (4.) ____________ are paid and collected by the (5.) ________. They may be involved in (6.) ____________ the future profitability of the enterprise. The bookkeeper might also be responsible for the (7.) ____________ of the enterprise, so that it is able to pay its bills on time.

Übung 2:

Übersetzen Sie!

1. computer literacy ______________
2. income ______________
3. expenses ______________
4. liquidity ______________
5. predict ______________
6. enterprise ______________

Übung 3:

Welche der folgenden fünf Beispiele gehören zur Aufgabe eines Buchhalters? Kreuzen Sie an.

1. Forecasting the future liquidity of an enterprise.
2. Buying and selling the assets of an enterprise.
3. Paying and collecting invoices.
4. Payment of wages and salaries.
5. Negotiating the costs of services given to the enterprise.

Rechnungswesen

Alle Unternehmen müssen ihre Finanzen kontrollieren, um darüber Rechenschaft ablegen zu können. Buchprüfer oder Wirtschaftsprüfer sind dafür verantwortlich, über die finanzielle Situation einer Firma Auskunft zu geben.

Accounting can be described as the process of classifying and recording the transactions of a company. However, the current roles of accountants far exceed this limited definition.

Look at some of the roles accountants perform: Financial reporting: the accountants of a company are responsible for the preparation of the financial statements of the company. They may also be asked to prepare management reports on the profitability of certain operations.

Auditing: many companies are required by law to include an auditors report with their year-end accounts. The auditors must sign-off that they have audited the accounts in accordance with the law, and that the accounts were prepared in accordance with generally accepted accounting principles, and give a true and fair view of the financial position of the company.

Tax Advice: some accountants specialise in the preparation of tax returns for their clients. They may also give tax advice to enterprises.

Insolvency: when a company is unable to pay its debts, accountants may be called in to oversee the operations of the company. They will try to manage the business so that all or most of the legal obligations are met.

Financing: due to their financial expertise, accountants may be involved in general financing questions.

They can also give advice on financing strategies.

Vokabeln

absorption costing	Vollkostenrechnung
accounting	Buchhaltung
administrative costs	Verwaltungskosten
appropriation account	Gewinnverteilungsrechnung
auditor	Bilanzprüfer
auditing	Buchprüfung
break-even point	Kostendeckungspunkt
Chartered Accountant	staatlich geprüfter Bilanzbuchhalter
classify	klassifizieren
debts	Schulden
exceed	über etwas hinausgehen
financial	finanziell
financial position	Finanzlage
financing	Finanzierung
insolvency	Insolvenz
marginal costing	Teilkostenrechnung
profitability	Rentabilität
profit and loss account	Gewinn- und Verlustrechnung
solvency	Solvenz
wages office	Lohnbüro

Infobox

In most English speaking countries, there are various exams to be passed before qualifying as a Chartered Accountant (known as Certified Practising Accountant in the US). After the degree at university, one must sit further exams while working at an accountancy firm. After this process, the accountant could possibly work in any of the areas described in the text above.

Übung 4:

Vervollständigen Sie die Sätze!

1. Look ____________ some of the roles accountants perform.
2. They may also be asked to prepare management reports ____________ the profitability of certain operations.
3. The auditor report will say that the accounts of the company give a ____________ and ____________ view of the financial position.
4. When a company is unable to pay its debts, accountants may be called ___________ to oversee the operations.
5. There are various exams to be passed ____ _____ qualifying as a Chartered Accountant (US: Certified Practising Accountant).

Übung 5:

Ordnen Sie folgende Vokabeln den entsprechenden Übersetzungen zu!

1. chartered	☐ Bilanzbuchhalter
2. tax adviser	☐ Bilanzprüfer
3. auditor	☐ Steuererklärung
4. insolvency	☐ Buchhaltung
5. accounting	☐ Insolvenz

6. tax return ☐ staatlich geprüft

7. accountant ☐ Steuerberater

Übung 6:
Übersetzen Sie!

1. finanzieren, 2. Transaktion, 3. klassifizieren,

4. Bericht, 5. Bilanzprüfer, 6. Steuererklärung,

7. Schulden, 8. Insolvenz, 9. Universität,

10. Liquidität

1. _ _ _ ☐ _ _ _

2. _ _ _ _ _ _ _ ☐ _ _ _ _

3. ☐ _ _ _ _ _ _ _ _

4. _ _ _ ☐ _ _

5. _ ☐ _ _ _ _ _ _

6. _ _ _ _ _ _ _ _ ☐ _

7. _ _ _ ☐ _

8. ☐ _ _ _ _ _ _ _ _ _ _

9. _ ☐ _ _ _ _ _ _ _ _ _

10. _ _ _ _ _ _ _ _ _ ☐ _

Mystery Word ☐☐☐☐☐☐☐☐☐☐

Steuern

Jede einkommensteuerpflichtige Person und jedes Unternehmen müssen eine Steuererklärung abgeben und bezahlen indirekte Steuern wie z. B. Mehrwertsteuer. Mit Hilfe eines Steuerberaters lässt sich die Steuerlast jedoch reduzieren.

Have you ever heard the saying that in life only two things are certain, death and taxation? Against the former, there's not much we can do. Against taxation, we can hire tax accountants. Taxation is not only a matter of paying a sizeable part of our income to the government. On a personal level, every year we must complete and send a tax return to the tax office (US: Inland Revenue). It is our duty to declare all of our income, from which we can deduct certain expenses. The tax we must pay (income tax) is calculated on the basis of the figures we report in the tax return. Companies must also complete a tax return every year. The financial statements produced are used as the basis for the calculation of taxable income. After certain adjustments, the corporate tax rate is then levied. The various and complex transactions of companies provide opportunities for tax planning. International companies can take advantage of different tax rates in the different countries of operations. Transactions can sometimes be structured in ways which lead to lower levels of taxation. It is worth considering the financial structure of a business, and consulting a tax specialist who may be able to help reduce the tax liability. Unfortunately, it doesn't end with personal taxation and corporate taxation, the so-called direct taxes. There are also a myriad of indirect taxes, such as the VAT (Value Added Tax) in Britain. This tax is levied on the sale of goods or provision of services to other parties. Many of the indirect taxes have their own disclosure requirements, and returns which must be handed in every year.

Vokabeln

allowable against tax	steuerlich absetzbar
allowance	Steuerfreibetrag
assessment	Veranlagung
burden	Belastung
casual income	Nebeneinkünfte
declare	angeben
deduct	abziehen
depreciation	Abschreibung
disclosure	Mitteilung
duty	Pflicht
evasion	Hinterziehung
expenditure	Ausgaben
fiscal	steuerlich, Fiskal-
income tax	Einkommensssteuer
levy	erheben
liable to corporation tax	körperschaftssteuerpflichtig
tax code	Steuernummer
taxable income	steuerpflichtiges Einkommen
tax office (US: Inland Revenue)	Finanzamt
VAT (Value Added Tax)	Mehrwertsteuer

Infobox

The taxation systems of countries differ greatly. It is not possible to say that because a structure in one country is good for tax purposes, it must therefore be good also in other countries. This makes it even more difficult to operate international businesses, with different disclosure and reporting requirements.
It does however allow for tax planning which takes advantage of the laws in different countries.

Übung 7:

Wie lauten die Sätze richtig?

1. Companies return also year a tax complete every must.

____

____

2. It of financial considering worth structure is business the a.

____

____

3. Unfortunately, taxation it taxation and with personal corporate end doesn't.

____

____

4. The of greatly taxation differ countries systems.

_ _

Übung 8:

Welches Wort kann auf das gegebene folgen? Vergleichen Sie mit dem Text.

1. reporting _ _ _ _ _ _ _ _ _ _ _ _ _ _ _ _
2. income _ _ _ _ _ _ _ _ _ _ _ _ _ _ _ _
3. Inland _ _ _ _ _ _ _ _ _ _ _ _ _ _ _ _
4. tax _ _ _ _ _ _ _ _ _ _ _ _ _ _ _ _
5. personal _ _ _ _ _ _ _ _ _ _ _ _ _ _ _ _
6. direct _ _ _ _ _ _ _ _ _ _ _ _ _ _ _ _

Übung 9:

Vervollständigen Sie die Sätze!

1. Have you _ _ _ _ _ _ _ _ _ _ _ heard the saying that in life only two things are certain, death and taxation?

2. It is our _ _ _ _ _ _ _ _ _ _ _ to declare all of our income.

3. After certain adjustments, the corporate tax rate is then _ _ _ _ _ _ _ _ _ _ _.

4. It is _ _ _ _ _ _ _ _ _ _ _ considering the financial structure of a business.

5. The taxation systems _ _ _ _ _ _ _ _ _ _ _ countries differ greatly.

Übung 10:

Übersetzen Sie!

1. income tax _ _ _ _ _ _ _ _ _ _ _ _
2. disclosure _ _ _ _ _ _ _ _ _ _ _ _
3. VAT (Value Added Tax) _ _ _ _ _ _ _ _ _ _ _ _
4. duty _ _ _ _ _ _ _ _ _ _ _ _
5. tax office _ _ _ _ _ _ _ _ _ _ _ _
6. Inland Revenue _ _ _ _ _ _ _ _ _ _ _ _
7. declare _ _ _ _ _ _ _ _ _ _ _ _
8. deduct _ _ _ _ _ _ _ _ _ _ _ _
9. levied _ _ _ _ _ _ _ _ _ _ _ _

Infobox

For the calculation of corporate income tax, the financial statements are used as the starting point. There can be significant differences between the accounting profit and the taxable income. For example, in many countries, the depreciation allowed on assets by generally accepted accounting principles is different than what is allowed under the tax laws. There may also be vast differences between what expenditure is considered to be capital expenses, as opposed to normal operating expenses of the company. Accountants and tax advisers need to be aware of the potential differences between the treatment of transactions under accounting and tax laws.

Übung 11:

Sind die Sätze richtig oder falsch?

1. The accounting profit of a company is always equal to its taxable income.

☐ richtig ☐ falsch

2. Bookkeepers are responsible for the preparation of tax returns.

☐ richtig ☐ falsch

3. Differences in tax laws between countries offer tax planning opportunities.

☐ richtig ☐ falsch

4. The financial statements of companies listed on the stock exchange must be audited.

☐ richtig ☐ falsch

5. The financial statements are the basis for calculation of taxable income.

☐ richtig ☐ falsch

Übung 12:

Formulieren Sie die Sätze im Passiv!

1. Auditors must audit the financial statements of companies.

____

____

____

2. The government levies V.A.T. in Britain on the sale of goods.

____

____

____

3. Everyone must declare all of their income in a tax return at the end of the year.

____

____

____

4. The law requires companies to prepare financial statements.

____

____

____

Übung 13:

Bilden Sie sinnvolle Paare!

1. indirect and direct	☐ expenses
2. depreciation on	☐ report
3. deduct	☐ tax return
4. complete a	☐ statements
5. generally accepted	☐ taxes
6. financial	☐ accounting principles
7. auditors	☐ assets

Verträge, Kündigungen und Lizenzen 23

„Kostenlos“ klingt gut, aber man sollte auch das Kleingedruckte lesen. Geschriebene Vereinbarungen beinhalten oft Überraschungen für den Unaufmerksamen.

Verträge

Ein Vertrag ist eine Vereinbarung zwischen zwei oder mehreren Parteien. Im folgenden Dialog erklärt ein Manager einem neuen Angestellten seinen Arbeitsvertrag.

Manager: Ok. So the first part is your job title. You are a commercial clerk.

Employee: Ok.

Manager: Remuneration comes next – in other words – how much we'll be paying you.

Vokabeln

annual leave	Jahresurlaub
clerk	Angestellter
confidentiality	Vertraulichkeit
core	Kern
days off	freie Tage
delete	streichen
duty	Aufgabe
earnings	Verdienst
employment contract	Arbeitsvertrag
entitlement	Berechtigung
flexitime	Gleitzeit
full-time/part-time worker	Voll-/Teilzeitkraft
grievance	Beschwerde
medical ensurance	Krankenversicherung
option	Option
overtime	Überstunden
probationary	auf Probe
take-home pay	Nettolohn
work permit	Arbeitserlaubnis
working hours	Arbeitszeit

Employee: Salary?

Manager: Exactly. But there's more to it than just your basic salary. You need to know about your expenses – what you are entitled to claim for, for example, and what you're not.

Employee: Ok. You mean like travel claims.

Manager: Exactly. Except you won't be travelling.

Employee: Oh.

Manager: The next clause is about pensions – you know we pay a certain amount of your salary into a pension fund which later pays your company pension.

Employee: Right.

Manager: It's not much, so you'll need to have your own pension plan too. We can delete the bit about stock options – it doesn't apply to you.

Employee: I see.

Manager: Your holiday entitlement comes next. You see here you have 10 days paid leave in your first year, and 15 days a year after that.

Employee: Great. Does that include all the public holidays like Christmas?

23 Verträge, Kündigungen und Lizenzen

Manager: No, no. You get those too. Now, this clause here is about what happens when you are sick – you see that you need to see a doctor if you're away for more than 2 days. And here's the maternity clause.
Employee: Ok. Excuse me. What's probationary period.
Manager: That's where we watch you for the first 3 months to see if we like you. And of course you see if you like us. Both of us can terminate the contract within 48 hours during this time.
Employee: Ok.
Manager: Now comes the confidentiality clause. You can't tell other companies about our products and customers, for example. Intellectual property rights, trade secrets, sensitive documents that sort of thing.
Employee: Sure.
Manager: And if you ever leave us you can't provide similar services for any of our customers or direct competitors for up to six months.
Employee: Ok.
Manager: Grievance procedures cover what you need to do if you think we're treating you badly, for example.
Employee: All right.
Manager: And the last section here gives details of working hours, lunch breaks, core working times, that sort of thing.
Employee: Ok.
Manager: I suggest you go away and read this carefully, and if you don't have any questions after that we'll sign it and you can start work immediately.
Employee: Thank you.

Übung 1:

Ordnen Sie folgende Vokabeln den entsprechenden Übersetzungen zu!

1. clerk	☐ Vertraulichkeit
2. entitlement	☐ streichen
3. grievance	☐ Option
4. probationary	☐ Kern
5. confidentiality	☐ auf Probe
6. option	☐ Beschwerde
7. core	☐ Berechtigung
8. delete	☐ Angestellte

Übung 2:

Finden Sie die Wortverbindungen, wie sie im Text vorkommen. Der erste Teil ist vorgegeben.

1. direct _____________
2. working _____________

3. lunch ______________

4. holiday ______________

5. stock ______________

6. probationary ______________

7. confidentiality ______________

8. commercial ______________

9. travel ______________

Übung 3:

Vervollständigen Sie die Sätze! Die passenden Wörter finden Sie im Text.

1. Another word for trial period is ________ ________ period.

2. Companies normally want to keep things secret, so contracts often include a _______ _________ clause.

3. A person who works in an office is sometimes called a ________________.

4. Managers often have a basic salary which is supplemented by stock ______________.

5. Everyone has to be at work during ______ __________ working hours.

6. In Germany most people are entitled to 30 days ________________.

7. The works council will normally help you in the case of ________________.

Kündigungen

Eine Firma kann auf zwei Wegen verlassen werden: Entweder man kündigt, oder man wird gekündigt. Im ersten Fall heißt der Kündigungsbrief im Englischen *letter of resignation*, im zweiten Fall *letter of dismissal*. Hierzu je ein Beispiel.

Dear Mr Gonnarth

As required by my contract of employment, I hereby give you three months notice of my intention to leave Gonnarth Brothers at the end of September.

The decision to leave has not been easy. My partner and I have decided to move to Thailand, where we plan to set up a company specialising in the export of exotic wildlife.

I am grateful for all the experience and skills I have gained while a member of Gonnarth Brothers, and I will do my best to ensure that my handover to the nominated employee is as smooth as possible.

With best wishes

Jennifer Klasson

Dear Mr Smith

You have now received two verbal warnings and a written warning about the quality of your work, and the situation has not improved. Unfortunately this leaves us with no alternative. You are hereby informed that your employment contract with us is to terminate with effect from 30 November 2002. If you require any further information, or wish to appeal against your dismissal please contact me personally within the next few days.

Yours sincerely
E. Jackson, HR Manager

Vokabeln

appeal	Einspruch
dismissal	Entlassung
early retirement	Vorruhestand
gain	gewinnen
handover	Übergabe
industrial law	Arbeitsrecht
intention	Absicht
job cuts	Stellenkürzungen
make sbd redundant	jdn entlassen
nominate	nominieren
notice	Kündigungsfrist
resignation	Kündigung
terminate	enden, lösen, kündigen
trades union	Gewerkschaft
warning	Abmahnung
with effect from	mit Wirkung vom

Übung 4:

Verbessern Sie folgende Sätze.

1. Your contract will terminated with immediate effect.

_ _

_ _

2. I need to give you 30 days' noticed before I can leave the job.

_ _

_ _

3. I want to appeal for my dismissal.

_ _

_ _

4. I have gain a lot of experience during my time here.

_ _

_ _

5. I planning to hand over the accounts next week.

_ _

_ _

6. He wasn't dismiss: he resigned.

_ _

_ _

7. My intention is to taking three weeks' holiday in summer.

____

____

8. He was nominate at yesterday's meeting.

____

____

Infobox

Dismissal, notice etc.

Note that "Kündigung" can also be translated as termination, cancellation, dismissal or notice. Here are some examples:
He cancelled the contract with effect from July 15.
The contract was automatically terminated by the completion and handover of the new buildings.
He said that I would risk dismissal if I didn't come in on Saturday.
The landlord gave me three months' notice to leave the flat.

Lizenzen

Zwei Kollegen besprechen die Lizenzbedingungen einer neuen Software.

Jennifer: Hi John. I'm just reading through this licence agreement for the new software; can I ask you a couple of questions?

John: Sure. No problem. I went through it yesterday.

Jennifer: What do you think they mean by commercial and authorized users?

John: Let's have a look. Ah, see here. They're defined. Authorized users are basically employees of this company, whereas commercial users are people who use the software for commercial gain.

Jennifer: In other words to earn money?

John: Right.

Jennifer: Ok, that's fair enough. It says that the license does not include any commercial users.

John: Yes, and it also says that you'll have to keep full and up-to-date records of all authorized users and their access details.

Vokabeln

authorize	autorisieren, erlauben
define	definieren
expiry	Ablauf
gain	Gewinn
goods manufactured under license	In Lizenz gefertigte Ware
grant a license	Lizenz erteilen
illegal	rechtswidrig
license	Lizenz
license holder, licensee	Lizenznehmer
lincensor	Lizenzgeber
nullify	annullieren
renew	prolongieren
subscription	Abonnement
wade through	durchackern

Jennifer: That's a lot of work.

John: Yes, but failure to do so could nullify the license.

Jennifer: Ok. Moving on. Subscription period? Does that mean that we need to renew, every year?

John: Yes, exactly. In fact it says here that you need to do this at the start of each calendar year, otherwise the license will be terminated automatically.

Jennifer: And if I forget?

John: We'll be using the software ille-gally.

Jennifer: Ah. I'd better put the expiry date in my diary.

John: Yes, indeed. Have you looked at paragraph 3 yet?

Jennifer: No, not yet. Exciting, is it?

John: Sarcasm. Sarcasm. But there's an interesting point about copyright. It's all in the small print.

Jennifer: I think I'll go and wade through this again! See you later.

Übung 5:

Übersetzen Sie!

1. wade through ________________
2. define ________________
3. subscription ________________
4. expiry ________________
5. renew ________________
6. gain ________________
7. illegal ________________
8. nullify ________________
9. licensee ________________

Übung 6:

Bilden Sie sinnvolle Paare.

1. subscription	☐ through
2. expiry	☐ agreement
3. wade	☐ users
4. licence	☐ year
5. authorised	☐ period
6. calendar	☐ point
7. interesting	☐ date

Infobox

Years

A calendar year starts at the beginning of January and ends at the end of December.
An accounting or financial year covers the period covered by the annual accounts of an organization. In some countries it does not have to cover 12 months.
A sabbatical year is a year away from work, normally unpaid.
A fiscal year is the same as a tax year, and refers to the government's financial year. In Britain this runs from 6 April to 5 April. In the USA it is from 1 July to 30 June.

Klage und Gerichtsverfahren

Schlichtungsverfahren werden in Auseinandersetzungen im Geschäftsleben immer beliebter, da sie relativ kostengünstig und schnell sind. Viele internationale Verträge beinhalten Vereinbarungen wie die folgenden:

All disputes arising out of or in connection with the present contract shall be referred to and finally settled under the Rules of Arbitration of the Tinbuksani Chamber of Commerce by three arbitrators appointed in accordance with the said Rules. The language to be used in the arbitral proceedings shall be English. There are three common reasons for arbitration in the business world. First of all there is commercial arbitration, involving the resolution of disputes between two companies, for example. Secondly there is consumer arbitration, where the dispute is between a supplier and a consumer.
Finally there is labour arbitration, which involves employment related disputes. One of the main advantages for both parties is that the decisions are final and binding, and will be complied with without delay. Another advantage concerns with how much control the parties have over the proceedings. They can influence key procedural matters such as names and numbers of arbitrators, venues, language, timetables and so on. Finally, unlike litigation in national courts, arbitration is conducted in private, which may be essential for companies wishing to preserve trade secrets.

Vokabeln

arbitration	Schlichtungsverfahren
attorney	Rechtsanwalt
binding	verbindlich
comply	entsprechen
court	Gericht
defendant	Beklagter
dispute	Streit
judge	Richter
litigation	Rechtsstreit
petitioner	Kläger
procedural	verfahrenstechnisch
proceedings	Verfahren
refer	verweisen
venue	Verhandlungsort

Übung 7:

Finden Sie für die gegebenen Wörter die Entsprechungen im Text.

1. verweisen ____________
2. verbindlich ____________
3. verfahrenstechnisch ____________
4. Verhandlungsort ____________

5. Streit ___________
6. Rechtsstreit ___________
7. entsprechen ___________
8. Verfahren ___________
9. Gericht ___________
10. Schlichtungsverfahren ___________
11. Vertrag ___________

Übung 8:

Es haben sich acht Fehler eingeschlichen. Berichtigen Sie die Rechtschreibung.

All dispites arising out of or in connectin with the present contrect shall be referred to and finally settled under the Rules of Arbitation of the Tinbuksani Chamber of Commers by three abitrators appointed in accordance with the said Rules. The lenguage to be used in the arbitral proceeedings shall be English.

1. _________________________
2. _________________________
3. _________________________
4. _________________________
5. _________________________
6. _________________________
7. _________________________
8. _________________________

Übung 9:

Übersetzen Sie und enträtseln Sie das Lösungswort!

1. verfahrenstechnisch, 2. verbindlich, 3. Verfahren, 4. entsprechen, 5. Verhandlungsort, 6. Rechtsstreit, 7. verweisen

1. _____☐____
2. _☐_____
3. __________☐
4. ___☐__
5. ___☐_
6. __☐_______
7. _☐___

Mystery Word ☐☐☐☐☐☐☐

Fit im technischen Englisch? Ob es sich um technische Produktbeschreibungen, Beschreibungen technischer Abläufe oder um die Bereiche Computer und E-Commerce handelt, dieser Lernschritt ermöglicht einen raschen Einstieg in die technische Terminologie.

Technische Produktbeschreibungen

Ein Vertreter der Firma Compudot präsentiert die neueste Produktentwicklung.

Good morning everyone, thanks for coming. Today I'd like to tell you something about our latest product, the K23 Supreme. I've brought one with me so that you can see it for yourself. Let me tell you the exact measurements – you won't believe how we managed to make it so small. It's only 8.3 cm wide, 3.4 cm thick, and 10.2 cm long. It's by far the smallest product of its kind on the market. But the small size doesn't mean that it lacks power. Quite the opposite – inside the K23 you'll find a powerful 800 MHz Quantium processor. And it's easy to operate too. If you look here you'll see the user display screen, which is 6.5 cm square. It's a colour LCD screen, so very easy to read. You can use the K23 to send and receive email and surf the Internet. And the full keyboard makes inputting your data child's play. Of course, with a product of this kind, it's essential that you can transfer data to your home or office PC. That's why we've provided two ways to connect to your PC – either by infra-red or by USB cable. Finally, the casing is made of high-quality shock-resistant plastic, so you can drop it on the floor and it'll still work. So I'm sure you'll agree the K23 Supreme is a guaranteed success.

Vokabeln

display screen	Bildschirm
cable	Kabel
casing	Gehäuse
child's play	Kinderspiel
function	Funktion
infra-red	infrarot
LCD screen	LCD-Bildschirm
measurement	Maß, Abmessung
operate	bedienen
range	Auswahl
screen	Bildschirm
shock-resistant	schlagfest
square	im Quadrat
surf the Internet	im Internet surfen
transfer	übertragen

Infobox

British people increasingly use metric measurements. Americans still use imperial measurements. One inch is 2.54 cm, and one foot (12 inches) is 30.48 cm. Note that we use a point to show fractions, e.g. 2.54 cm (English) = 2,54 cm (German).

24 Technik und IT

Übung 1:

Übersetzen Sie die folgenden Sätze einer technischen Produktbeschreibung ins Deutsche.

1. The monitor is 32 cm wide.

____

____

2. The computer tower is 79 cm high.

____

____

3. The card is 2 mm thick.

____

____

4. The screen is 10 cm square.

____

____

5. The casing is shock-resistant.

____

____

6. You can transfer data to your PC using infra-red.

____

____

7. The processor is very powerful.

____

____

Übung 2:

Bilden Sie sinnvolle Paare.

1. the exact	☐ functions
2. on the	☐ processor
3. a powerful	☐ plastic
4. easy to	☐ success
5. a wide range of	☐ measurements
6. transfer	☐ operate
7. shock-resistant	☐ market
8. a guaranteed	☐ data

Beschreibung technischer Abläufe

Ein Angestellter der Firma Nakayama Technologies führt eine Besuchergruppe durch eine Chipfabrik. Vor der Führung erklärt er seinen Besuchern den Herstellungsprozess.

Hello everybody. Welcome to Nakayama Technologies. Before we tour the factory, I would like to give you a brief overview of how we make chips. This will help you to understand the different stages in the manufacturing process when we see everything in action.
So, our starting point for manufacturing chips is silicon wafer. This is prepared by cutting slices of wafer from large cylin-

der-shaped silicon crystals. The slices are then polished before use.
The first stage in the manufacturing process is called "dielectric deposition". This simply means that a layer of insulating material is put on to the surface of the chip.
The next stage is called "photolithography". The chip is covered with a light-sensitive chemical. A microscopic circuit pattern is projected onto the wafer surface. This stage will be repeated many, many times during the production process, to build up the different layers of the chip.

Vokabeln

bombard	beschießen
coat	beschichten
cover	bedecken
conductivity	elektr. Leitfähigkeit
heat	erhitzen
in a nutshell	kurz und bündig
insulating	isolierend
manufacturing process	Produktionsprozess
material	Stoff
polish	polieren
prepare	vorbereiten
property	Eigenschaft
protect	schützen
purification	Reinigung
remove	entfernen
repeat	wiederholen
slice	Scheibe
stage	Phase
strength	Festigkeit
surface	Oberfläche

Then comes the stage known as "etching". During this stage, certain material is removed from the surface of the chip, in order to create the device structures.
Next we have "ion implantation". This involves bombarding the wafer surface with ions in order to change the film's conductivity.
In the following stage, "rapid thermal processing" or RTP, the wafer is heated to a high temperature very quickly, changing the properties of the deposited film.
The steps dielectric deposition, photolithography and etching are then repeated as often as is required.
The wafer is then electroplated with copper, and finally coated with a ceramic or plastic material in order to protect it from the atmosphere.
So there we have it – the chip manufacturing process in a nutshell. Any questions before we begin the tour?

Infobox

In English, we often use the passive voice when describing technical processes. (This stage will be repeated many times.) The passive voice is constructed using the appropriate form of the verb "to be" plus the third form (past participle) of the main verb.

Übung 3:

Formulieren Sie die Sätze im Passiv!

1. We prepare silicon wafer by cutting slices of wafer from silicon crystals.

____

____

2. We polish the slices before use.

____

____

3. We put a layer of insulating material on to the surface of the chip.

____

____

4. We cover the chip with a light-sensitive chemical.

____

____

5. We will repeat this stage many times.

____

6. We remove material from the surface of the chip.

____

____

7. We heat the wafer to a high temperature.

____

____

Übung 4:

Ordnen Sie diese Vokabeln ihren entsprechenden Übersetzungen zu!

1. cover	☐ polieren
2. protect	☐ wiederholen
3. prepare	☐ erhitzen
4. repeat	☐ beschichten
5. polish	☐ entfernen
6. heat	☐ schützen
7. coat	☐ vorbereiten
8. remove	☐ bedecken

Wartungs- und Bedienungsanleitungen

Der folgende Text ist ein Auszug aus einer Bedienungsanleitung, in der erklärt wird, wie ein Tintenstrahldrucker installiert wird.

HOW TO INSTALL YOUR PRINTER

Step 1: Unpacking your printer

1 Open the top cover.

2 Remove the packing material from the inside of the printer.

3 Close the top cover.

Step 2: Connecting the power

1 Open the door on the back of the printer.

2 Plug one end of the power cable into the back of the printer.

3 Plug the other end of the power cable into the wall socket.

Step 3: Inserting the print cartridges

1 Turn on the printer.

2 Open the top cover. The cartridge holder will move to the centre of the printer.

3 Remove the print cartridges from the packaging.

4 Insert the black print cartridge in the right holder,
and insert the colour print cartridge in the left holder.

5 Close the top cover.

Step 4: Loading paper in your printer

1 Pull out the paper tray.

2 Remove the paper from its packaging.

3 Load the paper into the paper tray.

4 Slide the paper tray all the way back in.

Step 5: Connecting the USB cable

1 Plug one end of the USB cable into the USB port on the back of your printer.

2 Plug the other end of the USB cable into any USB port on the computer.

Step 6: Installing the software

1 Insert the software CD into your CD-ROM drive.

2 The installation program will start automatically. Simply follow the onscreen instructions to install the software.

Vokabeln

cartridge	Patrone
connect	anschließen
cover	Deckel
follow	befolgen
holder	Halter
insert	einlegen
install	installieren
instructions	Anweisungen
load	laden
packaging	Verpackung
paper tray	Papierschacht
plug	stecken
port	Anschluss
power	Strom
power cable	Stromkabel
slide	schieben
tape	Klebeband
unpack	auspacken
wall socket	Wandsteckdose
wear	Verschleiß

Übung 5:

Übersetzen Sie ins Englische.

1. Papierschacht ______________
2. Patrone ______________
3. schieben ______________
4. auspacken ______________
5. installieren ______________
6. Deckel ______________

IT-Berufe

Der folgende Zeitschriftenartikel gibt einen Überblick über einige gebräuchliche Berufe der IT-Branche.

IT is a very broad field, and is getting broader. The list of IT professions is continuously growing, with new professions being created all the time. When most people think of IT professions, they think of programmers or software engineers, namely people who design and write software. Another common profession is system administrator. This is the person responsible for maintaining the organisation's computers and operating systems. A related profession is network administrator, who is responsible for managing and maintaining an organisation's LAN (Local Area Network). Similarly, a network engineer is responsible for planning, designing, and implementing LANs and WANs (Wide Area Networks). One very important profession is technical support specialist, who assists end users with computer management, maintenance and troubleshooting. This can be done either remotely or in person. One relatively new profession is web designer – a person who designs web sites. Normally websites also have a webmaster, who administers and maintains the site.

Vokabeln

administer	administrieren
end user	Endnutzer
implement	implementieren
maintain	warten
maintenance	Wartung
management	Verwaltung
network administrator	Netzwerkadministrator
network engineer	Netzwerkingenieur
operating system	Betriebssystem
profession	Beruf
programmer	Programmierer
responsible for	verantwortlich für
software engineer	Software-Ingenieur
specialist	Fachmann / Fachfrau
system administrator	Systemadministrator
technical support	technische Unterstützung
troubleshooting	Fehlersuche

Übung 6:

Kreuzen Sie die zutreffenden Aussagen an.

1. The list of IT professions is always getting longer.
2. Programmers write software.
3. A software engineer maintains operating systems.

4. A network engineer plans networks.
5. A technical support specialist always helps the end user in person.
6. The profession of web designer is quite new.
7. Websites always have a webmaster.

Übung 7:

Bilden Sie sinnvolle Paare.

1. end	☐ a network
2. software	☐ user
3. system	☐ end users
4. technical	☐ engineer
5. operating	☐ support
6. maintain	☐ administrator
7. assist	☐ system

Computeranwendungen

Ein Universitätsdozent erklärt einer Anfängergruppe verschiedene Computeranwendungen.

So now I want to tell you something about the different applications you can use with your PC. Probably the most widely-used applications belong to what is known as an "office suite". The best known office suite is of course Microsoft Office. An office suite normally contains all the programs the average office worker needs: a word processor for writing documents, an email program, a spreadsheet for doing calculations, a database for storing information, and a presentations program for preparing slides for a presentation. Another common program is a web browser, which allows you to visit sites on the World Wide Web. Other software is more specialised and tends to be used by certain professions. For example, graphic designers use image editing programs like Photoshop to manipulate

Vokabeln

anti-virus program	Antivirenprogramm
application	Anwendung
calculation	Kalkulation
computer-aided design CAD	computergestütztes Entwerfen
computer-aided manufacturing CAM	computergestützte Fertigung
database	Datenbank
edit	bearbeiten
firewall	Firewall
image	Bild
image editing	Bildbearbeitung
manipulate	manipulieren
presentation	Präsentation
slide	Dia
spreadsheet	Tabellenkalkulationsprogramm
word processor	Textverarbeitungsprogramm

photographs and other images. Architects use computer-aided design (CAD) software. And of course, one very important piece of software is an anti-virus program – it's essential to have one in order to protect your PC from viruses.

Übung 8:

Füllen Sie die Lücken mit Wörtern aus dem Text.

1. Architects use _ _ _ _ _ _ _ _ _ software to design buildings.
2. You use a _ _ _ _ _ _ _ _ _ program to protect your PC from viruses.
3. You use a _ _ _ _ _ _ _ _ _ to write documents.
4. You use a _ _ _ _ _ _ _ _ _ program to prepare slides.
5. You use a _ _ _ _ _ _ _ _ _ to do calculations.
6. You use a _ _ _ _ _ _ _ _ _ to store information.

New Economy

Der folgende Artikel erzählt die Geschichte der kurzlebigen "New Economy".

In the late 1990s there was a lot of hype about the so-called "new economy". New economy companies were often unfavourably contrasted with "old economy" firms (also known as "bricks and mortar" firms). Some firms tried to combine the best of old and new economies, and were known as "clicks and mortar" firms. Many new economy firms went to IPO very quickly, and share prices went through the roof. Employees often became rich very quickly, due to the inflated value of their share options. However, few new economy firms ever showed a profit, and the majority went to the wall. After the stock market crash, the supply of venture capital available to e-business firms dried up.

Vokabeln

brick	Ziegel
cautious	vorsichtig
dry up	versiegen
go through the roof	die Schallmauer durchbrechen
go to the wall	Bankrott machen
hype	Medienrummel
investor	Investor(in)
IPO (Initial Public Offering)	Börsengang
mortar	Mörtel
profit	Gewinn
share	Aktie
share price	Aktienkurs
stock market crash	Börsenkrach
venture capital	Risikokapital

Was passt am besten in die Lücken?

1. It's been a _ _ _ _ _ doing business with you.
a) wonder b) pleasure c) fun d) great

2. Nice to meet you, Brian. We've _ _ _ _ _ a lot about you.
a) listened
b) found
c) heard
d) watched

3. This is Susanne. She's _ _ _ _ _ for marketing.
a) in charge
b) responsible
c) dependable
d) reliable

4. I'm calling _ _ _ _ _ our order.
a) about
b) on
c) around
d) because

5. _ _ _ _ _ I've got you on the line, there was something else I wanted to ask you.
a) It
b) When
c) During
d) While

6. May I ask the _ _ _ _ _ for your call?
a) reason
b) motive
c) ground
d) intention

7. I would like to learn more about what you do, in _ _ _ _ _ your consulting services.
a) especially
b) example
c) regards
d) particular

8. I am enclosing details of previous IT projects which will give you some idea of our main _ _ _ _ _ in this field to date.
a) performances
b) success
c) wins
d) achievements

9. Can you put this report in the _ _ _ _ _ cabinet, please?
a) filing
b) recording
c) folder
d) filling

10. Some staff members are becoming _ _ _ _ _ about computer security.
a) weak
b) relax
c) cool
d) lax

11. I won't get there in time for lunch, but I could _ _ _ _ _ to be there by 2 pm next Monday.
a) manage
b) get
c) go
d) achieve

12. Our monthly meeting with the _ _ _ _ _ committee is next week.
a) driving
b) steering
c) turning
d) routing

13. This ink jet printer is not _ _ _ _ _ with my computer.
a) harmonious
b) compatible
c) friendly
d) companionable

14. It'll be easier to keep everybody on _ _ _ _ _ during the meeting, if they know beforehand what we need to accomplish.
a) road
b) train
c) track
d) rails

15. Please be sure to _ _ _ _ _ time for each item on the agenda.
a) allocate
b) divide
c) share
d) distribute

16. This _ _ _ _ _ chart shows our sales broken down by country.
a) cake
b) pie
c) tart
d) doughnut

17. I would greatly _ _ _ _ _ it if you could hold all questions until the end.
a) appreciate
b) enjoy
c) like
d) value

18. I was wondering if you could _ _ _ _ _ on the percentage of cases that are actually won by us.
a) explain
b) elaborate
c) describe
d) express

19. We are looking for a sales executive. This _ _ _ _ _ is ideal for an ambitious, well-qualified candidate.
a) position
b) place
c) spot
d) point

20. I would be pleased to meet you and Mr Arthur Simons to discuss how I could _ _ _ _ _ to your company.
a) provide
b) contribute
c) assist
d) help

21. I will call you next week to see when is a _ _ _ _ _ time for us to meet.
a) convenient
b) comfortable
c) polite
d) conventional

22. In our company, all our employees are _ _ _ _ _ to make decisions, even at lower levels.
a) powerful
b) mighty
c) forceful
d) empowered

23. I left school at 15, and went straight into a(n) _ _ _ _ _.
a) apprenticeship
b) training
c) education
d) building

24. In the UK, public companies _ _ _ _ _ capital by selling shares.
a) rise
b) higher
c) lift
d) raise

25. The project will be completed in _ _ _ _ _ with the plan we worked out in the last status meeting.
a) harmony
b) accordance
c) unity
d) accord

26. An action plan will help you _ _ _ _ _ your objectives.
a) achieve
b) complete
c) follow
d) arrive

27. Successful time management will enable you to _ _ _ _ _ the tasks which are important to you within the given time.
a) achieve
b) perform
c) present
d) make

28. Ink _ _ _ _ _ for printers are normally quite expensive.
a) cartridges
b) patrons
c) holders
d) containers

29. Let me give you my _ _ _ _ _ card to keep in touch.
a) visit
b) business
c) travel
d) trade

30. _ _ _ _ _ users are not allowed to use a company intranet.
a) Unprotected
b) Incompatible
c) Unauthorized
d) Inaccessible

31. The next stage in the process is to screen the concept, to make sure that it is _ _ _ _ _.
a) sufficient
b) handy
c) convenient
d) feasible

32. Applied research aims to _ _ _ _ _ knowledge in order to solve a particular problem or meet a specific need.
a) acquire
b) reach
c) order
d) make

33. Hopefully the initial investment will be _ _ _ _ _ at some point in the product lifecycle.
a) remarked
b) recouped
c) regained
d) repeated

34. You normally have to pay import _ _ _ _ _ on imported goods.
a) fees
b) monies
c) duties
d) gains

35. It is not always easy to obtain _ _ _ _ _ to import goods into a country.
a) permit
b) convenience
c) visas
d) permission

36. Wholesalers and retailers work together to minimize _ _ _ _ _ chain costs.
a) delivery
b) supply
c) purchasing
d) logistics

37. Often an agent will earn a _ _ _ _ _ on the work he or she does.
a) charge
b) discount
c) duty
d) commission

38. You should emphasise the _ _ _ _ _ to the customer in your sales pitch.
a) benefits
b) paybacks
c) profits
d) rewards

39. There's a 30 per cent _ _ _ _ _ on the price at the moment.
a) charge
b) rebate
c) fee
d) discount

40. Thank you for your letter in which you expressed interest in our current _ _ _ _ _ of products.
a) scope
b) assortment
c) range
d) collection

41. I would be pleased to show you our production lines and shipping _ _ _ _ _.
a) facilities
b) conveniences
c) factories
d) amenities

42. You drive a _ _ _ _ _ bargain!
a) solid
b) hard
c) stiff
d) rigid

43. I'm just _ _ _ _ _ in for the secretary who's off sick.
a) standing
b) making
c) looking
d) taking

44. Our normal terms of payment are 30 days net, subject to _ _ _ _ _.
a) usability
b) ability
c) accessibility
d) availability

45. We would be grateful if you could _ _ _ _ _ the amount owing within the next few days.
a) mend
b) settle
c) reconcile
d) resolve

46. Customers take basic after sales service from suppliers for _ _ _ _ _.
a) approved
b) settled
c) decided
d) granted

47. Many businesses think of complaints as an unwelcome _ _ _ _ _ on their time.
a) invasion
b) interruption
c) intrusion
d) disturbance

48. There are many tricks of the _ _ _ _ _ which professional salespeople use.
a) trade
b) industry
c) deal
d) job

49. I had to make some last minute changes to my travel _ _ _ _ _.
a) itinerary
b) programme
c) tour
d) journey

50. We _ _ _ _ _ for up to 400 visitors a day.
a) supply
b) organize

c) arrange
d) cater

51. The hotel you booked for me was still under construction, which caused considerable _ _ _ _ _.
a) problem
b) nuisance
c) difficulty
d) inconvenience

52. It's _ _ _ _ _ that our trade fair stand be portable, lightweight, and flexible.
a) urgent
b) imperative
c) central
d) decisive

53. I need a cold drink! Where is the _ _ _ _ _?
a) toaster
b) refrigerator
c) cupboard
d) cooker

54. I have heard that your firm is the _ _ _ _ _ in this technology.
a) ancestor
b) predecessor
c) forebear
d) forerunner

55. Our biggest _ _ _ _ _ on this project are Bloggs and Co.
a) contestants
b) competitors
c) contenders
d) opponents

56. The _ _ _ _ _ is still out on exactly how useful the internet is for advertisers.
a) jury
b) judges
c) adjudicators
d) panel

57. Word-of-_ _ _ _ _ can be a very useful form of marketing.
a) jaws
b) lips
c) voice
d) mouth

58. A team has to be able to _ _ _ _ _ upon each other in difficult situations.
a) cope
b) agree
c) rely
d) stand

59. A company might hold a trip to _ _ _ _ _ its employees.
a) prize
b) incentive
c) return
d) reward

60. Sometimes excursions are used to _ _ _ _ _ teamwork.
a) sponsor
b) promote
c) endorse
d) uphold

61. At the end of every fiscal year, every public listed company is required to prepare an annual _ _ _ _ _.
a) report
b) description
c) story
d) statement

62. Globalisation has led to the _ _ _ _ _ of major finance centres, in New York, London, Frankfurt and Tokyo.
a) opening
b) materialization
c) emergence
d) surfacing

63. In order to be listed on one of the stock exchanges, the company has to issue a _____ and a listing application.
a) pamphlet
b) list
c) prospectus
d) catalogue

64. A bookkeeper's responsibilities include the collection and payment of _____.
a) demands
b) invoices
c) charges
d) duties

65. Some accountants specialize in the preparation of tax _____ for their clients.
a) accounts
b) returns
c) proceeds
d) earnings

66. It is our duty to _____ all of our income to the tax office.
a) pronounce
b) assert
c) declare
d) affirm

67. Companies normally want to keep things secret, so contracts often include a(n) _____ clause to stop employees giving away company secrets.
a) confidentiality
b) isolation
c) secret
d) suspicion

68. Managers often have a basic salary which is supplanted by stock _____.
a) options
b) choices
c) alternatives
d) preferences

69. As required by my contract of employment, I hereby give you three months _____ of my intention to leave Monarch Brothers at the end of June.
a) examination
b) note
c) observation
d) notice

70. The full keyboard makes inputting your data _____.
a) child's play
b) kid's play
c) children's play
d) child's games

71. So there we have it – the chip manufacturing process in a _____.
a) nut
b) shell
c) doughnut
d) nutshell

72. Plug one end of the power cable into the wall _____.
a) hollow
b) opening
c) socket
d) hole

Englisch-Deutsch

A

a pile of stuff eine Menge Arbeit
above-mentioned oben angegeben
absorption costing Vollkostenrechnung
access Zugang
accessible zugänglich
account Konto
accounts payable Verbindlichkeiten
accounts receivable Forderungen
accounting Buchhaltung
accuracy Genauigkeit
achievement Leistung, Ergebnis
acquire erwerben
action Klage
action plan Aktionsplan
adjusted angepasst
administer administrieren
administrative costs Verwaltungskosten
advance Vorschuss
advertisement Anzeige
advertiser Inserent
agenda Tagesordnung
agent Vertreter
agree vereinbaren
agreement Übereinkunft
agriculture Landwirtschaft
all included alles in allem
allocate zuteilen
allowable against tax steuerlich absetzbar
allowance Steuerfreibetag
alternatively alternativ
ambition Ehrgeiz
ambitious ehrgeizig
amenity Einrichtung
announcement Durchsage
Annual General Meeting Jahreshauptversammlung
annual leave Jahresurlaub
annual report Jahresbericht
anti-virus program Antivirenprogramm
appeal Einspruch
applicable umsetzbar
application 1. Bewerbung; 2. Anwendung
application form Anmeldeformular
applied research angewandte Forschung
appointment book Terminkalender
appreciated anerkannt
apprenticeship Lehre
appropriation account Gewinnverteilungsrechnung
arbitration Schlichtungsverfahren
arrange aufstellen
artwork Grafik
assemble montieren
assembly Montage
assets Vermögenswerte
assist assistieren
associate Teilhaber
assortment Auswahl
assurance Versicherung
attorney Rechtsanwalt
attribute to zuschreiben
auditing Buchprüfung
auditor Revisor, Bilanzprüfer
authorization Berechtigung
authorize autorisieren, erlauben
availability Verfügbarkeit
available verfügbar
award Auszeichnung, Stipendium

B

back up unterstützen
background Werdegang
balance Kontostand, Saldo
balance sheet Bilanzaufstellung
ban Verbot
bank transfer Banküberweisung
banker's draft Bankwechsel
banking Bankwesen
bankrupt bankrott
bankruptcy Konkurs
banner Fahne, Banner
bargain günstiger Kauf
basic research Grundlagenforschung
behavioural traits Verhaltensmerkmale
benchmark vergleichen

benefit Vorteil, Nutzen
benefit begünstigen
bespoke maßgeschneidert
best practice optimales Verfahren
bid Angebot
bill Rechnung
bill of exchange Wechsel
bill of lading Konnossement
billboard Reklametafel
binder Hefter
binding verbindlich
blue chip erstklassige Standardaktie
board Vorstand
bond Obligation
booking Buchung
bookkeeper Buchhalter
boost Auftrieb geben
booth Stand
brainstorming Brainstorming, Gedankenaustausch
brand Sorte, Marke
break down (UK), ~ off (US) scheitern, abbrechen
break even ausgeglichener Geschäftsabschluss
break-even point Kostendeckungspunkt
brick Ziegel
brochure Broschüre
budget Budget, Etat
burden Belastung
burn oneself out sich völlig verausgaben
business card Visitenkarte
bust pleite
busy beschäftigt
buzz-word Modewort
by-product Neben-/Abfallprodukt
by return so schnell wie möglich

C

cable Kabel
calculation Kalkulation
campaign Kampagne
cancel ausfallen lassen
candidate Bewerber
capital growth Kapitalzuwachs
car rental Autovermietung
cardboard box Pappkarton
career Karriere
career objective Karriereziel
carnet Zollbegleitschein
carpenter Zimmermann
carrier Spediteur
cartridge Patrone
case study Fallstudie
cash flow Cashflow
cash in advance Vorauskasse
cash on delivery Nachnahme
casing Gehäuse
casual income Nebeneinkünfte
cater for versorgen
caterer Lieferfirma
cc (carbon copy) Durchschlag
C-corporation (US) Gesellschaft mit beschränkter Haftung (GmbH)
CD-ROM drive CD-ROM-Laufwerk
CEO (chief executive officer) Vorstandsvorsitzender
certificate of origin Ursprungszeugnis
CFO (chief financial officer) Finanzdirektor
chair leiten
chairperson Leiter(in)
challenge Herausforderung
change request Änderungswunsch
channel Kanal
charge berechnen
charge Gebühr
charisma Charisma, Ausstrahlung
chart Diagramm, Schaubild
chartered accountant staatlich geprüfter Bilanzbuchhalter
check überprüfen, testen
checkout Kasse
chemicals Chemieindustrie
CIO (chief information officer) EDV-Direktor
circulation Verteilung
claim back zurückfordern
claims Ansprüche
clarification Klarstellung
classify klassifizieren
clause Klausel

clerk Angestellter
client Kunde/Kundin
close of play Feierabend
coach trainieren
coat beschichten
coin Münze
cold application Blindbewerbung
colleague-bashing Mobbing
colour scheme Farbzusammenstellung
column Spalte
comments Kommentare
commission Provision
commitment Selbstverpflichtung
committed engagiert
commodity market Warenbörse
company Firma
company policy Unternehmenspolitik
compatible vereinbar
compensation Entschädigung, Ausgleich
competitive wettbewerbsfähig
competitor Konkurrent(in)
complaints Beschwerden
comply entsprechen, erfüllen
comprehensive insurance Vollkaskoversicherung
compromise Kompromiss
compromise Kompromisse schließen
computer aided manufacturing CAM, computergestutzte Fertigung
computer literacy Computerwissen
computer aided design CAD, computergestütztes Entwerfen
concept Konzept
concession Zugeständnis
condition Zustand
conduct durchführen, einberufen
conductivity elektrische Leitfähigkeit
conference Konferenz
confidentiality Vertraulichkeit
confirm bestätigen
confusion Verwirrung
connect anschließen
consignee Warenempfänger
consignment Lieferung
consignor Verfrachter
consolidation Konsolidierung
constraint Beschränkung
construction industry Baugewerbe
consumer Verbraucher
consumer durables langlebige Gebrauchsgüter
consumer goods Konsumgüter
consumer rights Verbraucherrecht
consumption Verbrauch
container Container
contraband Schmuggelware
contract Vertrag
contractor Auftragnehmer
contractual problems vertragsrechtliche Probleme
convenience store 24-Stunden-Geschäft
convert umtauschen
convey überbringen
conveyor belt Förderband
coordinate koordinieren
copy Text
core Kern
core product Haupterzeugnis
corporation Körperschaft
cost-effective kostenwirksam
counter Ladentisch
country of origin Herkunftsland
court Gericht
cover letter Anschreiben
credit card Kreditkarte
cross reference Gegenbuchung
crucial wesentlich
currency Währung
currency fluctuation Kursschwankung
current aktuell
curriculum vitae Lebenslauf
cursory oberflächlich
custom designed spezialangefertigt
customer base Kundenstamm
customer service Kundendienst
customised nach Kundenwunsch (gefertigt)
customs invoice Zollfaktura, ~rechnung
customs officer Zollbeamter

D
data Daten
database Datenbank
days off freie Tage
deadline Abgabetermin, letzter Termin
dealer Händler
debts Schulden
decision maker Entscheidungsträger
declare angeben
decline nachlassender Bedarf
deduct abziehen
default interest Verzugszinsen
defect Mangel
defendant Beklagte(r)
define definieren
delay Verspätung, Verzögerung
delete löschen, streichen
delivery Zustellung, Lieferung
delivery terms Lieferbedingungen
demand Forderung
demo Demo
demonstrate zeigen
department Abteilung
department head Abteilungsleiter
departure lounge Abflughalle
dependencies Abhängigkeiten
depreciate an Wert einbüßen
depreciation Abschreibung
derivative Derivat
design Design, Gestaltung
destination Ziel
destination country Bestimmungsland
detail-oriented detailverliebt
develop entwickeln
development Entwicklung
device Gerät, Vorrichtung
direct mail advertising Postwurfsendung
direct marketing Direktvertrieb
disclosure Mitteilung
discount Rabatt, Preisnachlass
dismissal Entlassung
display screen Bildschirm
distributor Zwischenhändler
dividend Dividende
division Abteilung, Geschäftsbereich
document Dokument
documentary letter of credit Dokumentenakkreditiv
doorstep selling (UK) Haustürverkauf
double-entry bookkeeping doppelte Buchführung
draft entwerfen
drawback Rückerstattung
drawee Bezogene(r)
drawer Aussteller(in)
drive aushandeln
due date Fälligkeitsdatum
duty Pflicht, Aufgabe
DVD player DVD-Spieler

E
early retirement Vorruhestand
earnings 1. Ertrag; 2. Verdienst
economics Volkswirtschaft
edit bearbeiten
edition Ausgabe
education Ausbildung
elaborate on näher ausführen
electrician Elektriker
email address E-Mail-Adresse
embargo Handelsverbot
embark anfangen
employee Angestellter
employment contract Arbeitsvertrag
empowered ermächtigt
enclose beifügen
encrypted verschlüsselt
end user Endnutzer
end-consumer Endverbraucher
energetic energisch
enforced durchgesetzt
engaged besetzt
enhance verbessern
enquiry Anfrage, Nachfrage
entail beinhalten
enterprise Betrieb, Unternehmen
entitlement Berechtigung
envelope Briefumschlag

environment Umwelt
equipment Ausstattung
essential unentbehrlich
establish festlegen
estimate Kostenvoranschlag
ETA (estimated time of arrival) geschätzte Ankunftszeit
evaluate evaluieren, bewerten
evasion Hinterziehung
evidence Beweis
exceed überwiegen, hinausgehen über
exchange tauschen
exchange rate Wechselkurs
execute ausführen
exhibition Ausstellung
expectations Erwartungen
expenditure Ausgaben
experience Erfahrung
expiry Ablauf
exposure Aussetzung
extension cord Verlängerungskabel

F
face sich stellen
facilitate erleichtern
facilities Ausstattung, Einrichtung
factory shop Fabrikverkauf
failure Versäumnis, Misserfolg
fancy goods Neuheit
FAO (for attention of) zu Händen von
fast-selling umsatzstark, leicht verkäuflich
fax Fax
feasible möglich
feature Merkmal, Bestandteil
field Gebiet
field experiment Feldexperiment
field survey Feldstudie
file einreichen
file-card box Karteikasten
filing cabinet Aktenschrank
final quality inspection Endkontrolle
financial records Rechnungsunterlagen
financing Finanzierung
finished product Fertigerzeugnis
firewall Zugangsschutzsystem, Firewall
firm offer festes Angebot
fiscal steuerlich, Fiskal-
fiscal year Geschäftsjahr
fixed assets Anlagevermögen
fixture 1. Vorrichtung; 2. Grundausstattung
flawed fehlerhaft, defekt, mangelhaft
flexitime Gleitzeit
flip chart Flipchart
floppy disk drive Floppy-Laufwerk
fluctuate fluktuieren
fluctuation Fluktuation
FOB (free on board) frei an Bord
folder Aktenmappe
follow befolgen
foodstuff Nahrungsmittel
forecast Prognose
forecast vorhersagen
foreman Vorarbeiter
forerunner Marktführer
forge schmieden
form Formular
formal qualification offiziell anerkannte Qualifikation
formulate formulieren
freelance freiberuflich
full-time/part-time worker Voll-/Teilzeitkraft
function Funktion

G
gain gewinnen
gain Gewinn
generate erzeugen
give in nachgeben
go over besprechen
go public an die Börse gehen
go through the roof die Schallmauer durchbrechen
go to the wall Bankrott machen
goal Ziel
good for kreditwürdig
goods manufactured under license in Lizenz gefertigte Ware
goodwill Geschäftswert, Firmenwert
Gov (governor) Direktor

grant a license Lizenz erteilen
graphic panel Bildtafel
graphics card Grafikkarte
grievance Beschwerde
grill in die Zange nehmen
gross brutto
group dynamics Gruppendynamik
growth Wachstum
guideline Vorschrift

H
handle behandeln
handover Übergabe
hard disk drive Festplatte
hard earned cash sauer verdientes Geld
hard sell aggressive Verkaufstaktik
hard-working fleißig
have it customised angepasst den Bedürfnissen
have over Vorsprung haben
head of department Abteilungsleiter
health and safety Gesundheit und Sicherheit
healthcare Gesundheitswesen
hedge against absichern gegen
hoax Presseente
holder Halter
hole puncher Locher
home page Homepage
hospitality area Begegnungsfläche
house mail Hauspost
human element menschliches Element
human resources Personal
hype Medienrummel
hypothesis Hypothese

I
illegal unzulässig, rechtswidrig
image 1. Image; 2. Bild
image editing Bildbearbeitung
imaginative kreativ
implement realisieren, implementieren
implement Gerät
implementation stage Realisierungsphase
implication Implikation
import duty Einfuhrzoll
impose verhängen
impression Eindruck
improvement Verbesserung
in accordance with in Übereinstimmung
in advance im Voraus
in bond Zollverschluss
Inc (incorporated) eingetragen
incentive Anreiz
incl (including) einschließlich
income tax Einkommenssteuer
incoming mail Posteingang
inconvenience Unannehmlichkeit
Incoterms International Commercial Terms
increase vergrößern
indication Hinweis
induction Einführung (in den Beruf)
industrial law Arbeitsrecht
information flow Informationsfluss
infra-red infrarot
ink cartridge Tintenpatrone
Inland Revenue (US) Finanzamt
innovative innovativ
input Beitrag
inside cover Umschlaginnenseite
insist insistieren, bestehen auf
insolvency Insolvenz
inspiring ermutigend
install installieren
instalments Raten
instruction Anweisung
insurance Versicherung
intangible (assets) immaterielle Vermögenswerte
intention Absicht
interaction Interaktion
interest Zins(en)
intermediary Zwischenhändler
intermodal transportation Transport mit mehreren Verkehrsmitteln
internal post interne Post
international money order internationale Zahlungsanweisung
Internet Internet

internship Praktikum
interruptions Unterbrechungen
intrusion Störung
inventories Warenbestandswert
invest anlegen, investieren
investment Anlage, Anlagekapital
investment bank Investmentbank
investment income Kapitalerträge
investment scheme Anlageplan
investor Investor(in)
invoice Warenrechnung, Rechnung
IPO (Initial Public Offering) Börsengang
irrevocable unwiderruflich
issue Angelegenheit, Thema, Frage
issue ausgeben, ausstellen
item Tagesordnungspunkt
item number Artikelnummer
itinerary Reiseroute

J/K/L
jig Spannvorrichtung
job cuts Stellenkürzungen
judge Richter
judgement Beurteilung
jury Schöffe
keep at it nicht lockerlassen
keep sbd on track jmdn. in der Spur halten
key people Schlüsselfiguren
keyboard Tastatur
keyword Schlüsselwort
knock off nachlassen
knowledgeable Kenntnisse haben
knowledge-based fundiert, wissensbasiert
label beschriften
laboratory Labor
laser pointer Laserpointer
last minute changes Änderungen in letzter Minute
lathe Drehbank
LCD screen LCD-Bildschirm
leaflet Prospekt
legal tender gesetzliches Zahlungsmittel
lend leihen
let down im Stich lassen
levy erheben (Steuern)
liabilities Verbindlichkeiten
liability Haftung
liable to corporation tax körperschaftssteuerpflichtig
liaison Zusammenarbeit
license Lizenz
license holder, licensee Lizenznehmer
licensor Lizenzgeber
life cycle Lebenszyklus
light box Leuchtkasten
light fixture elektrische Anschlüsse
limited beschränkt
limited liability company (UK) Gesellschaft mit beschränkter Haftung (GmbH)
link Verknüpfung
liquidity Liquidität
literature stand Prospektstand
litigation Rechtsstreit
load laden
location Ort
logo Firmenzeichen, Logo
lorry (UK) Lastkraftwagen
lost property office Fundbüro

M
mail-order catalogue Versandhauskatalog
maintain 1. fortsetzen; 2. instand halten
maintenance Instandhaltung, Wartung
major burden Hauptbelastung
make sbd redundant jmdn. entlassen
manage schaffen
management Verwaltung, Unternehmensführung
managing director geschäftsführender Direktor
manipulate manipulieren
manufacturer Hersteller
manufactures Industrieware
manufacturing process Produktionsprozess
marginal costing Teilkostenrechnung
market Markt
market vermarkten
market need Nachfrage
market research Marktforschung
marketing Marketing

material Stoff
mature fällig werden
maturity Reife
measurement Maß, Abmessung
media advertising Werbung in Medien
medical insurance Krankenversicherung
meeting Besprechung
memorandum Notiz, kurze Mitteilung
memory Speicherplatz
merchandise Ware
merger Fusion
metal detector Metalldetektor
milestone Meilenstein
milling machine Fräsmaschine
mind map Mind Map, Gedankendiagramm
mining Bergbau
minutes Protokoll
modification Änderung
modify modifizieren
modular modular, zusammensetzbar
Mom and Pop store Tante-Emma-Laden
mortar Mörtel
motivated motiviert
mouse Maus
multimedia projector Beamer

N
natural resources Rohstoffe
necessity Notwendigkeit
need Bedürfnis
negotiate verhandeln
negotiation Verhandlung
net netto
network Netzwerk
network administrator Netzwerkadministrator
network engineer Netzwerkingenieur
nominate nominieren
note Geldschein
notebook Notizbuch
notepad Notizblock
notice Kündigungsfrist
novelties Krimskrams, Neuheiten
nullify annullieren

O
objective Absicht
of value von Wert
office supplies Büromaterial
OHT (overhead transparency) Folie
on approval zur Ansicht
on demand auf Nachfrage
on receipt nach Eingang
on someone's books in einer Kartei
on the move unterwegs
operate operieren, funktionieren, bedienen
operating system Betriebssystem
operation Arbeitsweise
operator Bediener
option Option
order Bestellung, Auftrag
order anordnen, bestellen
organisational chart Organigramm
oriented orientiert
origin Herkunft
out of bounds verboten
outcome Ergebnis
outdoor advertising Außenwerbung
outgoing mail Postausgang
outlet 1. Steckdose; 2. Verkaufsstelle
outlook Vorhersage
outstanding obligations Verbindlichkeiten
outward investment Auslandsinvestition
over the limit über das erlaubte Maß
overdue fällig
overhead projector Tageslichtprojektor
overheads Nebenkosten
overtime Überstunden
overview Überblick

P
PA (personal assistant) persönlicher Assistent
package Paket
packing Verpackung
pamphlet Broschüre
paper tray Papierschacht
paperclip Büroklammer
paperwork Papierkram

paramount höchst, ausschlaggebend
parent Mutterfirma
partnership Partnerschaft
party selling Partyverkauf
password Passwort
past due im Rückstand
pay zahlen
pay particular attention auf etwas achten
payee Zahlungsempfänger(in)
payment Zahlung
peak time Hauptbelastungszeit
perform ausführen
performance Tagespensum
perk Vergünstigung
permission Genehmigung
personal development Personalentwicklung
Personal Equity Plan (PEP) persönlicher Aktiensparplan
personalized stationery persönliches Briefpapier
persuade überzeugen, überreden
pertain to etw betreffen
peruse sorgfältig durchsehen
petitioner Kläger(in)
pharmaceuticals Pharmaindustrie
photocopier Kopiergerät
pie chart Kreisdiagramm
pigeonholes Fächer
pitch zum Kauf drängen
place platzieren
plot aufzeichnen
plug stecken
pocket calculator Taschenrechner
podium Podium
point man Anführer
pop-up aufklappbar
port Anschluss
portable tragbar
position 1. Standpunkt; 2. Stelle
postage Porto
postpone verschieben
power Strom
power cable Stromkabel
predict voraussagen
prefabricated vorgefertigt
prefer bevorzugen
preliminary vorläufig
preparation stage Vorbereitungsphase
prepare vorbereiten
presence Präsenz
present anwesend
presentation Präsentation
presentation markers Stifte für Flipcharts
press conference Pressekonferenz
press kit Pressemappe
press release Presseerklärung
press spokesman Pressesprecher
pressure Druck
pretend vortäuschen
previous vorangegangen
price increase Preiserhöhung
primary primär
printer Drucker
priority list Prioritätenliste
probationary auf Probe
procedural verfahrenstechnisch
proceedings Verfahren
processing plant Aufbereitungsanlage
processor Prozessor
procurement Beschaffung
productive produktiv
profession Beruf
professional experience Berufserfahrung
profit Gewinn
profit and loss (or income) statement Gewinn-und-Verlustrechnung
profitability Rentabilität
programmer Programmierer
progress Fortschritt
project projizieren, vorausplanen
project manager Projektmanager
projection screen Bildschirm
promote fördern, werben
promoted befördert
promotion Beförderung
promotion strategy Werbestrategie
proof Beweis
property Eigenschaft

propose vorschlagen
proprietor Inhaber
prospect Aussicht
prospective zukünftig
prospectus Prospekt
protocol Protokoll
prototyping Entwicklung eines Prototyps
provide sorgen
provider Anbieter
provision Bereitstellung
provoke provozieren
PS (postscript) Postskriptum
public company (UK) Aktiengesellschaft
publish veröffentlichen
purification Reinigung
purpose Zweck

Q
qualification Qualifikation
qualitative qualitativ
quality assurance Qualitätssicherung
quality control Qualitätskontrolle
quantitative quantitativ
quarter Vierteljahr
query Anfrage
questioner Fragesteller
questionnaire Fragebogen
quota Quote

R
R&D (research and development) Forschung und Entwicklung
rack Gestell
raise beschaffen
raise finance einen Finanzierungsplan erstellen
range Sortiment, Auswahl
rate Preis, Steuersatz
raw material Rohstoff
re (regarding) hinsichtlich
reach Reichweite
read studieren
reassure versichern
recap rekapitulieren
receipt 1. Eingang, Empfang (von Waren); 2. Quittung
receipts Einnahmen
receptionist Empfangsdame
recognise anerkennen
reduce senken
Ref (reference) Aktenzeichen
refer verweisen
reference Referenz
refine verbessern
refund Geld zurück
registered mail Einschreiben
regulation Regelung
reimburse rückvergüten
release onto the market auf den Markt bringen
reliability Zuverlässigkeit
rely upon each other sich aufeinander verlassen
reminder Mahnung
remittance Geldsendung
remuneration Bezahlung
renew prolongieren
renewable erneuerbar
rent mieten
repay zurückzahlen
reply Antwort
report findings Ergebnisse/Befunde berichten
report on berichten über
reporter Reporter
representative Vertreter
representative repräsentativ
reps (representatives) Vertreter
reputation Reputation, guter Ruf
request bitten, ersuchen
researcher Forscher
resignation Kündigung
resource Hilfsmittel
respondent Befragter, Proband
responsibility Verantwortung
responsible for verantwortlich für
restriction Beschränkung
result in führen zu
retailer Einzelhändler
retailing Einzelhandel
return Rendite

return on investment (ROI) Kapitalrendite
revalue aufwerten, neu bewerten
revenue Einnahmen
review überarbeiten, durcharbeiten
review nochmalige Prüfung
reward belohnen
rewarding lohnend
risk analysis Risikoanalyse
run leiten
run Ansturm, erhöhte Nachfrage

S
salary Gehalt
sale Verkauf
sale or return Kauf mit Rückgaberecht
sales pitch Kundenansprache
sales research Verkaufsforschung
sample Warenprobe, Stichprobe
satisfaction Zufriedenstellung
satisfy befriedigen
save sparen
savings bank Sparkasse
scanner Scanner
schedule planen, ansetzen
S-corporation (US) Aktiengesellschaft (AG)
screen überprüfen
screen Bildschirm
seal Dichtung
search engine Suchmaschine
second Ware zweiter Wahl
secondary sekundär
secretary Sekretär(in)
section Unterabteilung, Sektion
sector Branche
security Sicherheit
seek anstreben
sell verkaufen
semifinished product Halberzeugnis
Sen (senator) Senator
send schicken
service charge Bedienungsgeld
session Sitzung
set up a meeting eine Besprechung organisieren
settle bezahlen
settlement Bezahlung
settlement date Zahlungstermin
share verteilen
share Aktie
share price Aktienkurs
shareholder Aktionär
shareholders equity Eigenkapital
shelf Regal
shipment Versandeinheit
shipper Befrachter
shock-resistant schlagfest
shoot up hochschnellen
shop 1. Geschäft, Laden; 2. Werkhalle
shuttle Pendelverkehr
sick-leave krankgeschrieben
sight deposit Sichteinlagen
single-source einzelne Quelle
skill Fähigkeit
slice Scheibe
slide Dia
slide projector Diaprojektor
slogan Slogan
slum im Wert stark fallen
soft sell diskrete Verkaufstaktik
software engineer Software-Ingenieur
sole trader Einzelunternehmer
solution Lösung, Einigung
solvency Solvenz
sophisticated anspruchsvoll
sort sortieren
sound card Soundkarte
source Quelle
source country Herkunftsland
source of funds Kapitalquelle
speaker Redner
speaking am Apparat
special offer Sonderangebot
specialist Fachmann/Fachfrau
specification genaue Angaben
speculate spekulieren
speculative letter Blindbewerbungsanschreiben
spreadsheet Tabellenkalkulationsprogramm

square im Quadrat
staff Belegschaft
stage Phase
stake Beteiligung
stand in vertreten
stapler Tacker
statistics Statistik, Statistiken
status meeting Projektbesprechung
steady zuverlässig
steering committee Lenkungsausschuss
stipulate (that) es zur Bedingung machen, dass
stock exchange Börse
stock market crash Börsenkrach
stockbroking Wertpapierhandel
stocked with gut eingedeckt mit
stockist Fachhändler, ~geschäft
store Laden
strength Stärke, Festigkeit
Subj (subject) Thema
submit vorlegen
subscription Abonnement
subsidiary Tochterfirma
substantial wesentlich
subtotal Zwischensumme
succumb erliegen
suggest vorschlagen, empfehlen
summarise zusammenfassen
summary Zusammenfassung
supply chain Lieferkette
surface Oberfläche
survey 1. Umfrage; 2. Untersuchung
system administrator Systemadministrator
systematic systematisch

T

take care of erledigen
take for granted sich auf etwas verlassen
take into consideration berücksichtigen
take legal action rechtliche Schritte einleiten
take notes sich Notizen machen
take on übernehmen
take-home pay Nettolohn
talent Begabung
talk Vortrag
tape Klebeband
target country Bestimmungsland
tariff barrier Zollbarriere
tax adviser Steuerberater
tax break Steuervergünstigung
tax code Steuernummer
tax office (US Inland Revenue) Finanzamt
tax return Steuererklärung
taxable income steuerpflichtiges Einkommen
tax-free benefit steuerfreie Vergünstigung
team Arbeitsgruppe, Team
team player Teamplayer
teamwork Zusammenarbeit
technical literature Fachliteratur
technical support technische Unterstützung
temp Aushilfe
term deposit Termineinlagen
terminal Endstelle
terminate enden, lösen, kündigen
tertiary tertiär
the former/latter die erste/zweite Möglichkeit
third party Dritte, Unbeteiligte
thoroughly gründlich
time management Zeitplanung
timeframe Zeitrahmen
to date bis jetzt
tool Werkzeug
Total Quality Management TQM, totales Qualitätsmanagement
tracing Ablaufverfolgung
tracking and tracing facilities Nachvollziehbarkeit des Transportwegs
trade fair Handelsmesse
trade publication Veröffentlichung
trade union Gewerkschaft
trading partner Handelspartner
training Weiterbildung
transaction Transaktion
transcontinental transkontinental
transfer übertragen
trend Trend, Tendenz
tricks of the trade Kniffe

troubleshooting Fehlersuche
truck (US) Lastkraftwagen
trust vertrauen
try probieren

U/V
unauthorized unberechtigt
unforeseen unerwartet
unlimited mileage unbegrenzte Kilometerzahl
unpack auspacken
unsettled ungeklärt
update aktualisieren
up-to-date aktuell
urgent dringend
URL URL-Adresse (Website-Adresse)
user Benutzer
vacancy offene Stelle
valid gültig
validity Gültigkeit
value Wert
VAT (Value Added Tax) Mehrwertsteuer
venture capital Risikokapital
venue Verhandlungsort
version Fassung
video recorder Videorekorder
virus Virus (Computer)
visa Visum
visit Besichtigung
vital lebenswichtig, unbedingt notwendig
vulnerability Anfälligkeit

W/X/Y
wage Lohn
wages office Lohnbüro
waive charges auf Gebühren verzichten
wall mounting Wandaufhängung
wall socket Wandsteckdose
warehouse Lagerhaus
warning Abmahnung
waste verschwenden
weakness Schwäche
wear Verschleiß
website Website
weigh wiegen
well-qualified hochqualifiziert
whiteboard Whiteboard
wholesale Großhandel
wholesaler Großhändler
winner Verkaufsschlager
with effect from mit Wirkung von
without obligation unverbindlich
word processor Textverarbeitungsprogramm
work environment Arbeitsatmosphäre
work permit Arbeitserlaubnis
workforce Arbeitskräfte, Belegschaft
working hours Arbeitszeit
x-ray durchleuchten, röntgen
year under review Berichtsjahr

Der wichtigste Wortschatz

Deutsch-Englisch

A

Abflughalle departure lounge
Abgabetermin deadline
Abhängigkeiten dependencies
Ablauf expiry
Ablaufverfolgung tracing
Abmahnung warning
Abonnement subscription
Abschreibung depreciation
absichern gegen hedge against
Absicht intention, objective
Abteilung department, division
Abteilungsleiter head of department
abziehen deduct
administrieren administer
aggressive Verkaufstaktik hard sell
Aktenmappe folder
Aktenschrank filing cabinet
Aktenzeichen Ref (reference)
Aktie share
Aktiengesellschaft (AG) S-corporation (US), public limited company (UK)
Aktienkurs share price
Aktionär shareholder
Aktionsplan action plan
aktualisieren update
aktuell current, up-to-date
alles in allem all included
am Apparat speaking
Anbieter provider
Änderung modification
an die Börse gehen go public
Angestellter employee
an Wert einbüßen depreciate
Änderungen in letzer Minute last minute changes
Änderungswunsch change request
anerkannt appreciated
anerkennen recognise
Anfälligkeit vulnerability
anfangen embarking
Anfrage query, enquiry
Anführer point man
angeben declare
Angebot bid
Angelegenheit issue
angepasst adjusted
angepasst den Bedürfnissen customised
Angestellter clerk
angewandte Forschung applied research
Anlage investment
Anlageplan investment scheme
Anlagevermögen fixed assets
anlegen invest
Anmeldeformular application form
annullieren nullify
anordnen order
Anreiz incentive
anschließen connect
Anschluss port
Anschreiben cover letter
Ansprüche claims
anspruchsvoll sophisticated
anstreben seek
Ansturm run
Antivirenprogramm anti-virus program
Antwort reply
Anweisung instruction
Anwendung application
anwesend present
Anzeige advertisement
Arbeitsatmosphäre work environment
Arbeitserlaubnis work permit
Arbeitsgruppe team
Arbeitskräfte workforce
Arbeitsrecht industrial law
Arbeitsvertrag employment contract
Arbeitsweise operations
Arbeitszeit working hours
Artikelnummer item number
assistieren assist
auf den Markt bringen release onto the market
auf etwas achten pay particular attention
auf Gebühren verzichten waive charges
auf Nachfrage on demand

auf Probe probationary
Aufbereitungsanlage processing plant
aufklappbar pop-up
Auftrag order
Auftragnehmer contractor
Auftrieb geben boost
aufwerten revalue
aufzeichnen plot
Ausbildung education
ausfallen lassen cancel
ausführen execute, perform
Ausgabe edition
Ausgaben expenditure, expenses
ausgeben issue
ausgeglichener Geschäftsabschluss break even
aushandeln drive
Aushilfe temp
Auslandsinvestition outward investment
auspacken unpack
Außenwerbung outdoor advertising
Aussetzung exposure
Aussicht prospect
Ausstattung equipment, facilities
Aussteller(in) drawer
Ausstellung exhibition
Auswahl assortment, range
Auszeichnung award
autorisieren authorize
Autovermietung car rental

B

bankrott bankrupt
Bankrott machen go to the wall
Banküberweisung bank transfer
Bankwechsel banker's draft
Bankwesen banking
Banner banner
Baugewerbe construction industry
Beamer multimedia projector
bearbeiten edit
bedeutende Leistung achievement
bedienen operate
Bediener operator
Bedienungsgeld service charge
Bedürfnis need
befolgen follow
befördert promoted
Beförderung promotion
Befrachter shipper
Befragter respondent
befriedigen satisfy
Begabung talent
Begegnungsfläche hospitality area
begünstigen benefit
behandeln handle
beifügen enclose
beinhalten entail
Beitrag input
Beklagte(r) defendant
Belastung burden
Belegschaft staff
belohnen reward
Benutzer user
berechnen charge
Berechtigung authorization, entitlement
Bergbau mining
berichten über report on
Berichtsjahr year under review
berücksichtigen take into consideration
Beruf profession
Berufserfahrung professional experience
beschaffen raise
Beschaffung procurement
beschäftigt busy
beschichten coat
beschränkt limited
Beschränkung constraint, restriction
beschriften label
Beschwerde complaint, grievance
besetzt engaged
Besichtigung visit
besprechen go over
Besprechung meeting
bestätigen confirm
Bestellung order
Bestimmungsland destination country, target country

Beteiligung stake
Betriebssystem operating system
Beurteilung judgement
bevorzugen prefer
Beweis evidence, proof
Bewerber candidate
Bewerbung application
bezahlen settle
Bezahlung remuneration, settlement
Bezogene(r) drawee
Bilanzaufstellung balance sheet
Bilanzprüfer auditor
Bild image
Bildbearbeitung image editing
Bildschirm projection screen, display screen
Bildtafel graphic panel
bis jetzt to date
bitten request
Blindbewerbung cold application
Blindbewerbungsanschreiben speculative letter
Börse stock exchange
Börsengang IPO (Initial Public Offering)
Börsenkrach stock market crash
Brainstorming brainstorming
Branche sector
Briefumschlag envelope
Broschüre brochure, pamphlet
brutto gross
Buchhalter bookkeeper
Buchhaltung accounting
Buchprüfung auditing
Buchung booking
Budget budget
Büroklammer paperclip
Büromaterial office supplies

C

CAD, computergestütztes Entwerfen computer aided design
CAM, computergestützte Fertigung computer aided manufacturing
Cashflow cash flow
CD-ROM-Laufwerk CD-ROM drive
Charisma charisma
Chemieindustrie chemicals
Computerwissen computer literacy
Computervirus virus
Container container

D

Daten data
Datenbank database
definieren define
Demo demo
Derivat derivative
Design design
detailverliebt detail-oriented
Dia slide
Diagramm chart
Diaprojektor slide projector
Dichtung seal
die erste/zweite Möglichkeit the former/latter
Direktor Gov (governor)
Direktvertrieb direct marketing
diskrete Verkaufstaktik soft sell
Dividende dividend
Dokument document
Dokumentenakkreditiv documentary letter of credit
doppelte Buchführung double-entry bookkeeping
Drehbank lathe
dringend urgent
Dritte third party
Druck pressure
Drucker printer
durcharbeiten review
durchführen conduct
durchgesetzt enforced
durchleuchten x-ray
Durchsage announcement
Durchschlag cc (carbon copy)
DVD-Spieler DVD player

E

EDV-Direktor CIO (chief information officer)
Ehrgeiz ambition

ehrgeizig ambitious
Eigenkapital shareholders equity
Eigenschaft property
Eindruck impression
Einführung (in den Beruf) induction
Einfuhrzoll import duty
eingetragen Inc (incorporated)
Einkommenssteuer income tax
Einnahmen revenue, receipts
einreichen file
Einrichtung amenity, facility
einschließlich incl (including)
Einschreiben registered mail
Einspruch appeal
Einzelhandel retailing
Einzelhändler retailer
einzelne Quelle single-source
Einzelunternehmer sole trader
elektrische Leitfähigkeit conductivity
Elektriker electrician
elektrische Anschlüsse light fixture
E-Mail-Adresse email address
Empfangsdame receptionist
enden terminate
Endkontrolle final quality inspection
Endnutzer end user
Endstelle terminal
Endverbraucher end-consumer
energisch energetic
engagiert committed
Entlassung dismissal
Entschädigung compensation
Entscheidungsträger decision maker
entwerfen draft
entwickeln develop
Entwicklung development
Entwicklung eines Prototyps prototyping
Erfahrung experience
Ergebnis outcome
Ergebnisse achievements
erheben (Steuern) levy
erledigen take care of
erleichtern facilitate
erliegen succumb
ermächtigt empowered
ermutigend inspiring
erneuerbar renewable
erstklassige Standardaktie blue chip
Ertrag earnings
Erwartungen expectations
erwerben acquire
erzeugen generate
es zur Bedingung machen, dass stipulate (that)
etwas betreffen pertain to
evaluieren evaluate

F

Fabrikverkauf factory shop
Fächer pigeonholes
Fachhändler, ~geschäft stockist
Fachliteratur technical literature
Fachmann/Fachfrau specialist
Fähigkeit skill
fällig overdue
fällig werden mature
Fälligkeitsdatum due date
Fallstudie case study
Farbzusammenstellung colour scheme
Fassung version
Fax fax
fehlerhaft flawed
Fehlersuche troubleshooting
Feierabend close of play
Feldexperiment field experiment
Feldstudie field survey
Fertigerzeugnis finished product
festes Angebot firm offer
Festigkeit strength
festlegen establish
Festplatte hard disk drive
Finanzamt tax office (US Inland Revenue)
Finanzdirektor CFO (chief financial officer)
Finanzierung financing
Firewall firewall
Firma company
Firmenzeichen logo

fleißig hard-working
Flipchart flip chart
Floppy-Laufwerk floppy disk drive
Fluktuation fluctuation
fluktuieren fluctuate
Folie OHT, overhead transparency
Förderband conveyor belt
fördern promote
Forderung accounts receivable, demand
Formular form
formulieren formulate
Forscher researcher
Forschung und Entwicklung R&D (research and development)
Fortschritt progress
fortsetzen maintain
Fragebogen questionnaire
Fragesteller questioner
Fräsmaschine milling machine
frei an Bord FOB (free on board)
freiberuflich freelance
freie Tage days off
Fundbüro lost property office
fundiert knowledge-based
Funktion function
Fusion merger

G

Gebiet field
Gebühr charge
Gegenbuchung cross reference
Gehalt salary
Gehäuse casing
Geld zurück refund
Geldschein note
Geldsendung remittance
genaue Angaben specification
Genauigkeit accuracy
Genehmigung permission
Gerät implement, device
Gericht court
geschäftsführender Direktor managing director
Geschäftsjahr fiscal year
Geschäftswert goodwill
Geschäftsjahr fiscal year
Geschäftswert goodwill
geschätzte Ankunftszeit ETA (estimated time of arrival)
Gesellschaft mit beschränkter Haftung (GmbH) C-corporation (US), limited liability company (UK)
gesetzliches Zahlungsmittel legal tender
Gestell rack
Gesundheit und Sicherheit health and safety
Gesundheitswesen healthcare
Gewerkschaft trade union
Gewinn gain, profit
gewinnen gain
Gewinn- und Verlustrechnung profit and loss (or income) statement
Gewinnverteilungsrechnung appropriation account
Gleitzeit flexitime
Grafik artwork
Grafikkarte graphics card
Großhandel wholesale
Großhändler wholesaler
Grundausstattung fixture
Grundlagenforschung basic research
gründlich thoroughly
Gruppendynamik group dynamics
gültig valid
Gültigkeit validity
günstiger Kauf bargain
gut eingedeckt mit stocked with

H

Haftung liability
Halberzeugnis semifinished product
Halter holder
Handelsmesse trade fair
Handelspartner trading partner
Handelsverbot embargo
Händler dealer
Hauptbelastung major burden
Hauptbelastungszeit peak time
Haupterzeugnis core product
Hauspost house mail
Haustürverkauf doorstep selling (UK)

Hefter binder
Herausforderung challenge
Herkunft origin
Herkunftsland country of origin, source country
Hersteller manufacturer
Hilfsmittel resource
hinsichtlich re (regarding)
Hinterziehung evasion
Hinweis indication
hochqualifiziert well-qualified
hochschnellen shoot up
höchst paramount
Homepage home page
Hypothese hypothesis

I/J
im Quadrat square
im Rückstand past due
im Stich lassen let down
im Voraus in advance
im Wert stark fallen slum
Image image
immaterielle Vermögenswerte intangible (assets)
Implikation implication
in die Zange nehmen grill
in einer Kartei on someone's books
in Lizenz gefertigte Ware goods manufactured under license
in Übereinstimmung in accordance with
Industrieware manufactures
Informationsfluss information flow
infrarot infra-red
Inhaber proprietor
innovativ innovative
Inserent advertiser
insistieren insist
Insolvenz insolvency
installieren install
Instandhaltung maintenance
Interaktion interaction
International Commercial Terms Incoterms
internationale Zahlungsanweisung international money order
interne Post internal post
Internet Internet
Investmentbank investment bank
Investor(in) investor
Jahresbericht annual report
Jahreshauptversammlung Annual General Meeting
Jahresurlaub annual leave
jmdn. entlassen make sbd redundant
jmdn. in der Spur halten keep sbd on track

K
Kabel cable
Kalkulation calculation
Kampagne campaign
Kanal channel
Kapitalerträge investment income
Kapitalquelle source of funds
Kapitalrendite return on investment (ROI)
Kapitalzuwachs capital growth
Karriere career
Karriereziel career objective
Karteikasten file-card box
Kasse checkout
Kauf mit Rückgaberecht sale or return
Kenntnisse haben knowledgeable
Kern core
Klage action, lawsuit
Kläger(in) petitioner
Klarstellung clarification
klassifizieren classify
Klausel clause
Klebeband tape
Kniffe tricks of the trade
Kommentare comments
Kompromiss compromise
Kompromisse schließen compromise
Konferenz conference
Konkurrent(in) competitor
Konkurs bankruptcy
Konnossement bill of lading
Konsolidierung consolidation
Konsumgüter consumer goods
Konto account

Kontostand balance
Konzept concept
koordinieren coordinate
Kopiergerät photocopier
Körperschaft corporation
körperschaftssteuerpflichtig liable to corporation tax
Kostendeckungspunkt break-even point
Kostenvoranschlag estimate
kostenwirksam cost-effective
krankgeschrieben sick-leave
Krankenversicherung medical insurance
kreativ imaginative
Kreditkarte credit card
kreditwürdig good for
Kreisdiagramm pie chart
Krimskrams novelties
Kunde/Kundin client
Kundenansprache sales pitch
Kundendienst customer service
Kundenstamm customer base
Kündigung resignation
Kündigungsfrist notice
Kursschwankung currency fluctuation

L
Labor laboratory
laden load
Laden store (US), shop (UK)
Ladentisch counter
Lagerhaus warehouse
Landwirtschaft agriculture
langlebige Gebrauchsgüter consumer durables
Laserpointer laser pointer
Lastkraftwagen truck (US), lorry (UK)
LCD-Bildschirm LCD screen
Lebenslauf curriculum vitae
lebenswichtig vital
Lebenszyklus life cycle
Lehre apprenticeship
leihen lend
leiten chair run
Leiter(in) chairperson
Lenkungsausschuss steering committee
Leuchtkasten light box
Lieferbedingungen delivery terms
Lieferfirma caterer
Lieferkette supply chain
Lieferung consignment
Liquidität liquidity
Lizenz license
Lizenz erteilen grant a license
Lizenzgeber licensor
Lizenznehmer license holder, licensee
Locher hole puncher
Lohn wage
Lohnbüro wages office
lohnend rewarding
löschen delete
Lösung solution

M
Mahnung reminder
Mangel defect
manipulieren manipulate
Markt market
Marketing marketing
Marktforschung market research
Marktführer forerunner
Maß measurement
maßgeschneidert bespoke
Maus mouse
Medienrummel hype
Mehrwertsteuer VAT (Value Added Tax)
Meilenstein milestone
menschliches Element human element
Merkmal feature
Metalldetektor metal detector
mieten rent
Mind Map mind map
mit Wirkung von with effect from
Mitteilung disclosure
Mobbing colleague-bashing
Modewort buzz-word
modifizieren modify
modular modular
möglich feasible

Montage assembly
montieren assemble
Mörtel mortar
motiviert motivated
Münze coin
Mutterfirma parent

N
nach Eingang on receipt
nach Kundenwunsch (gefertigt) customised
Nachfrage market need
nachgeben give in
nachlassen knock off
nachlassender Bedarf decline
Nachnahme cash on delivery
Nachvollziehbarkeit des Transportwegs tracking and tracing facilities
näher ausführen elaborate on
Nahrungsmittel foodstuff
Neben-/Abfallprodukt by-product
Nebeneinkünfte casual income
Nebenkosten overheads
netto net
Nettolohn take-home pay
Netzwerkadministrator network administrator
Netzwerk network
Netzwerkingenieur network engineer
Neuheit fancy goods, novelities
nicht lockerlassen keep at it
nochmalige Prüfung review
nominieren nominate
Notiz memorandum
Notizblock notepad
Notizbuch notebook
Notwendigkeit necessity
Nutzen benefit

O
oben angegeben above-mentioned
Oberfläche surface
oberflächlich cursory
Obligation bond
offene Stelle vacancy
offiziell anerkannte Qualifikation formal qualification
operieren operate
optimales Verfahren best practice
Option option
Organigramm organisational chart
orientiert oriented
Ort location

P
Paket package
Papierkram paperwork
Papierschacht paper tray
Pappkarton cardboard box
Partnerschaft partnership
Partyverkauf party selling
Passwort password
Patrone cartridge
Pendelverkehr shuttle
Personal human resources
Personalentwicklung personal development
persönlicher Aktiensparplan Personal Equity Plan (PEP)
persönlicher Assistent PA (personal assistant)
persönliches Briefpapier personalized stationery
Pflicht duty
Pharmaindustrie pharmaceuticals
Phase stage
planen schedule
platzieren place
pleite bust
Podium podium
Porto postage
Postausgang outgoing mail
Posteingang incoming mail
Postskriptum PS (postscript)
Postwurfsendung direct mail advertising
Praktikum internship
Präsentation presentation
Präsenz presence
Preis price, rate
Preiserhöhung price increase
Presseente hoax
Presseerklärung press release

Pressekonferenz press conference
Pressemappe press kit
Pressesprecher press spokesman
primär primary
Prioritätenliste priority list
probieren try
Produktionsprozess manufacturing process
produktiv productive
Prognose forecast
Programmierer programmer
Projektbesprechung status meeting
Projektmanager project manager
projizieren project
prolongieren renew
Prospekt leaflet prospectus
Prospektstand literature stand
Protokoll minutes, protocol
Provision commission
provozieren provoke
Prozessor processor
Prozentsatz percentage
Punkt item, point

Q
Qualifikation qualification
qualitativ qualitative
Qualitätskontrolle quality control
Qualitätssicherung quality assurance
quantitativ quantitative
Quittung receipt
Quote quota

R
Rabatt discount
Raten instalments
realisieren implement
Realisierungsphase implementation stage
Rechnung bill, invoice
Rechnungsunterlagen financial records
Rechtsanwalt attorney
rechtliche Schritte einleiten take legal action
Rechtsstreit litigation
Redner speaker
Referenz reference
Regal shelf
Regelung regulation
Reichweite reach
Reife maturity
Reinigung purification
Reiseroute itinerary
rekapitulieren recap
Reklametafel billboard
Rendite return
Rentabilität profitability
Reporter reporter
Repräsentant agent
repräsentativ representative
Reputation reputation
Revisor auditor
Rezension review
Richter judge
Risikoanalyse risk analysis
Risikokapital venture capital
Rohstoff raw material
Rohstoffe natural resources
Rückerstattung drawback
rückvergüten reimburse

S
sauer verdientes Geld hard earned cash
Scanner scanner
Schaubild chart
Scheibe slice
scheitern break down (GB), ~ off (US)
schicken send
schlagfest shock-resistant
Schlichtungsverfahren arbitration
Schlüsselfiguren key people
Schlüsselwort keyword
schmieden forge
Schmuggelware contraband
Schöffe jury
Schulden debts
Schwäche weakness
Sekretär(in) secretary
sekundär secondary

Selbstverpflichtung commitment
Senator Sen (senator)
senken reduce
sich auf etwas verlassen take for granted
sich aufeinander verlassen rely upon each other
sich Notizen machen take notes
sich stellen face
sich völlig verausgaben burn oneself out
Sicherheit security
Sichteinlagen sight deposit
Sitzung session
Slogan slogan
so schnell wie möglich by return
Software-Ingenieur software engineer
Solvenz solvency
Sonderangebot special offer
sorgen provide
sorgfältig durchsehen peruse
Sorte brand
sortieren sort
Sortiment range
Soundkarte sound card
Spalte column
Spannvorrichtung jig
sparen save
Sparkasse savings bank
Spediteur carrier
Speicherplatz memory
spekulieren speculate
spezialangefertigt custom designed
staatlich geprüfter Bilanzbuchhalter chartered accountant
Stand booth
Standpunkt position
Stärke strength
Statistik statistics
Steckdose outlet
stecken plug
Stelle position
Stellenkürzungen job cuts
Steuerberater tax adviser
Steuererklärung tax return
Steuerfreibetrag allowance
steuerfreie Vergünstigung tax-free benefit
steuerlich absetzbar allowable against tax
steuerlich fiscal
Steuernummer tax code
steuerpflichtiges Einkommen taxable income
Steuersatz rate
Steuervergünstigung tax break
Stichprobe sample
Stifte für Flipcharts presentation markers
Stoff material
Störung intrusion
Strom power
Stromkabel power cable
studieren read
Suchmaschine search engine
Systemadministrator system administrator
systematisch systematic

T

Tabellenkalkulationsprogramm spreadsheet
Tacker stapler
Tageslichtprojektor overhead projector
Tagesordnung agenda
Tagesordnungspunkt item
Tagespensum performance
Tante-Emma-Laden Mom and Pop store
Taschenrechner pocket calculator
Tastatur keyboard
tauschen exchange
Teamplayer team player
technische Unterstützung technical support
Teilhaber associate
Teilkostenrechnung marginal costing
Termineinlagen term deposit
Terminkalender appointment book
tertiär tertiary
Text copy
Textverarbeitungsprogramm word processor
Thema Subj (subject)
Tintenpatrone ink cartridge
Tochterfirma subsidiary
TQM, totales Qualitätsmanagement Total Quality Management

tragbar portable
trainieren coach
Transaktion transaction
transkontinental transcontinental
Transport mit mehreren Verkehrsmitteln intermodal transportation
Trend trend

U/V
über das erlaubte Maß over the limit
überarbeiten review
Überblick overview
überbringen convey
Übereinkunft agreement
Übergabe handover
übernehmen take on
überprüfen screen, check
Überstunden overtime
übertragen transfer
überwiegen exceed
Umfrage survey
umsatzstark fast-selling
Umschlaginnenseite inside cover
umsetzbar applicable
umtauschen convert
Umwelt environment
unbegrenzte Kilometerzahl unlimited mileage
Unannehmlichkeit inconvenience
unberechtigt unauthorized
unentbehrlich essential
unerwartet unforeseen
ungeklärt unsettled
Unterabteilung section
Unterbrechung interruption
Unternehmensführung management
Unternehmenspolitik company policy
unterstützen back up
Untersuchung survey
unterwegs on the move
unverbindlich without obligation
unwiderruflich irrevocable
unzulässig illegal
URL-Adresse (Website-Adresse) URL
Ursprungszeugnis certificate of origin
verantwortlich für responsible for
Verantwortung responsibility
verbessern enhance, refine
Verbesserung improvement
verbindlich binding
Verbindlichkeiten liabilities, outstanding obligations, accounts payable
Verbot ban
verboten out of bounds
Verbrauch consumption
Verbraucher consumer
Verbraucherrecht consumer rights
Verdienst earnings
vereinbar mit compatible with
Verfahren proceedings
verfahrenstechnisch procedural
Verfrachter consignor
verfügbar available
Verfügbarkeit availability
vergrößern increase
Vergünstigung perk
Verhaltensmerkmale behavioural traits
verhandeln negotiate
Verhandlung negotiation
Verhandlungsort venue
verhängen impose
Verkauf sale
verkaufen sell
Verkaufsforschung sales research
Verkaufsschlager winner
Verkaufsstelle outlet
Verknüpfung link
Verlängerungskabel extension cord
vermarkten market
Vermögenswerte assets
veröffentlichen publish
Veröffentlichung trade publication
Verpackung packing
Versandeinheit shipment
Versandhauskatalog mail-order catalogue
Versäumnis failure
verschieben postpone

Verschleiß wear
verschlüsselt encrypted
verschwenden waste
Versicherung assurance, insurance
versorgen cater for
Verspätung delay
verteilen share
Verteilung circulation
Vertrag contract
vertragsrechtliche Probleme contractual problems
vertrauen trust
Vertraulichkeit confidentiality
vertreten stand in
Vertreter agent, representative
Verwaltung management
Verwaltungskosten administrative costs
verweisen refer
Verwirrung confusion
Verzugszinsen default interest
Videorekorder video recorder
Vierteljahr quarter
Visitenkarte business card
Visum visa
Volkswirtschaft economics
Voll-/Teilzeitkraft full-time/part-time worker
Vollkaskoversicherung comprehensive insurance
Vollkostenrechnung absorption costing
von Wert of value
vorangegangen previous
Vorarbeiter foreman
Vorauskasse cash in advance
voraussagen predict, forecast
vorbereiten prepare
Vorbereitungsphase preparation stage
vorgefertigt prefabricated
Vorhersage outlook
vorläufig preliminary
vorlegen submit
Vorrichtung fixture
Vorruhestand early retirement
vorschlagen propose, suggest
Vorschrift guideline
Vorschuss advance, retainer
Vorsprung haben have over
Vorstand board
Vorstandsvorsitzender CEO (chief executive officer)
vortäuschen pretend
Vorteil benefit
Vortrag talk

W

Wachstum growth
Währung currency
Wandaufhängung wall mounting
Wandsteckdose wall socket
Ware merchandise
Ware zweiter Wahl second
Warenbestandswert inventories
Warenbörse commodity market
Warenempfänger consignee
Warenprobe sample
Warenrechnung invoice
Wartung maintenance
Website website
Wechsel bill of exchange
Wechselkurs exchange rate
Weiterbildung training
Werbestrategie promotion strategy
Werbung in Medien media advertising
Werdegang background
Werkhalle shop
Werkzeug tool
Wert value
Wertpapierhandel stockbroking
wesentlich crucial, substantial
wettbewerbsfähig competitive
Whiteboard whiteboard

Z

zahlen pay
Zahlung payment
Zahlungsempfänger(in) payee
Zahlungstermin settlement date
zeigen demonstrate
Zeitplanung time management
Zeitrahmen timeframe

Ziegel brick
Ziel destination, goal
Zins(en) interest
Zollbarriere tariff barrier
Zollbeamter customs officer
Zollbegleitschein carnet
Zollfaktura, ~rechnung customs invoice
Zollverschluss in bond
zu Händen von FAO (for attention of)
Zufriedenstellung satisfaction
Zugang access
zugänglich accessible
Zugangsschutzsystem firewall
Zugeständnis concession
zukünftig prospective
zum Kauf drängen pitch
zur Ansicht on approval
zurückfordern claim back
zurückzahlen repay
Zusammenarbeit teamwork, liaison
zusammenfassen summarise
Zusammenfassung summary
zuschreiben attribute
Zustand condition
Zustellung delivery
zuteilen allocate
zuverlässig steady
Zuverlässigkeit reliability
Zweck purpose
Zwischenhändler distributor, intermediary
Zwischensumme subtotal
24-Stunden-Geschäft convenience store

1

Übung 1: 1. I'm looking forward to working with you. 2. I didn't catch your name. 3. We've heard a lot about you. 4. We're all on first names here. 5. She's responsible for all things financial.
Übung 2: 1. introduce 2. meet 3. pleased 4. pleasure 5. acquaintance 6. from 7. before
Übung 3: 1. It's pretty humid today, isn't it? 2. Does it always rain like this here? 3. Quite warm, isn't it?
Übung 4: 1. I saw you in the audience. 2. Did you enjoy it? 3. Don't know enough about it. 4. Have you come far for the conference? 5. It took me about 20 minutes. 6. I'm Harold Wilson, but people call me Harry. 7. Pleased to meet you Harry. 8. I didn't catch your name.
Übung 5: Sam tries to start talking business before a relationship is built up, eats pork, insists on alcoholic drinks, insults him by saying this one is on me.
Übung 6: 1. a list of food items in a restaurant 2. part of a contract 3. violent, irregular motion of air 4. suggest 5. demand 6. someone who checks the accounts 7. written agreement
Übung 7: 1. order 2. menu 3. recommend 4. nothing 5. insist
Übung 8: 1. taxi near here? 2. in writing. 3. for today? 4. in touch. 5. just summarise. 6. doing business with you. 7. it, I guess.
Übung 9: 2., 9., 4., 5., 6., 1., 12., 8., 10., 11., 7., 3. 13.
Übung 10: 1. just 2. that 3. catch 4. that 5. for 6. get (catch) 7. when (next time) 8. been 9. keep (stay)
Übung 11: 1. Give me a ring next time you're in London. 2. I'd be delighted to show you around. 3. Keep in touch. 4. Let me give you my card. 5. Have you got my phone number? 6. You can reach me on ... 7. I look forward to receiving your offer/price list.
Übung 12: 1. Thank 2. It's been 3. talking 4. would like

2

Übung 1: 1. Hector speaking. 2. This is James Zinn from Seven Systems. 3. How can I help you? 4. How are you? 5. Fine, thanks. And you? 6. What can I do for you? 7. I wanted to ask if … 8. I'm calling about our order. 9. There was something else I wanted to ask you.
Übung 2: 1. How are you? 2. How can I help you? 3. What can I do for you? 4. I'm calling about our order. 5. I wanted to ask if you had despatched our order. 6. While I've got you on the line… 7. There was something else I wanted to ask you.
Übung 3: 1. reason 2. moment. 3. speak 4. calling 5. tell 6. from 7. about 8. through 9. line. 10. hear
Übung 4: 1. who's calling? 2. on the line. 3. about our bill. 4. put you through. 5. for your call? 6. your company? 7. from you. 8. please.
Übung 5: 1. afraid 2. will 3. back 4. leave 5. tell 6. call 7. catch 8. spell 9. called
Übung 6: 1. I'm afraid Sarah is on holiday at the moment. 2. When will he be back? 3. He'll be back this afternoon. 4. Would you like to leave a message? 5. Can you tell her that I called? 6. I'll call him again tomorrow. 7. I'm afraid I didn't catch your name. 8. Could you spell your name for me please? 9. I'll tell her you called.
Übung 7: 1. isn't here at the moment. 2. to go and meet with a client. 3. to call me back. 4. just in case. 5. I'm not in the office. 6. those numbers back to you. 7. for calling. 8. Bernard gets your message.
Übung 8: 1. I'm afraid he isn't here at the moment. 2. He just left to go and meet with a client. 3. Could you ask him to call me back? 4. I'll give it to you again just in case. 5. Let me just read those numbers back to you. 6. Thanks for calling. 7. I'll make sure Keith gets your message.
Übung 9: 2., 4., 1., 6., 8., 3., 7., 5.
Übung 10: 4.

3

Übung 1: Dear Ms Jackson, Thank you for your cv and letter of 24 June, in which you ask about possible employment as a computer programmer. I am pleased to inform you that the IT department is currently looking for additional staff. Could you please fill in the enclosed application form and send it to me by not later than 17 July. I look forward to hearing from you. Yours sincerely Harold Maudlin HR department
Übung 2: 1. Ergebnisse 2. vorangegangen 3. Handelsmesse 4. vor allem 5. beifügen 6. bis jetzt 7. Auftragnehmer
Übung 3: 1. implications 2. limit 3. infection 4. copies 5. area 6. security 7. parties 8. stickers 9. regulations 10. hours 11. heads
Übung 4: 1. over the limit 2. health and safety 3. area 4. working hours 5. arrange 6. suggest 7. noticed
Übung 5: 1. richtig 2. falsch 3. falsch 4. richtig 5. richtig 6. falsch 7. falsch
Übung 6: Mr Thompson reported on the <u>current</u> situation regarding the new <u>assembly</u> line; the <u>conveyor</u> belt had now been set up and was now undergoing tests. <u>Comments</u> and suggestions for improvements were being collected from all involved, and would be <u>distributed</u> to heads of departments by November 12. The new staff had already received their <u>induction</u> training on company procedures, and would be <u>provided</u> with safety equipment by November 16.
Übung 7:
<u>Subj</u>: Visitors
The <u>CEO</u> and <u>CIO</u> will be visiting this branch next Monday. They will be accompanied by <u>Gov</u> Timbles and <u>Sen</u> Collins. Their <u>ETA</u> will be 12:30; <u>dep</u> 16:00. Department heads are asked to submit suggestions for the afternoon programme, (<u>incl</u> names of staff members present), to my <u>PA</u> by no later than 14:00 on Thursday.
Kenneth Sambini
Branch Manager
Übung 8: 1. dep 2. CFO 3. re 4. reps 5. R & D

4

Übung 1: 1. filing cabinets (all others are office supplies) 2. folders (all others are furniture) 3. ordinance (all others pertain to a photocopier) 4. dilemma (all others relate to computers) 5. reception area (the others describe office equipment) 6. yoghurt containers (all others are standard household items)
Übung 2: 1. richtig 2. falsch 3. falsch 4. falsch 5. falsch 6. falsch 7. richtig
Übung 3: 1. ordered 2. dishwasher 3. cabinets 4. files/folders/binders
Übung 4: 1. engaged 2. shall 3. manage 4. assist 5. rather
Übung 5: 1. Thank you for your time. 2. How may I be of help? 3. I am certain that he would want to schedule an appointment. 4. Could you assist me on this matter? 5. I believe we spoke on the phone this morning. 6. Shall I put you through to his secretary? 7. Hmm, that is not ideal for me, but is that the only time he has free? 8. I understand you are only here for a week, is that correct?
Übung 6: 1. Would; like 2. May 3. staying 4. When; possible 5. manage 6. ideal 7. Follow
Übung 7: 1. Good day, this is Troy from Human Resources calling. 2. That is not an ideal time for me. 3. It is urgent that I schedule an appointment with him any time today. 4. The line is engaged at the moment. 5. If you would have a seat, this will just take a moment. 6. I would love a tea, if it is no trouble.
Übung 8: 1. Posteingang 2. sich ergeben 3. Paket 4. Zustellung 5. intern 6. Postausgang 7. Fach 8. wiegen
Übung 9: 1. The postage must be paid. 2. The rates should be lowered. 3. The parcels are to be picked up today. 4. The outgoing mail is weighed by Heather. 5. The envelopes will be stuffed by Jerome. 6. The task has been finished. 7. By when will the pigeonholes be installed?
Übung 10: 1. sort 2. placed 3. pigeonholes 4. been completed 5. house mail/internal post 6. delivered 7. arise 8. packages/letters.
Übung 11: 1. pointers 2. excuse 3. forms 4. number of 5. through/out 6. an end
Übung 12: 1. accurate 2. overtime 3. excuses 4. sick-leave 5. allotted 6. valid 7. vacation
Übung 13: 1. richtig 2. falsch 3. falsch

5

Übung 1: 1. David, can you come in here for a moment, please? 2. Have you prepared the agenda for circulation yet? 3. It'll be easier to keep everybody on track. 4. Also pay particular attention to the order. 5. You think that'll work?
Übung 2: 1. Have you prepared the agenda for circulation yet? 2. It'll be easier to keep everybody on track. 3. Yeah, ok. I'll write it now. 4. Ok. I will prepare and bring it in for you to look at right away. 5. A typical agenda has the following items.
Übung 3: 1. What has to be achieved during the meeting? 2. A clear structure of the meeting has to be given. 3. Sufficient time must be given to each item on the agenda. 4. The minutes of the meeting are taken. 5. Sometimes, professional external moderators are used.
Übung 4: 1. minutes 2. interruption 3. disgruntled 4. sufficient 5. chair 6. allocate 7. insist 8. accomplish 9. ensure. Mystery word: moderator
Übung 5: 1. to 2. at 3. across 4. element 5. picture 6. spent 7. run
Übung 6: 1. Ergebnis 2. übernehmen 3. überzeugen 4. vergrößern 5. optimal 6. verhandeln 7. fortsetzen
Übung 7: 1. It is my opinion that you accept a slightly higher price. 2. It is my impression that you would like to maintain our relationship. 3. The ability to negotiate solutions is crucial. 4. When we have found another solution, the price will return to normal. 5. Conflict partners try to convince the others of their position. 6. Perhaps you could take on some of the costs.
Übung 8: 1. convince 2. goods 3. consider 4. optimal 5. in my opinion 6. maintain 7. outcome
Übung 9: 1. If I could just summarise the main points that we've covered. 2. I would like to go over the decisions reached today. 3. Thank you all for coming. 4. You will all receive a copy of the minutes by Friday. 5. I would like to ask you for your comments on the effectiveness of this meeting. 6. That's it for today. 7. Many meetings in English start with a period of small talk.
Übung 10: 1. small talk 2. crucial 3. chairperson 4. go over 5. summarise 6. minutes
Übung 11: 1. at 2. at 3. grateful 4. go 5. summarise 6. contact 7. crucial

6

Übung 1: 1. dry erase markers, presentation markers, permanent markers 2. whiteboard, flipchart, transparency/OHT 3. slide projector, DVD player, video recorder/VCR, overhead projector/OHP, multimedia projector 4. extension cord, outlet 5. podium, laser pointer
Übung 2: 1. must know 2. require 3. insist on having 4. provide 5. supply 6. offer
Übung 3: 1. run into 2. check and see 3. count on 4. go through 5. let them know 6. set something up
Übung 4: 1. One moment please. 2. Do you have time to tell me ... 3. Pardon me, require a what? 4. Actually, I would like to know ... 5. So I must insist on having ... 6. Do you prefer ...
Übung 5: 1. has worked; for 2. has only existed; for 3. has been employed; since
Übung 6: 3., 2., 4., 5., 1.
Übung 7: 1. a) 2. b) 3. b) 4. b)
Übung 8: 1. attribute to 2. development 3. demonstrate 4. nearby 5. succumb to 6. quarter
Übung 9: 1. pie chart 2. plunged 3. shoot up 4. fluctuate 5. charts, rows, columns
Übung 10: 1. a) I would like to begin with ... b) These actions lead us to ... c) Now, I will move on to the final. 2. by asking them to draw a circle and then answer a question to involve them in the presentation personally 3. How did they fill these

spaces? 4. a) By asking for volunteers, b) by handing out blank pieces of paper and pens, c) by showing pie charts … 5. a) easy, risky, survival 6. a) higher, b) more consistent, c) climbing more rapidly than d) ever before 7. to express the importance of the point made in the comparison of the past and present profits in the preceding sentence
Übung 11: 1. I believe I have covered everything. 2. Thirdly, and finally, I led you through a case study. 3. Now I would just like to recap the main points from today. 4. The second point I made pertained to consumer rights. 5. I first spoke about the value of investing.

7
Übung 1: 1. look for 2. ambitious 3. essential 4. remuneration 5. candidate 6. position 7. responsibility 8. well-qualified 9. experience
Übung 2: 1. experience 2. hard-working 3. summary 4. excellent 5. career 6. energetic 7. skill 8. goal 9. talent. Mystery Word: education
Übung 3: 1. experience as an executive secretary. 2. include: MS office, Internet 3. Office Management
Übung 4: 1. skills 2. in training 3. higher profits 4. junior staff 5. other companies 6. satisfaction 7. development

8
Übung 1: 1. Erziehung 2. Versicherung 3. Bau 4. Gesundheitsfürsorge 5. im Grunde 6. Freizeit
Übung 2: 1. falsch 2. falsch 3. richtig 4. falsch 5. richtig 6. richtig
Übung 3: 1. Let's look at each category in turn. 2. Primary eco-nomic activity has to do with natural resources like 3. mining, oil, and agriculture. 4. Secondary activity is basically the manu-facturing sector, 5. in other words making things from what we get from the primary activities. 6. Here we are looking at the construction industry, for example, 7. or engineering, chemicals, and pharmaceuticals. 8. The tertiary activities group services together, 9. so this includes retailing for example, as well as 10. financial sectors like banking and insurance. 11. It also includes education, healthcare, communication 12. and the leisure industries.
Übung 4: 1. basically 2. partner 3. privatised 4. capitalist 5. investment 6. limit 7. owner
Übung 5: 1. proprietor 2. capital 3. partnership 4. risk 5. activities 6. sector 7. resources
Übung 6: 1. corporation 2. raise 3. partnership 4. sole trader 5. limited 6. proprietor 7. dividend 8. liability
Übung 7: 1. for 2. to 3. of 4. of 5. by 6. from 7. to
Übung 8: 1. achieve 2. decentralized 3. report 4. relationship 5. systematic 6. enforce 7. function 8. method 9. employee. Mystery word: hierarchy
Übung 9: 1. richtig 2. falsch 3. richtig 4. richtig 5. falsch 6. falsch 7. richtig
Übung 10: Downsizing is used to describe how companies reduce costs by reducing the size of their workforce; often middle management jobs are the first to go. Reengineering describes how companies redesign their processes in order to become more efficient. A virtual organisation refers to a temporary situation where two or more organisations come together to achieve a specific objective.
Übung 11: work on a project 2. take over a company 3. cut short a story 4. pay off a debt 5. end up as a manager 6. work out a solution
Übung 12: 1. school 2. read 3. straight 4. position 5. multinational 6. promoted 7. invested 8. lucky 9. millionaire
Übung 13: 1. apprenticeship 2. workers' council 3. board

9
Übung 1: 1. determine 2. function 3. perform 4. achieve 5. review 6. accomplished/achieved
Übung 2: 1. This year is flying by. 2. Have you ever taken the time to work out what is of value to you? 3. The future does not always bring what we expect. 4. Most people function better early in the morning, when they are fresh. 5. You should consider your performance level during a normal day. 6. 20% of my effort produces 80% of my results.
Übung 3: 1. Ziele 2. realistisch 3. von Wert 4. unvorhergesehen 5. überlegen 6. Rahmen 7. erreichen 8. überarbeiten
Übung 4: 1. I will write up your ideas around this topic. 2. Perhaps we can modify our existing software. 3. We could have it customised for our purposes. 4. That will be too expensive. 5. We could hire externals to develop the program.
Übung 5: A. 1. kreativ 2. Blick 3. verboten 4. Beitrag 5. unangemessen 6. provozieren 7. gemeinsame Problembewältigung B. 1., 3., 4., 6., 7.
Übung 6: 1. applicable 2. work environment 3. framework 4. input 5. glance 6. ideas 7. inappropriate 8. provoke 9. unforeseen 10. imaginative. Mystery word: brainstorm
Übung 7: 1. Resources are planned before embarking on a project. 2. It is important that the budget be allocated. 3. The time frame must be broken down into specific dates. 4. Human resources are allocated. 5. The plans and preparations are now carried out. 6. To assess the running of a project, a Gantt, PERT or CPM chart is often used.
Übung 8: The first step is to define the goal of the project, and the budget which can be allocated. This is the preparation stage. The project can then be planned in more detail. In the planning stage, human resources are allocated, and more specific time frames worked out. After the planning of the project is completed, comes the implementation stage. After completion, it is a good idea to evaluate the project.
Übung 9: 1. with 2. resources 3. phase 4. tool 5. oriented 6. dependencies 7. frame 8. term
Übung 10: 1. falsch 2. richtig 3. falsch 4. falsch 5. richtig 6. richtig
Übung 11: 1. guidelines 2. analysis 3. establish 4. nominate 5. delegate 6. status 7. evaluate

10

Übung 1: 1 hard disc drive 2. printer cartridge 3. type on a keyboard 4. scan in a picture 5. graphics card 6. floppy disc 7. artificial intelligence 8. data traffic 9. e-commerce 10. homepage 11. word processor
Übung 2: 1. printer 2. scanner 3. cartridge 4. keyboard 5. monitor 6. floppy drive 7. sound card 8. tower 9. mouse 10. CD-ROM drive 11. graphics card 12. modem
Übung 3: 1. Let me give you my business card. 2. Do you have an email address? 3. What's the URL of your home page? 4. I don't look at that account very often. 5. I'll send you an email within the next few days. 6. I don't check my email very often.
Übung 4: 1. website 2. your email 3. an email/a reply 4. address 5. card 6. a reply 7. page 8. email account
Übung 5: 1. richtig 2. falsch 3. falsch 4. richtig 5. richtig 6. falsch 7. falsch
Übung 6: 1. network 2. share 3. websites 4. authorization 5. accessible 6. access 7. Unauthorized 8. firewall
Übung 7: 1. gather 2. documents 3. submit 4. query 5. match 6. keywords 7. refine
Übung 8: 1. query 2. link 3. gather 4. submit 5. match 6. refine 7. information
Übung 9: 1. falsch 2. richtig 3. richtig 4. richtig 5. richtig 6. falsch
Übung 10: 1. bill 2. transaction 3. credit card 4. secure 5. security 6. balance 7. procurement 8. encrypted. Mystery word: Internet
Übung 11: 1. bill 2. balance 3. security 4. procurement 5. encrypted

11

Übung 1: 1. A product life cycle can be divided into four parts. 2. The first stage involves design and production. 3. During the growth stage the product is launched onto the market. 4. The product eventually stops being produced. 5. Finally the product goes into decline. 6. Clothing is sometimes produced for a single season. 7. Some foodstuffs show no sign of going into decline.
Übung 2: 1. divided 2. involves 3. launched 4. eventually 5. decline 6. produced 7. sign
Übung 3: 1. something you eat 2. going down 3. fully developed 4. technical changes 5. to get back 6. no ups or downs
Übung 4: 1. My car is very reliable. 2. We do experiments in the laboratory. 3. The main issue has to do with fees. 4. Is the data valid? 5. First we need to formulate a hypothesis. 6. Let's review the literature. 7. Children acquire knowledge at school.
Übung 5: 1. review 2. formulate 3. find 4. laboratory 5. analysed
Übung 6: 1. idea 2. concept 3. feasibility study 4. preliminary design 5. evaluation and improvements 6. prototyping 7. final design
Übung 7: 1. What 2. Where 3. What 4. What 5. What 6. When 7. Who; what
Übung 8: 1. points 2. shop 3. tools 4. materials 5. management 6. control 7. department 8. area
Übung 9: 1. assembly 2. shop 3. milling machine 4. lathe 5. jigs and fixtures 6. conveyor belt 7. casting 8. forge 9. walkway
Übung 10: 1. richtig 2. falsch 3. richtig 4. richtig 5. richtig 6. falsch

12

Übung 1: 1. falsch 2. falsch 3. richtig 4. richtig 5. richtig 6. falsch 7. richtig
Übung 2: 1. partner 2. barrier 3. country 4. break 5. import duty 6. duty 7. commission basis 8. on imports 9. trade 10. exports 11. outflow
Übung 3: 1. wholesaler 2. restrictions 3. duty 4. trading partner 5. commission 6. destination 7. origin
Übung 4: 1. richtig 2. falsch 3. falsch 4. richtig 5. falsch 6. richtig
Übung 5: 1. search 2. value 3. consignee 4. carnet 5. impose 6. sample 7. issue
Übung 6: 1. transportation 2. facilities 3. source 4. reach 5. container 6. service 7. provider 8. shipper 9. markets
Übung 7: 1. shipper 2. destination 3. fleet 4. carrier 5. truck 6. facility 7. reach 8. trailer 9. origin
Übung 8: 1. falsch 2. richtig 3. richtig 4. richtig 5. falsch 6. falsch 7. falsch
Übung 9: 1. consolidation 2. convenience store 3. satisfaction 4. supply chain 5. wholesaler 6. distributor 7. manufacturer
Übung 10: 1. intermediary 2. factory shops 3. customer base

13

Übung 1: 1. richtig 2. richtig 3. falsch 4. richtig 5. richtig 6. falsch 7. richtig
Übung 2: 1. maker 2. books 3. party 4. a commission 5. published 6. talks 7. to the press 8. basis
Übung 3: 1. freelance 2. third party 3. publish 4. commission 5. client 6. decision maker 7. on s.o.'s books 8. agent
Übung 4: 1. falsch 2. richtig 3. falsch 4. richtig 5. richtig 6. falsch 7. richtig
Übung 5: 1. pitch 2. confident 3. cake 4. convinced 5. persuasive 6. evidence 7. benefited 8. reputation 9. pretending
Übung 6: 1. of cake 2. pitch 3. argument 4. character 5. evidence 6. point 7. the benefits 8. weight 9. your reputation
Übung 7: 1. That would make sense. 2. There's a 10 per cent discount on the price. 3. In that case, I would suggest this model. 4. Can you tell me what you plan to use your phone for? 5. Shall I make out the contract for you? 6. That sounds like just what I need. 7. I would say this product will suit you better.
Übung 8: 1. times 2. offer 3. charges 4. case 5. discount 6. sense 7. move 8. need
Übung 9: 1. discount 2. suggest 3. seeing as 4. slightly 5. special offer 6. mainly 7. especially 8. charge. Mystery Word: customer

Übung 10: 1. benefits 2. hands up 3. a feeling 4. frustrated 5. time 6. hold of someone 7. care of something 8. you money

14

Übung 1: 1. Sortiment 2. zugehörig 3. Verfügbarkeit 4. wesentlich 5. Rabatt 6. Einrichtungen 7. umfassend
Übung 2: 1. products 2. availability 3. discounts 4. date 5. list 6. lines
Übung 3: 1. transfer 2. lading 3. demand 4. of credit 5. letter of credit 6. origin 7. certificate 8. a contract 9. in advance
Übung 4: 1. falsch 2. falsch 3. richtig 4. richtig 5. richtig
Übung 5: 1. You drive a hard bargain. 2. I'll send you the quotation by close of play tomorrow. 3. We could give you a discount if you agreed to buy over 500 units. 4. As long as you pay us in cash, we would be happy to forget the paperwork. 5. Let's look at what's included in the package. 6. Our warranty assumes we have done the installation ourselves.
Übung 6: 1. assumed 2. prefer 3. bargain 4. throwing 5. off
Übung 7: 1. I'd rather we summarised very briefly before you go. 2. There are still a couple of outstanding points on my list. 3. I'll be in touch. 4. Is there anything you'd like to add? 5. When will you get the licenses to us? 6. I think we'll need to set up another meeting. 7. We agreed on a price of $100,000.
Übung 8: 1. points 2. summary 3. meeting 4. touch 5. question. Mystery word: price

15

Übung 1: 2., 4., 5., 15., 6., 8., 3., 11., 13., 14., 12., 10., 9., 7., 1.
Übung 2: 1. about 2. person 3. supplies 4. like 5. copy 6. need 7. customer 8. website 9. help (assistance)
Übung 3: 1. I'm ringing to ask about ordering some office supplies. 2. Are you the right person to be speaking to? 3. I'd like to order some office supplies. 4. What would you like to order? 5. Do you have a copy of our catalogue? 6. You can order everything you need online. 7. Do I need a customer number or anything? 8. It's all on the website. 9. Just give me a call if you need any help filling in the order form.
Übung 4: 1. Please note that the prices do not include postage and packing. 2. We enclose a copy of our price list and terms of payment. 3. We are happy to offer a first order discount of 3%. 4. Please do not hesitate to contact me if you have any further questions. 5. Our normal terms of payment are 30 days net. 6. I have enclosed a copy of our latest catalogue. 7. Thank you for the above-mentioned enquiry. 8.These special terms are available until the end of July. 9. This offer is subject to stock availability.
Übung 5: 1. mentioned 2. payment/delivery 3. delay 4. draft 5. list 6. packing 7. availability 8. enquiry
Übung 6: 1. consignment 2. payment/delivery 3. order 4. payment/delivery/delivery date 5. the price 6. payment/delivery 7. 21 days for delivery
Übung 7: Thank you for your offer of 15 January 2006. Please supply us with 30 printers, item no 65Gh, by March 30. We note that the total price for the consignment is $6000, including delivery to our offices in Hamilton. Payment will be made on receipt of the goods. Could you also confirm delivery date by return.
Übung 8: 1. delivery terms 2. on receipt 3. label 4. delay 5. banker's draft 6. promise 7. consignment (delivery)
Übung 9: 1. reminder 2. payment/settlement 3. outstanding 4. overdue 5. reminder 6. payment/settlement 7. action 8. return
Übung 10: 1. discount 2. remittance 3. insist, settle 4. overdue 5. settlement 6. Failure
Übung 11: 1. Vorauskasse 2. per Nachnahme 3. Zahlungsbedingung 4. Proformarechnung

16

Übung 1: 1. b) 2. a) 3. b) 4. c)
Übung 2: 1. formulate 2. approach 3. needs 4. commitment 5. authority 6. expectations 7. interaction
Übung 3: 1. Customer service is the factor which companies claim to have over their competitors. 2. The management must provide training. 3. It is essential to understand the customer. 4. Every effort should be made to listen to customers. 5. It is important to consider the intercultural differences of the approach to customer service. 6. The customer is king.
Übung 4: 1. at 2. granted 3. beyond 4. cash 5. out 6. about 7. line
Übung 5: 1. erwähnen 2. anerkennen 3. untersuchen 4. unterscheiden 5. offenlegen 6. bemerken 7. verbessern
Übung 6: 1. from 2. will 3. to 4. about 5. point
Übung 7: 1. solve 2. imagine 3. persuade 4. by heart 5. hear 6. understand. Mystery word: listen
Übung 8: 1. Now that I have the customer, how do I keep them? 2. These consultants are now taught to listen to their customers. 3. Imagine the difficulty in a non-native language. 4. It is therefore very important to ask questions.
Übung 9: 1. inconvenience 2. bill 3. distance 4. compensation 5. conditioning 6. class 7. faithfully
Übung 10: 1. I am writing to complain about my hotel accommodation. 2. My room was dirty, 3. the air condition was broken, 4. and the restaurant only served cold meals. 5. In addition, the staff were extremely unfriendly. 6. Worst of all, the hotel was located 7. near the town rubbish dump, 8. which made the smell unbearable. 9. I would like to know 10. how you plan to compensate me 11. for this unacceptable situation. 12. Otherwise, you will be hearing from my lawyers.
Übung 11: 1. assure 2. inconvenience 3. claims 4. legible 5. compensation 6. refund 7. considerable

17

Übung 1: 1. planning 2. reserve 3. like 4. confirm 5. changed, will be arriving 6. stayed 7. be paying 8. Would you like

Übung 2: 1. a car 2. insurance 3. changes 4. room 5. mileage 6. thanks 7. return
Übung 3: 1. seat 2. a while 3. on 4. search 5. check 6. exit
Übung 4: 1. falsch 2. richtig 3. richtig 4. falsch 5. richtig 6. richtig 7. falsch
Übung 5: 1. source 2. cater for 3. locations 4. workforce 5. merchandise 6. founded
Übung 6: 1. warehouse 2. location 3. cater 4. souvenir 5. workforce 6. reliable 7. for
Übung 7: 1. The catering was first class. 2. I left a tip for the chambermaid. 3. There were two laundry bags in my cupboard. 4. Service charge is not included. 5. It was 5 star, so the amenities were excellent. 6. The beach was easily accessible from the hotel. 7. We booked a package tour.
Übung 8: 1. forgot 2. work out 3. believe 4. turned out 5. was 6. weren't 7. wished

18
Übung 1: 1. designed 2. carousel 3. area 4. decision 5. customers 6. rental 7. mounting
Übung 2: 1. We need to send in the order for our stand by the end of the day. 2. I'd like to run my conclusions by you. 3. If I could just cut in here, Ashley? 4. It's not simple to choose. 5. And don't forget the transportation and set up stages. 6. I guess you've got a point.
Übung 3: 1. in 2. by 3. up 4. between 5. in 6. of 7. with
Übung 4: 1. much 2. much 3. many 4 much 5. much 6. many 7. much
Übung 5: 1. electrician 2. printers 3. shelves 4. caterers 5. business card 6. pamphlet 7. invoice
Übung 6: 4., 8., 1., 6., 2., 7., 3., 9., 5.
Übung 7: 1. for 2 to 3. up 4. on 5. from 6. before 7. on
Übung 8: 1. Place the snacks on the table 2. Separate the damaged posters from those intact. 3. Check on the progress daily. 4. Open each meeting with a joke. 5. Erect the stand. 6. Reposition the light boxes. 7. Look at the refrigerator. 8. Share the work.
Übung 9: 1. above 2. right of/left of 3. right of/left of 4. on 5. over here 6. in 7. below
Übung 10: 1. drafted 2. specifications of 3. ideal 4. exchanged 5. think 6. benefits 7. works
Übung 11: 1. business cards 2. contact of 3. letter 4. relationships 5. impression 6. sales
Übung 12: 1. to see it first hand 2. That would be lovely. 3. try 4. browse 5. specifications 6. Can I tempt you with a drink? 7. Well done. 8. around the corner 9. You made it.

19
Übung 1: 1. There are a couple of things I want to talk to you about. 2. They're backed up by someone from the marketing department. 3. Can you just go over the promotion strategy again? 4. Basically we'll be running a two day campaign in the national press. 5. Emily said you wanted to see me. 6. What about the catalogue? 7. Who's doing the presentations?
Übung 2: 1. press 2. campaign 3. strategy 4. competitor 5. presence
Übung 3: 1. Konkurrent 2. verschieben 3. Werbekampagne 4. Rezension 5. Exemplar
Übung 4: 1. Hi John, good to see you. 2. It'll be available from our stand at all the major book fairs. 3. I'm sending (I'll be sending) around 300 copies out next week. 4. Oh, there is one other thing.
Übung 5: 1. customer 2. spend 3. number 4. write down 5. responses 6. discover
Übung 6: 1. b) 2. a) 3. a) 4. c)
Übung 7: 1., 2., 4., 6.
Übung 8: 1. richtig 2. richtig 3. falsch 4. richtig 5. richtig
Übung 9: 1. Verhältnis 2. Werbespots 3. Zuschauer 4. sich zum Ziel setzen 5. abhängig sein von 6. Kleinanzeige
Übung 10: 1. cinema (all the others are print media) 2. word of mouth (all the others are mass market media) 3. street furniture (all the others are online media) 4. leaflet (all the others are national media)
Übung 11: 1. message, 2. language, 3. challenge, 4. question, 5. expensive. Mystery word: sales
Übung 12: 1. challenge 2. form 3. page 4. problem 5. of you 6. the number
Übung 13: 1. in front of you 2. top of the page 3. meet the challenge 4. solve the problem 5. fill in the form
Übung 14: 1. with 2. do 3. that 4. want 5. allow 6. for

20
Übung 1: 1. magazine 2. come up 3. placing, media 4. isn't it 5. handle 6. would 7. stick
Übung 2: 1. Are you ready for our meeting? 2. Just give me a second. 3. Will we be placing it in any other media? 4. The plan is to air both radio and television spots beginning next month. 5. What kind of image are we looking to present? 6. I want you to handle the television campaign. 7. Do you think you can handle it?
Übung 3: 1. media 2. audience 3. characteristics 4. party 5. campaign 6. class 7. relations
Übung 4: 1. Just give me a second. 2. Did we come up with that? 3. That's what you wanted to speak to me about, isn't it? 4. Can you handle it? or Do you think you can handle it? 5. We thought that the print campaign would plant the seeds. 6. You'll be in charge of the whole show. 7. It sounds like a great project.
Übung 5: 1. What can I do for you? 2. I'd like to propose some softer initiatives as well. 3. Didn't I already tell you about the press conference? 4. We can only learn from our mistakes. 5. Don't worry about it. 6. You'll do fine. 7. The team will be there to back you up.
Übung 6: 3., 7., 2., 1., 4., 5., 6.

Übung 7: 1. held 2. media 3. direct 4. purpose 5. importance 6. trade 7. question 8. answer
Übung 8: 1. Why do companies hold excursions for their employees? 2. Where are excursions normally held? 3. Why do companies have motivational excursions? 4. Have you ever been on a motivational excursion? 5. Which factory or plant would you like to tour? 6. When did you begin your career here?
Übung 9: 1. investor 2. rival 3. pack 4. effective 5. colleague 6. goods 7. fair

21
Übung 1: 1. sheet 2. statement 3. meeting 4. equity 5. equipment 6. receivable/payable 7. year
Übung 2: 1. aufgelaufen 2. Vorhersage 3. Geschäftswert 4. immaterielle Vermögenswerte 5. Warenbestandswert 6. Haushaltsjahr 7. Arbeitsweise
Übung 3: 1. goodwill (all the others are in the profit and loss statement) 2. accounts payable (all the others are assets) 3. Shareholders Equity (the others are reports to be presented to the shareholders) 4. inventories (all the others are expenses)
Übung 4: 1. In the corporate world however, the face of banking changed enormously in the twentieth century. 2. Instead of keeping our money under the bed, we are all used to asking a bank to look after our money for us. 3. The latter part of the twentieth century saw the rapid expansion of investment banks. 4. This business has become more sophisticated in the last twenty years. 5. New banking products are invented almost every week. 6. Today, banks are required to serve international clients. 7. For many years in the United States of America commercial and investment banks were separated by law.
Übung 5: 1. under, look 2. lend 3. behalf 4. repeal 5. merger 6. sophisticated
Übung 6: 1., 2., 4., 5.
Übung 7: 1. dividend, 2. bond, 3. derivative, 4. share, 5. stock exchange, 6. capital growth. Mystery word: invest
Übung 8: 1. falsch 2. richtig 3. falsch 4. falsch 5. richtig
Übung 9: 1. Everybody who has travelled to another country knows of the problems associated with changing currencies. 2. The introduction of the euro has solved many of these problems. 3. The whole accounts of a foreign subsidiary must also be translated into the currency of the parent. 4. Companies should also take into consideration the currency exposure they have. 5. Also foreign travelling in the euro-zone has been made easier. 6. Time will tell how the peoples of Europe adapt to their new currency.
Übung 10: 1. Many of these problems have been solved by the introduction of the euro. 2. Careful consideration must be given to how these transactions are to be dealt with in the accounts. 3. Foreign currencies must be converted into our own currency 4. The accounts of subsidiaries are translated into the home currency of the parent company. 5. Foreign travelling has been made easier by the euro.

22
Übung 1: 1. bookkeepers 2. formal qualifications 3. enterprise 4. invoices 5. due date 6. forecasting 7. liquidity
Übung 2: 1. Computerwissen 2. Einkommen 3. Ausgaben 4. Liquidität 5. voraussagen 6. Unternehmen
Übung 3: 1., 3., 4.
Übung 4: 1. at 2. on 3. true, fair 4. in 5. before
Übung 5: 1. staatlich geprüft 2. Steuerberater 3. Bilanzprüfer 4. Insolvenz 5. Buchhaltung 6. Steuererklärung 7. Bilanzbuchhalter
Übung 6: 1. finance 2. transaction 3. classify 4. report 5. auditor 6. tax return 7. debts 8. insolvency 9. university 10. liquidity. Mystery word: accountant
Übung 7: 1. Companies must also complete a tax return every year. 2. It is worth considering the financial structure of a business. 3. Unfortunately, it doesn't end with personal taxation and corporate taxation. 4. The taxation systems of countries differ greatly.
Übung 8: 1. requirements 2. tax 3. Revenue 4. return/accountant/specialist/rate 5. taxation 6. tax
Übung 9: 1. ever 2. duty 3. levied 4. worth 5. of
Übung 10: 1. Einkommenssteuer 2. Mitteilung 3. Mehrwertsteuer 4. Pflicht 5. Finanzamt 6. Finanzamt 7. angeben
Übung 11: 1. falsch 2. falsch 3. richtig 4. richtig 5. richtig
Übung 12: 1. The financial statements must be audited. 2. VAT. is levied on the sale of goods in Britain. 3. All income must be declared in a tax return at the end of the year. 4. Companies are required to prepare financial statements.
Übung 13: 1. taxes 2. assets 3. expenses 4. tax return 5. accounting principles 6. statements 7. report

23
Übung 1: 1. Angestellte 2. Berechtigung 3. Beschwerde 4. auf Probe 5. Vertraulichkeit 6. Option 7. Kern 8. streichen
Übung 2: 1. competitor 2. hours 3. breaks 4. entitlement 5. option 6. period 7. clause 8. clerk 9. claim
Übung 3: 1 probationary 2. confidentiality 3. clerk 4. options 5. core 6. holiday (vacation) 7. grievances
Übung 4: 1. Your contract will terminate with immediate effect. 2. I need to give you 30 days' notice before I can leave the job. 3. I want to appeal against my dismissal. 4. I have gained a lot of experience during my time here. 5. I plan to handover the accounts next week. 6. He wasn't dismissed: he resigned. 7. My intention is to take three weeks' holiday in summer. 8. He was nominated at yesterday's meeting.
Übung 5: 1. durchackern 2. definieren 3. Abonnement 4. Ablauf 5. prolongieren 6. Gewinn 7. rechtswidrig 8. annullieren 9. Lizenznehmer
Übung 6: 1. period 2. date 3. through 4. agreement 5. users 6. year 7. point
Übung 7: 1. refer 2. binding 3. procedural 4. venue 5. dispute 6. litigation 7. comply 8. proceedings 9. court 10. arbitation 11. contract

Übung 8: 1. disputes 2. connection 3. contract 4. Arbitration 5. Commerce 6. arbitrators 7. language 8. proceedings
Übung 9: 1. procedural 2. binding 3. proceedings 4. comply 5. venue 6. litigation 7. refer. Mystery word: dispute

24
Übung 1: 1. Der Bildschirm ist 32 cm breit. 2. Der Computerturm ist 79 cm hoch. 3. Die Karte ist 2 mm dick. 4. Der Bildschirm hat 10 cm^2. 5. Das Gehäuse ist schlagfest. 6. Sie können Daten mittels Infrarot auf Ihren PC übertragen. 7. Der Prozessor ist sehr leistungsstark.
Übung 2: 1. measurements 2. market 3. processor 4. operate 5. functions 6. data 7. plastic 8. success
Übung 3: 1. Silicon wafer is prepared by cutting slices of wafer from silicon crystals. 2. The slices are polished before use. 3. A layer of insulating material is put on to the surface of the chip. 4. The chip is covered with a light-sensitive chemical. 5. This stage will be repeated many times. 6. Material is removed from the surface of the chip. 7. The wafer is heated to a high temperature.
Übung 4: 1. bedecken 2. schützen 3. vorbereiten 4. wiederholen 5. polieren 6. erhitzen 7. beschichten 8. entfernen
Übung 5: 1. paper tray 2. cartridge 3. slide 4. unpack 5. install 6. cover
Übung 6: 1 richtig 2. richtig 3. falsch 4. richtig 5. falsch 6. richtig 7. falsch
Übung 7: 1. user 2. engineer 3. administrator 4. support 5. system 6. a network 7. end users
Übung 8: 1. CAD 2. anti-virus 3. word processor 4. presentations 5. spreadsheet 6. database

Lösungen zum Abschlusstest

1. b) 2. c) 3. b) 4. a) 5. d) 6. a) 7. d) 8. d) 9. a)
10. d) 11. a) 12. b) 13. b) 14. c) 15. a) 16. b) 17. a) 18. b)
19. a) 20. b) 21. a) 22. d) 23. a) 24. d) 25. b) 26. a) 27. b)
28. a) 29. b) 30. c) 31. d) 32. a) 33. b) 34. c) 35. d) 36. b)
37. d) 38. a) 39. d) 40. c) 41. a) 42. b) 43. a) 44. d) 45. b)
46. d) 47. c) 48. a) 49. a) 50. d) 51. d) 52. b) 53. b) 54. d)
55. b) 56. a) 57. d) 58. c) 59. d) 60. b) 61. a) 62. c) 63. c)
64. b) 65. b) 66. c) 67. a) 68. a) 69. d) 70. a) 71. d) 72. c)